Class and Civil Society

Class and Civil Society:

The Limits of Marxian Critical Theory

Jean L. Cohen

The University of Massachusetts Press   Amherst 1982

Copyright © 1982 by Jean L. Cohen
All rights reserved
Printed in the United States of America
LC 82–11104   ISBN 0–87023–380–7
Library of Congress Cataloging in Publication Data
appear on the last printed page of this book.

For Cele with all my love

Acknowledgments

I would like to thank the Fulbright Commission for providing the financial support in 1975–76 for the early stages of this project. I am also grateful to Dr. Joseph Murphy, former president of Bennington College, for his intellectual encouragement and financial assistance for the final stages. My stay as a Visiting Fellow at the Max Planck Institute at Starnberg, West Germany, in the winter of 1981 provided the context for stimulating discussion, out of which the last chapter of this book was formed.

My conversations with a number of intellectuals and scholars over the years have been essential to the creation of this work. I shall mention only the most important among many: Cornelius Castoriadis, Claude Lefort, Agnes Heller, Mihaly Vajda, Ferenc Feher, George Markus, Claus Offe, Albrecht Wellmer, and, finally, Emil Oestereicher, my dissertation director. Neither this book, nor the intellectual and political development it bespeaks would have been possible without my ten-year affiliation with *Telos* as an associate editor, and discussions with other editors, especially, Paul Piccone and Dick Howard. Finally, and above all, I would like to thank Andrew Arato. Of all the above mentioned friends, his intellectual support, manifested in continuous discussions at nearly every stage of the manuscript, was the most important.

Contents

Preface

This book is not intended as a work in Marxology. Rather, I seek to make a contribution, however modest, to the development of a *new* critical theory of society.

Why a new critical theory of society? Why proceed through the oeuvre of Marx at all? The old Critical Theory, the project of the Frankfurt School, had, despite its many revisions of Marx, a deep orthodox Marxist strain. Its vision of the underlying contradictions of modern society involved the simple alternative: either the increasing crisis of capitalism and the victory of the industrial proletariat *or* a "one-dimensional" society containing all social change, occasioning the decline of the subject and of culture itself. The original Marxian project sought to assess, account for, and address the major social movement of its time, the workers' movement. The economic contradictions of capitalism, the social struggles of workers *against* capitalist rationalization and *for* the democratization of both economy and polity were the dominant themes. Despite the continuities between contemporary Western societies and their nineteenth-century counterparts—they are still capitalist, still civil societies, with states that are even more fully formally democratic than before—the transition from liberal to late capitalism has decisively altered all the key terms of the classical project. Yet clearly what we are confronted with is not the final vision of Critical Theory: a one-dimensional universe in which the culture industry and successful economic expansion and growth have succeeded in papering over all contradictions, suppressing conflict, and creating the happy consciousness.

On the contrary, social movements are proliferating in nearly every sector of society. New social actors are addressing an entirely original range of issues and challenging the cultural model (progress and growth) and hierarchical structures of contemporary Western society. Although the workers' movement has been "institutionalized," welfare-state reform strategies have not rendered the realm of production immune to radical social contestation nor prevented the development of alternative visions of the social organization of labor. The "legalization" of the working class and the emergence of new, nonclass social movements do mean, however, that the old theoretical explanations and guarantees of social transformations (above all, the theory of class and the philosophy of history) are no longer convincing. The concept of class can certainly point to forms of domination, inequity and potential social struggles over the division and control of labor time. Yet it is unable to provide the exclusive referent for an alternative vision of society or even for the dynamics of contestation and transformation in the present. More significant, the Marxian concepts of class, totality, system, and history cannot serve as the standpoint from which to unify, theoretically or practically, the plurality of social struggles and movements in contemporary society.

The absence, not of a radical workers' movement, but of a workers' movement with convincing universalistic claims, together with the presence of diverse, localized, and seemingly unconnected social movements (the women's movement, the ecology movement, citizens' initiatives, the peace movement, and so forth) have led some to revive the one-dimensionality thesis and to conclude that a new narcissism, anomie, and a narrow particularism are the most likely paths for social actors in contemporary Western society. To insist that contemporary social movements do not articulate universalistic values, that they are either anti- or unpolitical, that no unified alternative model of society is forthcoming from them, and that their collective identities are particularistic, is, however, strange on the part of critical intellectuals regardless of whether such statements accurately describe some strong trends. Such judgments reveal a failure of political will as well as nostalgia for the old theoretical model that located universality in a single subject and whose social vision (an alternative industrial society) was directly fused with the political project of taking state power. What this nostalgia obscures is that struggles of industrial workers took diverse forms and posed a variety of goals that had no self-evident unity. Rather, the workers' movement was unified through a process of mutual interaction between intellectuals and social groups in creating the theoretical and ideological significations that constituted the socialist project. Since we can no longer ground unity on the fact of labor or in the concept of class, what is needed now is a new theoretical reflection and interpretation of social contestation and political action. Indeed, the need for a critical theory with practical intent is based on the very plurality of social movements, each potentially in solidarity with one another and hence not antiuniversalistic, but also possessing some regressive and particularistic strains. In short, the task of the critical theorist is to accept the diversity of identities and movements while attempting to develop a theoretical framework capable of defending and promoting the potential complementarity of emancipatory struggles.

It should be clear that Marxism can no longer fulfill this function. The Marxist assumption that the institutions of modern civil society and the class relations of the capitalist mode of production are one and the same occludes the very aspects of society that must be interrogated and precludes any understanding of what is new about the new social movements. The corresponding vision of a future community that has abolished once and for all the duality of society and state conceals the positive institutional achievements of modernity. It also forecloses communication with social movements that seek the further democratization of a differentiated, hence modern, social structure. Finally, any attempt to transcend the sterile opposition of "reform" versus "revolution" that has been used by Marxists to evaluate social struggles since the nineteenth century with such poor results, is automatically blocked by a theory that aims at complete discontinuity with the institutions of "bourgeois" society. It is, however, precisely the task of critical theory to articulate the highly desirable interrelation between political and institutional reform, and social movements. A new theory of civil society is indispensable for such concerns.

Why then bother to reconstruct and criticize the Marxian theoretical project at all? Marxism is both a rich and antinomic theory hardly exhausted by its dogmatic presuppositions or interpreters. If the central weakness of Marx's vision is the occlusion of the *positive* achievements of modern civil society that are still well worth defending, he was the peerless critic of the *negativity* and ever-present dangers of the historically given form of this society. By discovering its genuinely new principle of stratification, i.e., *social* antagonism, by showing the reasons for the modern state's violation of its own principles, by retracing the journey of domination and hierarchy from the polity to the factory, Marx has quite evidently left us an unsurpassed model for critical thinking. But, using his own phrase, only a "ruthless criticism" of *his* work, has a chance to rescue the valid insights concerning the threat posed by capitalist rationalization to democratic politics and to the very existence of civil society, from the morass of an increasingly inadequate and impotent theory.

Introduction

It has become increasingly apparent to nondogmatic Marxist theorists that the Marxian class theory is in crisis. For many, the experiences of fascism, Stalinism, and the New Deal had already combined to crush the expectations of the classical version of the theory.[1] With fascism, the world economic crisis occasioned the movement of social strata, consigned by Marxism to a peripheral role, to the center of the political stage, while those who were expected to act in a progressive, revolutionary manner "failed" to do so. With Stalinism, the so-called socialist revolution did not lead to a free, classless society. Instead, it entailed the destruction of three particular classes—nobility, bourgeoisie, and peasantry—and led to the creation of a new system of stratification and domination unthinkable within the Marxian framework. With the New Deal in the United States, the economic crisis heralded an explicit form of state intervention that seemed to enable the most advanced capitalist systems to integrate the implicit challenge of the workers' movement (unionism) into one of its constituent elements. The welfare state in its various postwar versions reconstructed the capitalist system, everywhere complicating its internal stratification. Moreover, social movements proliferating in the West in the 1960s signaled the emergence of a "New Left" politics that articulated radical needs of a variety of groups distinct from the working class.[2] Recently, attacks on the welfare state from above and from below,[3] together with new social movements on the right and on the left that traverse class lines,[4] have occurred in every Western capitalist society. A reassessment of Marxian types of class theory is thus long overdue.

Within the existing range of neo-Marxism,[5] the dogma of the industrial proletariat as *the* revolutionary class and the one and only revolutionary subject has, accordingly, been more or less abandoned. Elaborate conceptual schemes have been developed to account for changes in the structure of production, a new relation between state and civil society, and the proliferation of new social strata in society and state. Attempts to explain these developments, however, have not involved a critical reassessment of the original theory. Neo-Marxian class analyses have either explicitly built upon the old paradigm or implicitly presupposed particular features of it. Despite the variety of theoretical strategies and political positions that make up the spectrum of neo-Marxian class theory, an unreflective relation to the Marxian original is characteristic of them all.

Unless the presuppositions of Marxism are reconstructed and immanently criticized, they are bound to constantly reemerge from the intellectual history of the past century to haunt those who seek to revise or transcend Marx in light of historical transformations. The purpose of this book is to provide such a critique. I hope to show that the problems inherent in developing a new class theory for contemporary society do not derive simply from unexpected historical change and new complexities but are rooted in the premises and project of Marxian class theory itself. The inability of the various neo-Marxian approaches to explain either the stratification or the global structure of contemporary society can be traced directly to their dogmatic assumptions.

This study will attempt to lay the groundwork for a *post-Marxist* critical *stratification* theory able to come to grips with the diversity and innovations of contemporary capitalist society without ignoring the Marxian achievement. By "post-Marxist" I mean an approach that reflects on, and frees itself from, dogmatic Marxian presuppositions but remains continuous with the project of a thorough critique of modern civil society.[6] This does not mean, however, that I accept the Marxian analysis of civil society. On the contrary, I shall argue that it is precisely this analysis, at the heart of the class theory, that must be reassessed and altered. Let me anticipate my main argument: The Marxian class theory was burdened from the start with an analysis of civil society torn between two opposing impulses: first, the effort to articulate the *social* character of the new relation between private (family) and public (state) in terms of an analysis of the major social movement of the time; and second, the tendency to reduce both the social sphere and the workers' movement to the logic and contradictions of a mode of production—the capitalist economy. The overall preponderance of the latter in Marx's work accounts for the transformation of an originally critical analysis of the specific modern principles of stratification into a dogmatic class theory. It would thus not be possible to develop a new critical stratification theory, to address social movements, or to assess structural contradictions without a revision of the theory of civil society on which the class analysis is based. Accordingly, I use the term *stratification* rather than *class*. The question as to which Marxian categories might continue to inform such a project can be answered only after an immanent critique of the theory as a whole.

Indeed, it should be apparent that neo-Marxist attempts to develop a new *class* theory of contemporary capitalism are biased from the outset. They presuppose, by definition, that the analysis of production relations, socioeconomic groups, capitalist reproduction mechanisms, and class struggles is the key to the logic of contemporary civil society and potential radical social movements. But it is precisely this prejudice that can no longer be maintained. I shall thus present in this introduction a typology of neo-Marxian theoretical strategies in order to illustrate the difficulties involved in all versions of Marxian class analysis.

Four basic types of neo-Marxian theory have been developed to address the changed practice of the workers' movement, the emergence of new social strata, and the implications of state intervention in the economy for class formation and struggle. They can be characterized as follows: theories seeking a revolutionary subject that is not a class to substitute for or spark the proletariat; "new working-class theories"; structuralist Marxist class analyses; and theories of the "new intellectual class." Although these approaches tend to succeed one another historically, my interest is not in their genesis but in the type of theorizing and specific Marxian presuppositions inherent in each.

1. The search for a substitute revolutionary subject to play the role formerly assigned to the proletariat and to lead or otherwise activate the former, is a telling witness to the crisis of Marxism. The work of Herbert Marcuse provides the paradigm for this approach.

Marcuse's theory of one-dimensional society must be seen as a response to the "failure" of the proletariat to become revolutionary and the success of advanced capitalism in reproducing itself. His theory postulated the emergence of an authoritarian technical rationality that has freed itself from the particular interests of capital and has become a political force capable of suppressing social contradictions, critical discourse, and radical needs.[7] It corresponds to the idea that the successes of the mixed economy of the welfare state have resulted in a "happy consciousness" (material satisfaction without freedom), a series of "repressive desublimations" (permissiveness without satisfaction), and the dissolution of the boundaries between the public, the private, and the social (typical of liberal capitalism) that were once the crucial loci of critique, individuality, and the condition of possibility of proletarian class consciousness.

Accordingly, Marcuse turned away from the critique of political economy and relied instead upon the philosophical presuppositions of Marx's oeuvre. He reconstructed the concept of radical need, the theory of alienation, and the concept of the revolutionary subject in the hope of locating a nonproletarian actor to which they might apply. There is thus a direct connection between Marcuse's specific type of Marxian orthodoxy and the unorthodox stance of the "great refusal," the seemingly romantic critique of industrialism, and the continual shifts in designating a suitable addressee of the theory. The limits of such an approach can be traced to the fusion of a relentlessly critical analysis of late capitalism and a failure to critically examine its own philosophical, Marxian premises. This makes itself felt in four domains: the class analysis; the theory of revolution; the primacy of labor and the economy; and the critique of civil society.[8]

The class analysis: The bourgeoisie and the proletariat remain the fundamental *classes* of modern society, although the bourgeoisie loses its preeminent control of the economy and state to the "technostructure," while the proletariat cannot carry out its revolutionary mission because its class consciousness is blocked by mass culture. Thus, rather than question the class theory that imputes such a mission to its addressee, Marcuse prefers to blame a derailed history for the failure of the Marxist project in the West.

The theory of revolution: To Marcuse, the proletariat was the revolutionary class par excellence because it embodied the absolute negation of bourgeois society. Its total misery, alienation, and exclusion from society pointed toward the radical revolution demanded by Marxist theory. Once it was assumed that the working class was integrated into society and into the political (electoral) system, the search for a substitute could commence. The turn to the underclasses—blacks, students, women, the "third world," and so on—and the effort to derive radical needs from psychological and anthropological (instead of economic) factors filled the gap.[9] This was perfectly consistent with the Marxian theory of revolution that requires a revolutionary subject to represent a complete refusal of capitalist society and a radically new mode of being. I would say that the most significant, new, non-Marxist element here—Marcuse's ability to positively validate the needs of non-working-class strata and to recognize their potential—is vitiated by the retention of the notion of a unified, revolutionary subject.

The primacy of labor and the economy: One could argue that from the beginning, and without change, the entire thrust of Marcuse's antipathy toward capitalism sprang from his emphasis on the concept of labor and the critique of *alienated labor*. This provides the key to his attack on both Soviet Marxism and Western capitalism. It also explains his affinity with one version of Marx's own model of communism: the model of the *Grundrisse*. According to Marcuse's interpretation of this text, automation abolishes (potentially) the need for alienated labor, and freedom is conceived in the nonpolitical terms of the extension of free time. Marcuse's idea of happiness as a free play of faculties, a reconciliation of man and nature, subject and object—to the exclusion of a concern with institutional forms and political freedom—derives from his concept of alienated labor. The theory of radical needs is thus disassociated from the proletariat gone reformist and attached to new revolutionary subjects without occasioning a reorientation toward issues of political alienation and domination.

The critique of civil society: What is most fateful in the continuity between Marx and neo-Marxists of this orientation is their dislike of the institutions of modern civil society and their reduction of these institutions to mere bourgeois culture and capitalist relations. Certainly, from the standpoint of administered mass democracy, Marcuse displayed a preference for an often idealized model of liberal capitalism, with its intact private sphere, family form, individuality, and autonomous culture. He concurred with Marx in embracing the underlying universalistic values of modernity. Like Marx, however, he tended to dismiss liberal political and economic institutions as bourgeois ideology —as structures that prevented the full realization of these values for everyone. Marcuse even spoke of liberal tolerance as repressive and (like Horkheimer, Adorno, and many groups of the New Left) located the seeds of fascism and one-dimensionality in liberal capitalist civil society and in the dialectic of "instrumental reason" it fostered.

To this decidedly Marxist view of modernity, Marcuse added an interpretation of Max Weber's concept of rationalization as the supposedly smooth, conflict-free extension of technical reason to all of society. This was to account for the failure of the Marxist project among its original addressees.[10] It generated a one-sided analysis that implied that total emancipation required the total abolition of civil society by a new revolutionary subject (or several such subjects) totally heterogeneous to the institutions of the present order.

One can get out of this theoretical morass only by taking seriously the original (but undeveloped) Marxian insights into the contradictory nature of all institutions of modern society. A recognition of the heterogeneity of civil society, an analysis of what is worth preserving of its institutional articulation, could break the circle of totalization. But an approach that rests on the presuppositions of the Marxian class theory, despite its willingness to dispense with the dogma of the industrial proletariat, will necessarily fail to grasp the new and be forced into the awkward position of chasing after various social movements with the badge of revolutionary subject.

2. The second version of neo-Marxian class theory, in part a challenge to the first,[11] focuses directly on changes in the structure of labor within welfare-state capitalist systems in order to provide a "strategy for labor." The "new-working-class" theorists[12] rejected the theses of the integration, embourgeoisement, and one-dimensionalization of workers by distinguishing between an old and a new working class. Serge Mallet and André Gorz pointed to the new types of strikes initiated by highly skilled technical strata in France in the 1960s as the sign of the emergence of potentially radical segments of the working class within the advanced sectors of capitalist industry. Taking *Das Kapital* as their model, new-working-class theorists engaged in an analysis of the labor process, assessing the requalification and retraining of sectors of the labor force as the basis for a new dialectic of labor. Like the original critique of political economy, the new one offered here sought to link changes in production to the history and objective possibilities of the workers' movement. The modernization of the university, the scientization and professionalization of the labor process, and the potentialities inherent in automation were assessed in terms of a new political economy of corporate capitalism. Accordingly, the social strata generated by these developments are seen as a new working class to which the radical potential formerly attributed to the proletariat is now imputed.

Although they draw on somewhat different aspects of the Marxian theory, it is illuminating to compare the first and second approaches to class analysis. Both Marcuse and Gorz/Mallet argue that the ability of advanced capitalism to meet the vital needs of the population undermines the formerly explosive contradiction between the old working class and capitalism. Both reject the usual Leninist solution and search for new "qualitative" or radical needs around which groups struggling for change might organize. The theory of alienation provides the common basis for the interpretation of needs for creative activity, meaningful work, fellowship, self-development, happiness, and freedom as radical needs, that is, inevitably generated and denied by the capitalist system. Despite their disagreement as to which groups develop these needs (for Marcuse, non-working-class strata; for Gorz/Mallet, the new working class), the key criterion of radicality is whether or not needs can be satisfied within capitalism. Finally, both rely on the *Grundrisse* for an alternative model, although the latter reject the Marcusian idea of the abolition of direct labor as utopian. Through a refinement of the analysis of labor as science/art/communication, the second approach locates the potential for nonalienated activity at the point of production. The new technical strata are interpreted as workers, able and willing to abolish the capitalist/bureaucratic stranglehold on production that prevents the realization of these needs. Gorz and Mallet argue, in short, that the new working class possesses a level of knowledge and education and engages in a type of labor that generates qualitative needs for autonomy, participation, and workers' control (autogestion) that cannot be satisfied within the framework of capitalist production relations.

The critique of science, technology, and the hierarchical division of labor does not imply for new-working-class theorists, as it does for Marcuse, that the realm of necessary labor either is doomed to perpetuate alienation or must be changed on the basis of an entirely new science and technology.[13] Rather, the objective possibility for abolishing the hierarchical, managerial, and capitalist subordination and constitution of technology must be tested empirically, from case to case. Nevertheless, regarding the agent of radical change, the theoretical strategy of locating radical needs within a particular group remains the same.[14] To be sure, they choose to preserve different aspects of the original Marxian theory to assess the new strata involved. Marcuse retains the Hegelian Marxist concept of subjectivity but abandons the focus on an economic class, whereas Gorz and Mallet drop the invidious distinction between productive/unproductive, mental/manual labor in order to expand the concept of a *universal* working class. The total lack of consistency on the part of Marcuse in asserting now the students, now marginal or suppressed ethnic groups, or perhaps women, as the bearers of radical needs and the inability of new-working-class theorists to specify precisely which sectors of the working class they have in mind reveal the difficulties of both approaches. That the identical strata are at times deemed to be the class/nonclass subject of radical change damns both of the theoretical approaches as well as the faulty sociology inherent in them.

The drawbacks of the second approach have become clear in the context of the denouement of the 1960s. The obvious has asserted itself: Like the old working class, the new has quite particular interests and is just as likely to embrace its privileged status above and distinct from the old workers as to present itself as their vanguard in the struggle against all privilege. This is not to say that Gorz and Mallet were not "onto something" when they rejected the consignment of the workers' movement to the dustbin of liberal capitalist history, or when they sought a strategy for labor adequate to the very real changes in the structure of production and to the demands for autogestion articulated by groups of workers themselves. The attempt to replace the sterile Marxist opposition of reform versus revolution with a theory of structural reform (Gorz) and to articulate a theory of counterpowers for the workplace was an important antidote to theories that tended to relinquish the sphere of production to the realm of necessity.[15] Yet the theoretical scaffolding on which these efforts were erected was built on sand. The critique of approaches that deny the possible emergence of radical struggles at the point of production loses its impact with the restriction of the "will to self-management" to a new working class on the dubious basis of its *mode* of labor. To root the potential "praxis subject" in the performance of unalienated labor—in other words, to once again reconceptualize struggles for democratization and counterpowers in terms of a class theory—is to reveal an unreconstructed *ouvrier*-ism that glorifies yet again the worker qua worker. Here too universality is inscribed in a particular group. The usual weaknesses of council communism[16] are repeated despite the different subject and despite the attempt to speak to the "needs" of nonproletarian strata in motion. Indeed, the pseudopluralism of the model becomes patently clear with the explicit projections for a future homogeneity of the working class (this time at the highest rather than the lowest common denominator). The very logic of the theory is antipluralist to the extent that it totalizes the disparate strata of professionals, scientists, students, etcetera, into a single new working *class* with universalistic qualities and needs.

The tensions in this approach between a nascent antiproductivist, ecological, "postindustrial" theory and another updated critique of political economy focusing on the structure of labor and workers' struggles were bound to erupt once the theorist became disappointed (as he had to be) by his designated addressees. It should come as no surprise, then, that André Gorz, the theorist of the new working class par excellence, has recently made a 180-degree about-face and said adieu to the proletariat, old or new.[17] Clearly, the third approach to class theory corrects the second only by going to opposite extremes.

3. The direct challenge to new-working-class theories can be found in "structuralist" Marxist class analyses, represented by Nicos Poulantzas and E. O. Wright.[18] Although in disagreement about particulars, Poulantzas and Wright attempt to bring the full force of a highly elaborate structuralist theory to bear on the emergence of new social strata and the new role of the state in advanced capitalism. Structuralist Marxists, however, reject out of hand the philosophical presuppositions of the Marxian class theory. The concepts of subjectivity, alienation, fetishism, consciousness,[19] and civil society are abandoned as Hegelian metaphysics. Instead they embrace Louis Althusser's "symptomatic" reading of the theory of historical materialism and of the structural analysis of the capitalist mode of production in Marx's *Capital*, denuded, of course, of any dialectic of labor or consciousness. On the other hand, this self-proclaimed scientific Marxism seeks to challenge the hegemony of empiricism and positivism in the social sciences through structuralist methods. But, precisely because they have chosen to rely on an extremely objectivistic reading of the Marxian categories (closer to the Marxism of the Second International and Engels than to Marx), the questions posed by Poulantzas and Wright, and the results of their analyses turn out to be both remarkably trivial *and* obscurantist.

It is quite distressing for the brave reader who has waded through the swamp of categories and charts that proliferate endlessly in the works of Poulantzas and Wright to discover that the issue of class theory boils down to a squabble over the "boundary problem." The question posed by this approach is: What criteria determine the boundary between classes? Who or, rather, which social categories are in which class? This exercise in pigeonholing is allegedly significant because "classes are social forces and have real consequences" and because "it is important for socialist strategy":[20] We are, accordingly, offered an elaborate analytic of the old categories, with some new ones thrown in, that supposedly explains the causal relations between them and the "level of appearances." In neither the works of Poulantzas nor those of Wright, however, do we ever really leave the realm of structures. It turns out that they operate not with two sets of variables—structural logic of capitalist reproduction/social class or class struggle (appearance)—but with only one, the former. The analysis always proceeds from the side of "structure," juggling and elaborating categories ad infinitum in order that they might mesh with the "realities" of social stratification. Yet it is unclear whether these realities are simply given or, worse, derived from the structures themselves. Since the old class concepts and prejudices are presupposed from the outset, the key dilemma endemic to any class theory based on *Das Kapital* cannot even be posed. I am referring to the fact that it is possible neither to deduce the classes or class struggles (social action) of any given capitalist society from the analysis of the capitalist system (structures) nor, inversely, to derive the structures from the "appearances" (social classes and social movements). The only question that concerns our structuralists, however, is where, in which structures, to place the intermediate strata between capital and labor, and the state. The prior (theoretical) issue of the ambiguous relation between system and class, or "objective structure" and social action, is systematically and necessarily obscured by the objectivistic bias of structuralist Marxist class theory. Since this version of Marxian orthodoxy seems to have made quite an impact, a brief discussion of its theoretical strategy is in order.

Poulantzas's structuralist definition of social classes shows more clearly than any possible commentary the objectivism and determinism of the overall approach: "More exactly, social class is a concept which shows the effects of the ensemble of structures, the matrix of a mode of production or of a social formation on the agents which constitute its supports. This concept reveals the effects of the global structure in the field of social relations." [21] Classes are defined as the effects of structures, determined not just by the economic structure but also by political and ideological structures. In other words, "economic" criteria (defined as the distinction between productive and unproductive labor) are insufficient to determine class position. In addition, we have to look at "political" criteria, or the distinction between supervisory and nonsupervisory roles, and "ideological" criteria, or the distinction between mental and manual labor.[22] This multiplication of class determinants is supposed to conjure away the charge of economic reductionism. Political and ideological structures are "relatively autonomous," the "economic" is determining only "in the last instance." What has not disappeared, however, is the (futile) effort to derive the inputs to social action from the analysis of structures.

It should come as no surprise, then, that Poulantzas vehemently denies any similarity between his consideration of political and ideological structures and the Hegelian Marxist formulations of the "class-in-itself/class-for-itself" problematic. For the structuralist Marxist, the issue is never "class consciousness" or autonomous political action of a self-constituted working class. The concern is solely with the analysis of the various objective factors that determine class positions. The relation between these class positions, the "objective" interests invariably imputed to their "carriers," and other inputs to social action, is left for the reader to deduce. To be sure, Poulantzas insists that one cannot define classes outside class struggle; but he banishes the ogre of "consciousness" by arguing that class struggle refers not to the conscious self-organization of a class as a social force but rather to the antagonistic and contradictory quality of social relations of production. The proletariat is not the *subject* of revolution but only its *agent*. With one stroke we are freed from the annoying problem of subjectivity that plagued so many neo-Marxists. Into its place steps the "problem" of identifying the potential members of the objectively revolutionary class, the proletariat. This is the *object*, in both senses, of scientific Marxist strategy and tactics.

The fruit borne by this structuralist construction are the criteria for deciding class boundaries and the concept of the "new petty bourgeoisie." If we take the three classificatory schematas described above, we find that the proletariat is that group which engages in productive, manual, nonsupervisory labor.[23] This distinguishes the proletariat from the new middle strata—engineers, technicians, foremen, civil servants —who comprise a class continuous with and inclusive of the remnants of the old declining petty bourgeoisie. Why? Because they bear the same ideological relationship to the class struggle of capital and labor as their nineteenth-century counterparts! Since they occupy positions of ideological control over the proletariat and perform mental labor, the new middle strata are not a new working class. Despite the fact that these strata are often productive wage workers, they are "structurally" a new petty bourgeoisie. Moreover, they are as politically suspect as the old one, that is, they are prone to reformism, power fetishism, and individualism. To round off the analysis, we are told that the bourgeoisie are those who have economic ownership (control) and de facto possession of the means of production. Formal legal criteria of property ownership are dismissed as "bourgeois."

Poulantzas's structuralist class theory occasioned a major reply from his American counterpart, Eric Olin Wright.[24] It seems that Poulantzas's argument has defeated its own purpose. The analysis that characterized the new middle strata as a new petty bourgeoisie in order to defend the purity of the proletarian basis of communist politics has the unfortunate result of reducing the working class to a minuscule proportion of the population.[25] Since Wright wants to defend the idea of a revolutionary proletariat, along with workers' control, while avoiding the Leninist implications of the above analysis, he subjects Poulantzas's work to a critique.

Wright's major theoretical innovation is his division of the theory of structural causality into six "modes of determination": structural limitation, selectivity, reproduction/nonreproduction, functional compatibility, transformation, and mediation.[26] This daunting array of categories allegedly allows one to create a model of determination of the relations among economic structures, state structures, state intervention, and class struggle. It does *not*, however, alter the objectivistic bias of the approach. Because Wright operates with the same Marxist interpretation as Poulantzas (derived from Althusser), his "discomfort"[27] with Poulantzas's dismissal of the problem of consciousness is not translated into a serious revision of the theoretical strategy as a whole. Only the boundaries are shifted.

In rejecting both the maximalist (all wage laborers are proletarians) and the minimalist (Poulantzas's version) views of who is a proletarian, Wright had to solve the "boundary problem" all over again. His breakthrough is the discovery that there is a discontinuity between occupational position in the division of labor and class position. But Wright does not choose to reflect upon the relation between structure and class in general; instead, he simply develops new formulas to fill in the gaps. Thus those positions in the division of labor that are not constitutive of class positions are called "objectively contradictory locations between classes." Class is still defined via structure, that is, in terms of "fundamental class interests" that involve the structure of social relations of a mode of production for which economic relations are primary. The "fundamental class interests" of the proletariat (that could be shared by others) are those potential objectives that could become actual objectives of struggle in the absence of mystifications and distortions of capitalist relations.[28] And, Wright insists, socialism is the class interest of workers not on moral or normative grounds but because workers would struggle for socialism if they had the scientific understanding of the contradictions of capitalism that, needless to say, he possesses. Thus the return of "consciousness" as a relevant factor leads directly to the Leninist position that Wright seems to want to avoid.

Control over labor power, control over the physical means of production, and control over investments/resources are Wright's substitutes for Poulantzas's criteria for determining the central class boundary. Bourgeoisie and proletariat occupy polar positions regarding each of these three "processes," and those positions that do not perfectly correspond to the basic class forces are contradictory class locations. Those not yet involved in the division of labor have their class position identified by their class trajectory, or the class to which they most likely will belong in the future. Finally, those employed by the political and ideological apparatuses (Althusser's term) are distinguished according to whether they create or merely disseminate state policy and bourgeois ideology. Every social stratum is thus assessed in terms of the division of labor and the concept of class. No other interests, groupings, needs, activities, or desires are deemed to be relevant.

Accordingly, the working class includes all those who occupy working-class positions in the social relations of production, those directly linked to the working class by their class trajectories, and those occupying working-class positions in political and ideological apparatuses. The trick succeeds; the proletariat grows to a size never dreamed of by Poulantzas. But there is another bonus. For it turns out that the new middle strata are not a new petty bourgeoisie but occupy contradictory class positions, many of which "carry" a "real interest" in socialism. They too can join the proletariat in the common struggle, provided that there is an enlightened socialist strategy able to reorient conflict over immediate interests toward fundamental interests. The illuminating aspect of the concept of "contradictory class position" is that the relevant strata can "go either way" in the struggle between capital and labor. One might point out, however, that this is precisely what Marx argued for the old petty bourgeoisie! Nothing ventured, nothing lost. Moreover, Wright claims that the fundamental interest of the proletariat is to obtain state power and establish ideological hegemony. He is interested *only* in the autonomous power of the *working class* in society—other groups are left to fend for themselves or to bask in the ideological hegemony of the proletariat. Clearly, such an approach is incapable of grasping what is new about the social strata and social movements proliferating in contemporary capitalist societies.

4. The version of neo-Marxian class analysis enjoying the greatest vogue is the theory of the new intellectual class. From standpoints as diverse as those of a self-defined left-Hegelian (Alvin Gouldner), leftist Eastern European dissidents (Georg Konrad and Ivan Szelenyi), remnants of the New Left in its Leninist version (Barbara and John Ehrenreich), and neoconservatives (Irving Kristol et al.),[29] echoes of the old theme of the treason of the clerks (Julien Benda), managerial revolution (James Burnham), and the new class (Milovan Djilas) have emerged in a new form. The red thread uniting this diversity is the transference of the class referent of the historical materialist theory of revolution from workers to intellectuals and the identification of their concerns for critique, emancipation, participation, egalitarianism, or social justice as an ideological bid for establishing their own class power against both capital and labor by taking control of the state. Although many of the proponents of this thesis are decidedly anti-Marxist, the theoretical strategy at issue here is informed by Marxian class theory. The theorists all go beyond stratification analysis[30] to assert that a particular interest exists for a wide spectrum of intellectuals that, often unbeknownst to them, teleologically unites them in a project of class rule. Thus, in this respect, a classically Marxist perspective pervades the work of the entire spectrum of "new-intellectual-class" theorists.

The political and theoretical conclusions reached by the application of the historical materialist theory of change and class relations to intellectuals are, to say the least, both ambiguous and contradictory. Gouldner and Szelenyi/Konrad employ the class concept against, among others, the historical carriers of the theory—Marxists/Leninists —yet see the coming to power of the intellectual class as inevitable. The Ehrenreichs use it to vindicate a quasi-Leninist strategy. The "New Right" wields the class concept against those intellectuals who are critical of the status quo, with the exception, of course, of themselves. But they all have as their model the historical materialist interpretation of the French Revolution as a dialectic of universal and particular class interests. Like the Marxian critique of "bourgeois ideology" (universalistic values used to conceal the rise to power of a particular class, the bourgeoisie), the "unmasking critique" of the claims of intellectuals to represent, articulate, or even think the universal seeks to reveal the particular interests of a class on the road to class power. I will discuss the dangerous implications of this self-satisfied critique of intellectual transcendence, and the implicit plea for the end of ideology, but let me first briefly address the more serious versions of the thesis as they bear on my central concern: the use and abuse of Marxian class theory to comprehend the new.

Gouldner's simple little book is the most faithful to the classic historical materialist theory of revolution and class. It deviates from the original only insofar as the class agent of the anticapitalist project is concerned. Indeed, it is quite reasonable to be confused as to whether the new intellectual class substitutes for the bourgeoisie or the proletariat in this analysis.[31] The intentions of the book are clear in one respect, however: Gouldner wants to dispense once and for all with any claims of intellectuals (specifically Marxists) to selflessly represent the interests of other strata. He thus throws down the gauntlet to the classic Marxian/Gramscian position that intellectuals are a stratum capable only of representing interests of other classes, while rejecting the Mannheimian view that they are free-floating, able to represent universality.[32] Instead, he maintains that intellectuals are a *class*, with specific interests, that already controls the means of production and violence in contemporary society through their monopoly of scientific and technical knowledge. Produced in the universities and reproduced on an expanding scale due to the education and communications revolutions, the knowledge class has, according to Gouldner, elaborated an ideology and a culture. Professionalism serves to justify the intellectuals' guildlike privilege and power. Their common "culture of critical discourse" distinguishes them linguistically from others and provides the focus around which their interests coalesce to devalue the authority claims of the old ruling class (capitalists or bureaucrats). The principles of discourse, voluntary consent, context-free knowledge, and scientific modes of justification of all truth claims, inherent in the culture of critical discourse, are the basis for the rejection of any authority other than the rules of reason and knowledge that it establishes. This culture is thereby the core of an ideology with universalistic claims for a potential new ruling class that is already a community—technical and humanist intellectuals.

Gouldner maintains that the particular interests of this new class are to increase its share of the gross national product, to acquire a position of power that will allow it to ensure its privilege, and to control its work setting. On the basis of a rather flimsy sociology of intellectuals, he imputes to them a telos of revolution and a class interest in becoming the dominant group in a future statist society in which both bureaucracy and capital will be "expropriated." In short, intellectuals cannot be content with their privilege in the given system because (1) they are alienated; (2) their upward mobility is artificially blocked by capitalists and bureaucrats; (3) they suffer a status disparity between their functional role in the system and their comparatively low enjoyment of power and wealth; (4) their technical interests are stymied; (5) they are underemployed and overproduced; and (6) their very culture urges them to a stance of permanent revolution and generates a moralizing commitment to represent the "social totality." Accordingly, their strategy to gain control will be a combination of vanguardism and alliance with all oppressed groups to overthrow capitalism. The revolutionary ideology of this class will fuse themes of workers' control (so much for the new-working-class thesis), meritocracy, and a principle of distributive justice based on the old socialist ideal of "from each according to his ability, to each according to his work," with intellectual work valued highest.

It would be a mistake, however, to take this class analysis of the new stratum as a warning against its Machiavellian designs. Despite the above, Gouldner argues that intellectuals are not simply a particularistic class that disguises its interests as universal but are actually a "flawed universal class." The utter confusion of orthodox Marxism and anti-Marxism in the overall approach yields this surprise ending. The new class is a flawed universal class because it cultivates its own particular guild interests but, at the same time, embodies the collective, or universal, interest. It turns out, after all, that the new intellectual class is the "most progressive force in history," that the culture of critical discourse is a harbinger of freedom, that the attack on the old order really represents the interests of almost everyone. From the heights of a historical materialist insight into future development, Gouldner claims that the intellectual class (like the rising bourgeoisie) is universal *and* progressive. Elitism and tendencies toward consolidation of privilege are its "flaw." Gouldner's work is thus only apparently a critique of Marxism.

It is difficult to see just what the *class* theory of intellectuals adds to the common analyses of the privilege and power of intellectual strata besides a deterministic evolutionism. Its sole new twist consists in the uninspiring exercise of applying the historical materialist version of the Marxian class theory to Marxists, among other intellectuals, who presume to selflessly articulate the needs of other oppressed groups. But the claim that principles of consent, egalitarianism, and critique are the class ideology of intellectuals disempowers Gouldner's own progressivist conclusions and, more seriously, undermines the legitimacy of any critical theory in advance.

The new-intellectual-class thesis has been formulated in a far more sophisticated manner by Szelenyi and Konrad.[33] Their book links an informative historical sociology of intellectuals[34] to a systemic analysis of the one social system to which they apply the thesis: Soviet-type state socialism. The historically new feature of these systems—the penetration of society by the state—inspires Szelenyi and Konrad to offer what they call a "post-Marxist" analysis of the new mechanisms of stratification and power to be found there. The post-Marxist impulse of their theory is manifested in two ways: The state is viewed as a stratification mechanism that does not *reflect* class relations of society; and civil society is analytically distinguished from capitalism in the context of a critical political project calling for a socialist civil society. It is thus all the more distressing to find these impulses continually frustrated by the presence of a reconstructed Marxian class theory and the use of Marxian formulas such as "mode of production," two-class model, and "appropriation and control of the surplus product" as the key criteria for class boundaries. Clearly, Szelenyi and Konrad wanted to present their work as a sort of *Das Kapital* of state socialist systems, but their systemic analysis (entirely lacking in Gouldner) is prevented from articulating what is new about the structures of domination and stratification in these societies by the repeated use of categories generated within the critique of an entirely different social system, capitalism, despite their post-Marxist intentions.[35] Their arguments for the presence of a new intellectual *class* in the East are, consequently, far less convincing than those they bring forth *against* the thesis regarding the West.

According to Szelenyi and Konrad, the market and the redistributive mechanisms of "state monopoly capitalism" are the two main principles of stratification responsible for the proliferation of intellectual strata between capital and labor. Defined as monopolistic proprietors of knowledge that society considers to be transcontextual, intellectuals in the West are divided into scientific/technical and managerial strata, bureaucrats, elite cultural and marginalized humanistic intellectuals. The key argument against viewing these strata as a class is, to be sure, a Marxian one: There does not exist in the West any principle or

structure that could homogenize their interests and unify the centrifu-
gal tendencies of the stratification mechanisms at work here. Moreover,
the principles that legitimate the privileged status of some sectors of
intellectuals—professionalism plus the culture of critical discourse—
must compete with others whose force is hardly spent: private property
and political representation of pluralities within a parliamentary state.
Despite the redistributive mechanisms of state intervention, it is *within*
the framework of the separation of state and civil society and the continued importance of the market that professionalism acquires the
force of a legitimating ideology for intellectual privilege. Only Gouldner's confusion of privilege with the locus and logic of power enabled
him to assert the dominance and class status of intellectuals in the
West.[36]

Obviously, the thesis that intellectuals form a class in state socialism
rests on the claim to have found precisely such a homogenizing, unifying principle and mechanism. For Konrad and Szelenyi, the ideological
principle of "teleological rational redistribution," together with the
central planning mechanism of a state that has thoroughly penetrated
civil society, carries out this function. Instead of pursuing the theme
of the "primacy of the political," however, our authors focus on the
political/economic function of the planner/redistributor. Control over
and distribution of the surplus remains the key to their class analysis.
Stratification is thus analyzed in traditional Marxian categories. This
bias distorts the stratification theory as well as the critique of intellectuals.

Although it is conceded that only one sector of the dominant class
of intellectuals rules—the estatelike political bureaucracy of the party
—the presence of the structure of central planning is viewed as the
locus from which a class interest to rule is imputed to all intellectuals.
The fusion of telos (goal positing) and techne, state and society, allegedly inherent in the structural position of redistributive central
planning, locates the source of all privilege and power in a single structure. Technical, managerial, bureaucratic, and humanistic intellectuals
are enclosed in the embrace of the system from which their advantages
derive vis-à-vis the other main class of society—the direct producers.
Despite power struggles among the various factions, Szelenyi and Konrad argue that the new intellectual class shares the legitimating ideology of "rational redistribution" and planning, for it is this structure
that justifies claims to superiority and privilege of intellectual positions.
The defense of this ideology is also in the interest of those seeking to

replace the party elite. Indeed, with a view to the future, Konrad and Szelenyi argue that the principle of rational redistribution would be fully consistent with the class power of intellectuals only in a technocracy.[37] Only if the scientific/technical sector of the new intellectual class displaced the old party elite and itself occupied the key power positions in the state, abolishing irrational political criteria in enterprise management, would the class power of intellectuals and their legitimating principles be fully reconciled. We have thus come full circle. A teleological two-class model opposing those who control the surplus to the direct producers reappears at the heart of the analysis.

The fundamental flaw in this approach, to be attributed directly to the method of Marxian class theory it employs, is the confusion of two rather different structures and principles of stratification. The structural position of "rational redistributor" obeys a political/economic logic (planning) that is not adequately distinguished from the "primacy of the political," or the penetration of civil society by the state and of the state by the party. Although each subordinates techne to telos, the goals of efficient expanded reproduction (planning) and expansion and duplication of the state structure (primacy of the political) are not identical. The point at issue here is that, whereas the "post-Marxist" impulse of Szelenyi and Konrad points to the state as *the* stratifying mechanism, their Marxist structuralist analysis reduces this insight to the observation that the state as economic actor, as planner, creates a hierarchy of income and privilege. Only the economic function of the state is addressed here, not its political dynamic. Were these authors really to get at the unique features of stratification in statist systems, they would have to focus on the *political* logic of centralization and appropriation of *power* and the suppression of any and all counterpowers (publics, unions, voluntary associations, etc.).[38] It is the primacy of the political, not planning, that requires the total abolition of an autonomous civil society. Here is a principle of stratification quite different from the political/economic issue of distribution of and control over the surplus product, however the two might be related. The "bureaucratic" bearers of this political principle, however, are recognized only sociologically, not in terms of structure and logic.

There is thus a persistent ambiguity as to whether the redistributor/ planner or the party is the principle of unity for the dominant groups. The state socialist system is not analyzed in terms of the two often noncomplementary stratification principles, for, as we know, Marxian class theory allows only one core structure per system—hence the view that the present party-state is transitional to the pure system of rational redistribution, with the odd implication that only the central planner, not the party, is a structural feature of the system.

The theory of an intellectual class thus prevents an adequate articulation of the stratification and structure of statist systems. Like its counterpart in the West, this approach leaves one with no means to address the needs and struggles of those challenging the system. Indeed, the analysis rejoins Gouldner's in the rejection of all appeals to universal norms and transcendence as the ideology of intellectuals on the road to class power. This leaves the critic of intellectual hubris and pretension with a dilemma. The culture of critical discourse is reduced to a particular, critique is denuded of its project to articulate universal values, knowledge is relativized and situated vis-à-vis a class. Accordingly, the author's own critical intentions are severely impaired, for the attack on any reference to universality as covert substitutionalism implies that the intellectual should articulate only his own particular interests. One is left with the arbitrary choice of defending the particular interests of a group or groups against the particular interests of those in power. Konrad and Szelenyi choose to embrace the particular interests of the "direct producer." Unlike their Marxist predecessors, however, they can claim neither the universality of the class nor the certainty of history nor morality as the basis of their choice. Even their advocacy of the reconstitution of civil society (in a socialist form) is disarmed by their insistent antiuniversalism and their reduction of immanent critique to techniques that unmask particular interests. For a socialist civil society, in which the particular interests of all strata could be articulated and publics and self-managing organizations permitted, would have to rest on universal principles of nonexclusion, democratic participation, individual rights, and so on. I shall argue in this book that no adequate theory of civil society is possible on the basis of Marxian class theory—hence the tensions in this best of all versions of the theory of the new intellectual class.

The self-hatred of genuine critical intellectuals gives ammunition to those who hate the intellect and who oppose critique. The attack on the culture of critical discourse from the left has the unintended consequence of reinforcing the arguments of the New Right proliferating in contemporary Western societies. It is, of course, granting too much to call the complaints about the rise of a new intellectual class raised by such neoconservatives as Lionel Trilling, Irving Kristol, Seymour Martin Lipset, David Bazelon, Aaron Wildavsky, Jeanne Kirkpatrick, and others a *theory* at all,[39] but it is certainly a powerful ideology with a very obvious political thrust. A *quasi-Marxist class construct* is used to attack the redistributive mechanisms of the welfare state (excluding those aiding corporations) and to stigmatize all (other) critics of the status quo as either Nietzschean anarchists out to discredit all authority or self-serving power seekers concerned with consolidating and expanding their own class dominance.

There is certainly nothing new in conservative attacks on intellectuals.[40] What *is* new about the recent neoconservative broadside is the clever use of Marxian formula to discredit social movements concerned with emancipation, egalitarian ideals, social justice, and political freedom. Indeed, the theory of a new intellectual class is a response to a feared breakdown of the stratification system in capitalist society that has justified, until now, forms of domination and inequality. Indeed, what is referred to with alarm as the dissolution of the work ethic, the new narcissism, the loss of respect for authority, if taken together with the theory of the new intellectual class, can be seen as an effort to resolve the crisis of integration in an authoritarian and regressive direction.[41]

The theories of the new intellectual class thus create strange bedfellows. If we add the neo-Leninist approach of the Ehrenreichs[42]—a defense of the proletariat against the power-hungry professional/managerial class—the circle is completed. The obvious response to such confusion should be that the concept of class, whether in the form of a refurbished, revised, or distorted Marxism, cannot come to grips with the phenomena addressed.

None of the four types of neo-Marxian class theory has attempted to critically assess the fundamental presuppositions of the original Marxian synthesis. Instead, each approach extracts a particular aspect of the class theory as the basis of a revised class analysis for contemporary society. I have tried to show how, in each case, the absence of a critical analysis of the theory as a whole prevents an adequate, nondogmatic assessment of new forms of stratification, social movements, and state/society relations. In what follows, therefore, I differentiate the philosophical, sociological, and systemic elements of the Marxian theory that inform Marx's concept of class. Through an immanent critique of the theory, I seek to distinguish those dimensions that can be either directly continued or, more likely, used heuristically to guide future work in critical stratification theory.

Chapter 1

Civil Society and Its Discontents

For Marx, the duality of state and civil society is the hallmark of modernity.[1] On the basis of this never-abandoned theoretical framework, Marx developed a theory of the specifically *modern* principle of stratification—socioeconomic class relations. The distinction between state and civil society also served as the underlying basis for his pathbreaking analysis of the capitalist mode of production as a *system* with its own internal dynamics, logic of development, and crisis tendencies. To be sure, Marx inherited the concept of civil society from his most important teacher and predecessor, G. W. F. Hegel,[2] but Marx's attitude toward civil society was both less apologetic and more ambivalent than that of Hegel. Thus, for Marx, the emergence and development of civil society could appear simultaneously as the sine qua non for freedom, autonomy, individuality, and social justice and as the basis for new forms of domination, restriction, alienation, and inequality. The vicissitudes of this concept within Marx's oeuvre, the gains and losses involved in his selective appropriation and critique of Hegel's theory of civil society, have crucial bearing on the class theory, the theory of revolution, and the various models of the communist future he developed. Moreover, the concept of civil society is crucial to Marxian methodology, for the object of investigation, the concept of ideology, and the method of analysis employed all shift according to *changes* in the interpretation of civil society.

An underlying assumption of my discussion is that any attempt to "save" Marx by extracting a specific method (or period) as the "true" one, be it a Marxian philosophy, science, or critique, can achieve coherence only at the price of misunderstanding the deep-seated antinomies in his work—antinomies that the class theory seems to but, as we will see, does not resolve. On the other hand, any analysis that traces the development of Marx's class theory in relation to changes in his concept of civil society implies a periodization of Marx's oeuvre as a whole. It will be clear from the following that I classify Marx's texts into the following periods: the critique of civil society prior to 1844; the first critique of political economy in 1844; the theory of historical materialism, 1845–57; and the systemic theory of capitalist development in the *Grundrisse* and *Capital*, 1857–83. But let me stress at the outset that neither a concern for Marxist philology nor political instrumentalism underlies this periodization. Unlike the series of Marx interpretations beginning with the official Communist position of the 1930s, I do not wish to argue either for the continuity of Marx's work as a whole or that the "real," "Marxist" Marx begins only with a certain period or theory.[3] Instead, I will focus on and explain the antinomies of method and assumptions pervading Marx's work. Through an immanent critique I show that each new period can be grasped as an attempt to develop solutions or alternatives to problems arising in previous formulations of the critique of civil society—problems that the class theory both occasions and, through corresponding shifts, responds to.

At stake are theoretical and political issues that transcend mere Marxology. If Marxism remains one of the most influential theories of modernity, if it still functions as a powerful ideology of modernization in developing countries, it nevertheless fails to provide an adequate theoretical framework to account for the highly differentiated structure of advanced Western societies or to inform the variety of social movements proliferating therein. An important reason for this failure can be located in Marx's conception of civil society and the class analysis. His impressive theory of the organizing principle of the economy—the wage labor/capital relation—was accomplished at the price of identification of civil society with its most important historical manifestation, capitalism. Never having examined the heterogeneous origins or institutionalization of civil society, Marx identified modernity with capitalism, assuming that the logic of capitalism would stamp its form on all social relations. In a sense, social, political, private, and legal institutions were treated as the environment of the capitalist system, to be transformed by its logic but without a dynamism of their own. The analysis that linked economic categories and social classes into a totalizing system logic vitiated the insight into the differentiated character of modern civil society and the state. This remains the Marxian legacy, perpetuated above all by the class theory.

Compared with the richness of the institutional articulation of civil society, the state, and their interrelation offered by Hegel, Marx's analysis seems quite impoverished. Hegel excelled in grasping the "positive side" of the emergence of civil society; Marx's main contribution consisted in accounting for its "negative side"—the new forms of domination and stratification proliferating on its terrain. Nevertheless, although Hegel's understanding of the latter was inadequate, he provided the general parameters of the problems to which Marx presented his class theory as the solution. *Bürgerliche Gesellschaft*, or civil society, was differentiated by Hegel into the following: the system of needs (a market economy); the system of law (*Rechtspflege*, or the administration of justice securing civil liberties and protection from arbitrariness); and the system of pluralities—a network of associations and public administration (corporations and police).[4]

For Hegel, the internal differentiation of civil society, as well as its formal separation from the state, constituted the basis on which the principle of free, self-determining individuality with a claim to satisfaction and autonomy emerged. But he also knew that this principle was concretized in the form of privatized individuals whose needs appear as conflicting self-interests that threaten ethical communal life in a war of each against all to attain satisfaction.[5] Hegel argued that the division of labor, the system of private property and exchange, and the concomitant social determination of needs as infinitely expandable result in the universal interdependence of members of civil society. This interdependence makes itself felt, however, not in the form of conscious cooperation but as external necessity. Interdependence takes the form of economic laws stemming from the framework of competition and the division of labor that force the individual to instrumentally calculate, *for the sake of his own interest*, the interests of others. Unlike classical liberals, however, Hegel understood that the price of general prosperity was the sacrifice of ethical life to market rationality.[6] The "invisible hand" of economic laws, extolled by political economists, rests on exclusion from the internal dynamic of civil society of activity oriented toward any principle other than self-interest (e.g., concern for the general interest or the goals of society at large). In the absence of a higher unity, the principle of self-determining personality resolves into the abstract freedom of the egoistic proprietor who necessarily treats others as means and whose fate depends on the external influence of lawlike economic relations.

Hegel presumed to have found a partial resolution to the antagonistic system of needs and the threat of fragmentation and disintegration of civil society in the countervailing tendency of individuals to become members of groups that affirm general over particular interests and generate forms of social solidarity and consciousness. This was the function of the corporations and the rational administration of justice by the guardians of social welfare—the police.[7] By integrating the individual into group structures, and by defending both property rights and group interests, these institutions allegedly mediate between the isolated and egoistic individual and the higher ethical community of the state, itself oriented solely to universality. They do so by providing a communal basis to which the individual can relate in a way other than that of pure self-interest.[8]

But Hegel's recognition of the importance of the "symbolic"—meanings, values, norms, and their institutional articulation—to ethical life, to the formation of social solidarity and a stable political community, took the form of an analysis that privileged those institutions and traditions that could effectively integrate civil society and the state (individual and collectivity) over those that could assure political freedom. Hegel's theory of civil society was a response to what he saw as the main danger of natural right theory embodied in Jacobinism (especially the Rousseauian model)—namely, the absence of intermediary institutions between the individual and the state and the possibility of terror precisely in the name of the "people," or "the citizen" against the individual.[9] He thus rejected the principles of popular sovereignty, general will, and parliamentary democracy as well as direct democracy based on "one man, one vote." In their place, he presented a plurality of intermediary organizations and a complicated system of estate and corporate representation, whose function it was to protect personal liberties, provide limits to arbitrariness, and secure universality (the general interest, public virtue). The principles of natural right theory were preserved in a depoliticized form (the system of abstract right) that secured the private sphere of social exchange and civil liberty without the individualist postulate of contractarianism. At the same time he sought to reintroduce the "ethical substance of community" to social and political life (which he saw as the fundamental contribution of the Greek polis to the historical unfolding of freedom), but without the concomitant participatory democracy of the citizenry.

Hegel, of course, must be credited with the discovery that the systematic tendency of modern civil society is to replace ethical interaction and social solidarity with interest-oriented action and to establish a gulf between riches at one end of the social spectrum and poverty at the other.[10] But what concerned Hegel far more than the plight of the poor or the inequalities of civil society was the threat to social integration entailed in the development of the market system and the danger of the exercise of arbitrary political power by the state. Moreover, what distinguished Hegel's assessment and solution of the problems of civil society from the philosophers of the Enlightenment (and from Tocqueville) was his ambivalence toward *public opinion*. He viewed the free expression of public opinion as the sine qua non for a "rational political order" and a free civil society, but it was also the potential vehicle of error, ignorance, and irrational mass politics. Instead of trying to identify institutions within civil society in which a rational public opinion could be formed, in which an informed political will could be generated and participation in public life assured for the member of civil society, Hegel affirmed the principle of publicity only as the right of the private individual to express his personal opinion and to be informed of the results of political action by others. He restricted participation in a politically functioning public sphere to members of the estate-constituted legislature. As such, the principle of public opinion was transformed from a potential critical power and mediator between individual and state into a mechanism of integration from above.[11]

Hegel's ambivalence toward public opinion and his antidemocratic stance explain his choice of the estate form of political participation and the corporation as the means of providing the atomized, egoistic, interest-oriented elements of civil society with stable organizational forms and educating the isolated individual toward larger group identity. Far from preparing the citizen for active political participation in a democratic polity (far from affording experience in the *vita activa*), however, the virtue acquired through the school of the corporation (a nonpolitical interest group, albeit legally established) served the task only of social integration, fostering identity with the group and the state (patriotism) of essentially *privatized* individuals.[12] This should come as no surprise, for what charmed Hegel in ancient Greece was not the vita activa or democratic participation with its corresponding centrality of public opinion, but *Sittlichkeit*, the effectivity of cultural norms, values, and customs that serve social integration.[13]

Marx's criticism of the corporate organization of civil society and the estate form of representation is well known. For Marx, the drawback of the Hegelian system of corporations and estates is not simply that they are anachronistic but that they run counter to the crucial principles of civil society uncovered by Hegel himself.[14] The stability attained through the institutionalization of voluntary associations as corporations requiring state recognition and representation of the state bureaucracy on their councils—that is, the closure achieved through group representation of civil society in the state via the estate system—fatally undermines the independence of civil society, whose principles are individuality, *free association*, and self-organization.

The successful critique of Hegel's system of mediations between civil society and the state, however, led Marx to assume, erroneously, that there are no significant countervailing tendencies to the system of needs and that the *function* as well as the *form* of mediating institutions is either ineffectual or anachronistic.[15] Marx rejected both the liberal and the Hegelian versions of political freedom that restricted political will formation to action *within* the institutions of the state. Both were the epitome of political alienation. But he inherited Hegel's formulation of the problem of civil society—the war of each against all in the conflict to satisfy opposing particular interests—while rejecting the corporate solution. Once "class" and "social relations" became *the* concepts for the new modern sociality of civil society, however, any interrogation of the potentiality of pluralities to attain forms of "public freedom" within the institutional framework of civil society, as distinct from and *in addition to* formal democratic representation within the state, was blocked. In effect, by rejecting Hegel's institutional solution to the problems of the modern order, Marx threw out the baby with the bathwater. All institutions of civil society were deemed unacceptable. This led Marx to radicalize the opposition between a totally fragmented civil society and the state (mediated only through class oppression) and to locate in the *future* (both in time and in structure) a solution to contradictions that would involve some form of *reunification* of political and social life.

Marx's insight into the depoliticization of civil society with its separation from the state, together with his epochal discovery that the legal articulation of modern society and the formal democracy of the modern state veiled the particular interests of a particular class, set the problematic for his theoretical and political project. His antipathy toward those structures that seemed responsible for egoistic particularity, domination, and exclusion (the market and the state) occasioned his search for the universal within a particular agent, able to abolish both alleged sources of interest antagonism. Instead of seeking to articulate an institutional structuration of civil society and the state that would be universal insofar as it allowed the formulation of *all* interests and the participation of *all* pluralities in sociopolitical life challenging the state's monopoly of politics, he sought an embodiment of universality within a particular class. In order to understand how the class concept developed as Marx's understanding of the systemic relations of domination deepened, it thus is crucial to trace the fate of his concept of civil society. Only then can one grasp the impact this problematic had on all of Marxism—namely, the hatred of civil society, presumed to be identical with capitalist domination, and the development of a revolutionary ideology geared to the abolition of both capitalism and civil society. If there is a link between Marxism and authoritarianism, its theoretical basis must be located here.[16]

The "immanent critique" of civil society

Marx originally arrived at a critical concept of class through an immanent critique of the normative claims of the state and civil society as articulated in Hegel's Rechtsphilosophie and in the democratic constitutions of France and the United States.[17] Since the formally democratic state contained the demands of reason insofar as its self-legitimations were the universalistic principles uncovered by philosophy, the task of the critic was to extract the norms of modern political institutions as their truth content (freedom, democracy, equality, justice, personhood, autonomous individuality) and to contrast them to the particular institutional forms that realized them only in part. Immanent critique thus had a dual project: (1) to thematize and open to discussion those normative principles inherent in modern political structures that should inform social and political praxis; and (2) to demonstrate the institutional constraints preventing their actualization in modern society (critique of domination and stratification).

To be sure, in his early writings Marx also makes use of the method of "invertive critique" borrowed from Feuerbach, but to dismiss his early works as being dominated by an essentially Feuerbachian "problematic" is to miss what is new in Marx's theory of civil society.[18] The invertive critique consists of a rejection of Hegel's speculative panlogism, that is, the eagerness to find reason in the world and the primacy given to theory or logic over history. This prevented Hegel from considering the real nature of the institutions he investigates, resulting in the apologetic replacement of a critical investigation by philosophy's self-satisfied discovery of itself everywhere.[19] According to Marx, Hegel's panlogical theory is the consequence of his proceeding with the "concept" (Begriff) as subject and reducing individuals and their modes of existence in the family, civil society, and the state to predicates. But Marx does not simply place "man" in that privileged space reserved by Hegel to the concept.[20] It is not an anthropological notion of man but the concept of civil society that constitutes the object of Marx's critique of the state and his transcendence of Feuerbach.[21] The invertive and immanent critiques are related as attempts to come to grips with the experience in everyday life of the inverted and doubled social relations unique to modern society. The contradictory emergence of the individual subject lacking subjectivity, the split of each into a "man" (bourgeois) and a "citizen," the separation of state and society, the atomization and isolation of individuals in civil society alongside their illusory communal existence as members of the state, and the subjugation of men to their own objectified social powers in the form of money constitute a description of the phenomenal forms of social life as experienced in the modern world.

Moreover, although *civil society* means to Marx primarily the *system of needs*, it was not at all at this point identified with what Marx was only later to call its anatomy—labor, or the mode of production. Because Marx had not yet reduced civil society and the state to determination by the economy, he was able through immanent critique to extract the universalistic normative principles of modern society from their ideological shell and to press for their realization in another form. Indeed, Marx agrees with Hegel that civil society, despite its lack of ethical integration, nonetheless presupposes an overriding normative principle unique to the modern world—the *universalistic* principle of free, self-determining, autonomous individuality with equal right to social justice and to attainment of satisfaction.[22] Both the internal legal structuration of civil society and the constitutional, formally democratic state are based on this principle.[23] It is in fact because of the assumption that philosophy has already been realized within the institutions of modern society, because the state and civil society have as their ground of legitimation the universalistic principles uncovered by philosophy, that critique can proceed from forms of empirical social institutions and immanently compare the claims with the institutional forms they legitimate. Immanent critique is thus a particular form of *ideology critique*[24] that extracts the normative principles of modern institutions (without placing primacy on any of them) as their truth content and makes it possible to contrast them to those institutions that systematically falsify their own principles by actualizing them only in part, or not at all.

The method of immanent critique does not entirely displace philosophy, however, despite Marx's famous assertion that philosophy can be overcome (*aufgehoben*) only if it is actualized.[25] Insofar as critique involves the tactic of dissolving those institutional blocks to the realization of philosophy, it implies a philosophical orientation that connects objectified norms to the presupposition of the practical possibility for individuals to institute new social relations that would conform to them. The *Contribution to the Critique of Hegel's Philosophy of Law* does, of course, contain the concepts of *man, alienation,* and *species being,* but they do not play the role that the structuralist interpretation (Althusser) attributes to them.[26] Neither does the "mature" Marx abandon the philosophical framework of his earlier texts. On the contrary, the counterargument to the structuralist interpretation, first propounded by the "socialist humanists," to the effect that the unity of Marx's oeuvre lies in a never-abandoned philosophy of praxis is cogent, with one proviso. The concept of praxis changes along with the concept of civil society in the various periods of Marx's works. In the earliest texts, *praxis* refers to political interaction. By 1844, it signifies primarily objectification. In the later texts its meaning varies between objectification and class struggle.[27]

Insofar as the first critique of civil society is concerned, the "essence of man," praxis, is located by Marx in political sociality, or the capacity for self-determination through interaction with others regarding the affairs of the community. Like the classic political philosophers, the critic of civil society considered the *differentia specifica* of humans to be political action. Accordingly, *participation* by individuals in their political life is the true expression of their humanity.[28] But this notion of "human essence," of praxis, is more an immanent and prescriptive norm than a concept of human nature; it is a *vérité à faire* rather than an eternal attribute of individuals. It plays the role of a regulative principle, a standard in terms of which particular forms of individuality and political and social structures could be evaluated. Like the later critique of alienated labor, the critique of political alienation refers to the separation of individuals from their "species life," taking the form of a critique of the separation of state and civil society as the institutional framework that prevents the active participation of individuals in their social political affairs.

In an extremely adept but fateful argument, Marx claims that the opposition of civil society and the state is the ground for the irreconcilable contradictions between norm and reality, particularity and universality. Whereas the modern state emerges as a network of distinct political institutions claiming universality (parliament, bureaucracy, army, police, courts), its simultaneous precondition and consequence are the emergence of civil society as the sphere consisting of unpolitical individuals united only through private need, interest, and mutual dependence through the division of labor and the market. The price for the achievement of individuality in the newly organized social sphere is its depoliticization, privatization and atomization (the individual as the bourgeois). Through the *monopolization* of political life the state signals both the loss of community and the denial of meaningful citizenship to the members of civil society. Thus "civil society" is Marx's concept of the depoliticization of modern individuality.

The critique of bureaucracy is instructive in this regard. Hegel had argued that universality is embodied in the state bureaucracy and that bureaucrats are a universal class insofar as they represent the will and interests of the community as a whole.[29] According to his model, a modern bureaucracy is freed from the particularistic material interests typical of strata within civil society because it is independent of both property qualifications and financial insecurity. The fixed salary, the career open to talents, the necessity of objective proof of knowledge and ability (examinations), the impersonality of the structure guided by the rule of law, the dispassionate behavior and sense of duty demanded of the bureaucrat, all these meant, for Hegel, that bureaucracy is a meritocracy standing above and protected against particular interests of civil society. He thus assumed that the bureaucracy has no particular interests of its own: It is universal in intent, structure, and social composition.

Marx's critique of this theory pursues two interdependent paths. On the one hand, he argues that, far from being the signs of its universality, the principles of secrecy and hierarchy, the fixed salary, and the requirement of examinations witness the particularity and privilege of modern bureaucracy. This does not mean, however, that bureaucracy is simply another class within civil society. Rather, it is a "castelike" entity located in the political apparatus whose particular interest is the accumulation of power and its own self-expansion. This is the first and last time that Marx analyzes a principle of stratification distinct from classes in terms that do not suggest that its power or logic derives from relations within civil society.[30]

On the other hand, state bureaucracy attests to the depoliticization of civil society and the political alienation of its members, because bureaucracy monopolizes access to and administration of the affairs of the political community. Authority is the basis of its knowledge, not the reverse; the examination requirement is a ritual that expresses the legal recognition of a knowledge of citizenship as a *privilege*.[31] In phrases reminiscent of Tocqueville and Weber, Marx argues that, even when open to any individual who qualifies, the bureaucracy's presence as a hierarchical structure demonstrates that political life resides not within but outside civil society. The presence of the bureaucracy (army, police, administration) reveals state and civil society to be *"two hostile armies, where every soldier has the 'opportunity' to become, by 'desertion,' a member of the 'hostile' army."* [32] Thus bureaucracy violates the universality of the state. It is worth noting that at this stage in Marx's work "universality" refers not to the interests of any group but to norms, law, and institutional structures.

Accordingly, Marx deemed the emergence of the modern state and civil society to be a gain, despite the political alienation involved. The loss of community, the unrestricted egoism of civil society, the incomplete universality of the polity make up the negative side, but the emergence of civil society and the democratic state entail an "increment in freedom." The universalistic norms of citizenship, sovereignty of the people, autonomy, equality, democracy, and so on, assure at least the formal/legal recognition of the individual as a *person* and *citizen* and the disassociation of *status* and *right*. They also establish the principle of political self-determination, a principle that is available to inform social movements against exclusion and political inequality:

The political revolution thereby *abolished* the *political character of civil society*. It broke up civil society into its simple component parts; on the one hand, the *individuals*; on the other hand, the *material* and *spiritual* elements constituting the content and the life and social position of these individuals. It set free the political spirit, which had been, as it were, split up, partitioned and dispersed in the various blind alleys of feudal society. It gathered the dispersed parts of the political spirit, freed it from its intermixture with civil life, and established it as the sphere of the community, the *general* concern of the nation, ideally independent of those *particular* elements of civil life. A person's *distinct* activity and distinct situation in life were reduced to a merely individual significance. They no longer constituted the general relation of the individual to the state as a whole. Public affairs as such, on the other hand, became the general affair of each individual, and the political function became the individual's general function.[33]

Political universalism is thus the major gain afforded by the birth of civil society and the formally democratic state.

It is also the reason for the appearance of the individual as a subject in a double sense. Posited as the self-determining source and ground for political and private life, one is also, as an empirical individual, subject to their laws and regulations. Herein lies the basis for inversion, doubling, or alienation in modern society. As member of the state, the individual is both a "citizen" participating in the determination of communal affairs and a "subject" (*Untertan*), the privatized object of political regulation. As member of civil society, despite or because of one's freedom to determine one's will, the individual is subject to those alien powers (economic laws) that determine his chances, impose an interest structure onto his needs, and deny autonomy in social life.

In his critique of the state, Marx sought to demonstrate that the depoliticization of the individual in his everyday life renders his "communal" life as a citizen formal, abstract, illusory. On the basis of his insight into the unfulfilled promise of civil society, it would seem that the practical task flowing from the immanent critique would be the establishment of an institutional framework that would not reproduce the schizophrenic split of individual/bourgeois, citizen/subject in its invidious form. A consistent version of civil society would, formally speaking, cntail the expansion of the newly emergent social sphere (as autonomous and self-instituting), the maintenance of the formal legality of the state, and the elaboration of public spaces in the institutions of society and state, guaranteeing the chance for open participation of all. The differentiation of roles—individual, citizen, public, private, social—would no longer be invidious in such a context. But because Marx viewed the very separation of state and society to be the *cause* of political alienation, because he saw in the countervailing tendencies to the system of needs (formation of voluntary associations and potential public spaces) *only* the expression of particular egoistic interests (determined by the market), this alternative was closed to him. The various solutions he proposed to the antinomies of modern society—individual versus community, public versus private, particular versus universal, freedom versus domination, equality versus inequality—had one theme in common: the reunification of state and civil society, of man and citizen:

only when the real individual absorbs in himself the abstract citizen . . . , only when man has recognized and organized his "forces propres" as social forces and consequently no longer separates social power from himself in the shape of political power, only then will human emancipation have been accomplished.[34]

Whatever form this vision might take (and Marx always avoided specifics regarding future institutions), its inherent danger is the violation of the autonomy of the social sphere. Oddly enough, Marx alerts us to this very danger in the same text in which the above quote appears. In the context of a critique of Jacobinism, he states:

At times of special self-confidence, political life seeks to suppress its prerequisite, civil society, and the elements composing this society, and to constitute itself as the real species-life of man devoid of contradictions. But it can achieve this only by coming into *violent* contradiction with its own conditions of life, only by declaring the revolution to be *permanent*.[35]

Only by terror. The theme of the reunification of man and citizen, state and civil society, is thus profoundly ambiguous, reflecting the ambivalence of Marx's attitude toward civil society. All of Marxism has been plagued with this ambivalence. This accounts for the curiously antimodern thrust of one of the most penetrating, future-oriented analyses of modernity, namely, the goal of de-differentiating state and society.

There is no question that Marx remained committed to the values of public freedom, democracy, autonomy, and equality, but only in his very earliest texts did he envisage a form of direct democracy based on the further development, rather than the abolition, of civil society—a form that would both protect the individual from and integrate him into society and state through his own active participation.[36] For the most part, however, the insight that modern civil society was "carried" by capitalism, that the modern democratic state fostered bureaucracy, blinded Marx to the heterogeneity of both institutions and pointed to a set of alternatives that either hearkened back to the premodern polis or pointed to a future statist/technocratic version of the reunification of social, communal, political life.[37] He sought to answer the development from the "democracy of unfreedom" (feudalism) to the state monopolization of political life with a stateless, direct democracy of freedom (society as community, political Rousseauianism) or a centrally planned, rationally administered society (Saint-Simonianism). In short, the assumption that the differentiation between state and civil society was the root of the loss of community condemned the Marxian theory of revolution to a vacillation between romanticism and scientistic rationalism. Class theory never transcended this archetypical antinomy of modern rationalization.

The immanent critique of civil society broached a recurrent problem for Marx: that of envisaging a social formation that would provide for individual autonomy on a basis other than capitalist private property as well as for participation in the social and political life of the community without reconstituting it in an alienated form. But the tendency to link the abolition of capitalism with the abolition of civil society led Marx to conceive a future as a total departure from the present, increasingly remote from the institutions and norms (and social movements) uncovered by critique.

Marx's conviction that the state/civil society duality implied the perversion of both by a false universality (bureaucracy and class) led him to search for the *embodiment* of a "true" universality able to reconcile community, society, individuality (the proletariat). This quest overburdened the class theory from the start and diverted Marx from seeking an institutional alternative to the "negative" aspects of modern civil society that could preserve its gains and operate on its own ground—that is, as a social space distinct from and embedding the state and economic apparatus. Like the system he criticized, Marx too tended to dissolve the social (civil society) into social relations of production, or to abstractly negate such reification by identifying the social with "the community" (the two sides of the class concept). As the problem of stratification moved to the center of his analyses, he focused increasingly on its economic rather than its social aspects (mechanisms of distribution, production relations versus reflection on legitimate norms of stratification, plurality, and institutional participatory spaces for their genesis), searching for the logic (of development and revolution) that would abolish mechanisms of stratification altogether. This search underlay the shifts in his concept of civil society, for as Marx began to focus on capitalism as the systematic cause of class, domination, inequality, the focus and method of analysis were altered.

The unmasking and transcendent critiques of civil society

The critique of civil society shifted ground. Although the immanent critique suffered from the absence of an adequate social theory able to account for the systematic character of relations of domination in modern society, it had the advantage of allowing for the distinction between universalistic norms and their ideological or legitimating functions. Its own norms could be situated historically. Simultaneously, the problem of revolutionary praxis as a practical political question involving reflec-

tion on social and political norms and on the institutional forms necessary to realize them could be posed. In the search for the basis on which
socioeconomic relations of inequality and domination are systematically
reproduced, Marx transformed his understanding of civil society as well
as his method of critique. The Paris *Manuscripts* of 1844 mark a major
turning point in Marx's work, not simply because they resulted from
his first confrontation with political economy but, above all, because
they signal a new approach to the analysis of civil society.[38] The introduction of the dualistic concept of labor (objectifying praxis/historically
specific wage labor)[39] as the unifying and active center of both civil
society and history occasions the transformation. The first critique
(1844) of political economy is no longer an immanent one (confrontation of norm with "reality"); civil society becomes analyzed in terms of
its "anatomy"—labor and class relations. The concept of ideology and
the method of its critique are radically altered.

The fundamental difference between the concept of civil society here
and previously lies in the reconstitution of its definitive representations
—the system of needs, legal relations, the egoistic individual—as the
surface expressions of a deeper reality: the labor/property relation. The
issue is no longer the thematization of the separation of state and civil
society but the analysis of what lies hidden beneath the surface appearances of conflicting interests, exchange, and political forms. The question has become that of the deeper organizing principle of the visible
relations. The thrust of the critique of political economy in the *Manuscripts* is not the contrast between norm and reality but the uncovering
of the structure of domination in the wage labor/property relation and
the exposure of political economy as an ideology of legitimation. I call
this method an "unmasking" critique. It has three basic attributes: It
reveals the internal contradictions within political economic theory; it
articulates the unexamined presuppositions of this "science/ideology";
and it attempts to speak to a set of "radical needs" generated within
capitalism that point to its transformation in a progressive direction.
Political economy is the privileged object of this critique, because it has
addressed, albeit inadequately, the organizing principle of civil society:
the labor/property relation. The "economics" of political economy are,
in short, the economics of capitalism.

The central contradiction of political economy, and of the society it
theorizes, is the positing of labor as the source of all wealth, while the
amassing of wealth and the increase of productivity condemn the worker
to poverty, dependence, and alienation.[40] The fundamental unexamined

presuppositions of political economy—the laws of competition, exchange, profit, accumulation, property—are presented as ahistorical, natural "facts"; they are not accounted for historically or systematically.[41] However, because civil society is now understood by Marx in terms of the underlying wage labor/property relation, the critique of presuppositions can no longer be oriented to those normative principles expressed but not realized in its institutions. The norms of political economy do not contradict its posture but confirm it. Frugality, sobriety, thrift, work, acquisition, self-interest—these are the proclaimed ethics of political economy that serve to complement its laws. If, as Marx points out, one claims that greed and self-interest are immoral or purely economic motives, one is applying standards from another sphere (religion, philosophy) that do not relate to the theory involved. To use Max Weber's phrase, the inner-worldly asceticism of political economy is not the renunciation of all ethics but the expression of moral laws in a political economic form.

Because the norms of this "science" confirm its premises and because Marx has not yet formed a developmental theory of capitalism, he is unable to ground the vision of an emancipated society in the analysis of its anatomy. The recognition that the attempt to create democracy through political will by the imposition of a "Spartan frugality" on the population must fail leads Marx to the conclusion that theory can be realized in a people only insofar as it is the realization of the *needs* of that people.[42] The task of critique thus becomes the identification of those needs (and their bearers) that capitalism systematically creates but cannot satisfy. It is in this context that the theory of alienation and the concept of praxis acquire a new meaning and, insofar as both are linked to a teleological philosophy of history, a new function. The famous discussion of alienated labor not only refers to the experience of the wage worker in capitalist society but presupposes a philosophical concept of labor as objectification (the dualistic concept of labor). The philosophical concept of praxis now refers to labor-as-objectification— the historical creativity of individuals that constitutes their needs as well as their products, social relations, culture, and institutions. It is a normative and future-directed concept that allows Marx to totalize history as alienation from the standpoint of the practical activity of future self-constituted subjectivity.[43] This model of human activity provides the foundation for a *transcendent* critique of political economy as a reductionist, economistic ideology. For, in addition to the critique that assumes the standpoint of its object (political economy) to reveal its internal contradictions, Marx evaluates the categories of political economy—above all, wage labor—from the transcendent position of species activity. He denounces the reductionist logic of political economy (and capitalism) that views the individual who labors as a working animal, an instrument of production, and reduces social relations to abstract economic laws.[44]

Nevertheless, the synthesis between philosophy and political economy through critique is a tenuous one. Because the critique of the new concept of civil society has taken the form of an unmasking critique, the philosophy of history and praxis must be seen as an alternative attempt to ground the now transcendent normative principles for an emancipated society in an abstract transhistorical dialectic. Moreover, once the speculative and eschatological character of this dialectic is pointed out,[45] one confronts the disadvantages of a critique of political economy that cannot adequately ground its norms. Nor can it argue for the objective possibility of the realization of its project, for there are no compelling reasons given either for the *choice* of an alternative future (absence of a political philosophy) or for the *probability* of communism appearing as the solution to the crisis tendencies of capitalism (absence of a theory of capitalist development).[46]

Even if one interprets the theory of praxis and alienation as a normative one rather than attributing to it a concept of human nature,[47] even if one grants that its function is to articulate the "meaning" of history as a practical task and a concept of communism that is normative, the charge of teleology is unavoidable. The link of the concept of objectification (continuous development of the powers and needs of the species) to a philosophy of history entails an evolutionary bias that projects standards and attributes of the present onto past and future. Two models of development are confused here. One refers to the unfolding of the productive capacities of mankind, or technological development and control of nature. The other refers to progress in the formative process of human beings in which personality is enriched by the increasing circle of objectifications (art, philosophy, ethics, needs, abilities) available for each successive generation.[48] They are fused insofar as development in the sense of overcoming the limits of nature is seen as the precondition for the full self-development of individuals. The drawbacks of this approach are of two sorts. The first is the illegitimate projection of the logic of objectification as continuous development of needs, capacities, and control out of its historical context within modern civil society onto the past and future as the principle of historicity per se.[49] This is false for precapitalist systems, and catastrophic (ecologically) as a logic for the future if it implies, as it too often does in Marxism, the unimpeded expansion of production. The second drawback of this approach lies in its proposing a notion of progress that is too absolute, which allows for no losses within the realm of value creation, symbolic meaning, and so on.[50]

In his subsequent writings, Marx offers two alternatives to this dilemma, each of which, as I shall show, is unsuccessful. The first emerges in the theory of historical materialism that seeks to substitute a more "concrete" theory of historical evolution for the philosophy of history described above. Within the framework of this theory, material production replaces the dualistic concept of labor, becoming the center of a new concept of civil society and a new method, "science," that purports to demonstrate the objective necessity of communism as the next stage in historical development. In the *Grundrisse* and *Capital*, on the other hand, the concept of alienation is historicized; the dialectic is taken out of history and placed within the internal framework of a developmental theory of capitalism. Let me briefly trace the implications of these shifts for Marx's theoretical and practical project.

Science and society

The immanent critique of the state/civil society duality had pointed to bureaucracy and social classes as the two historically specific forms of inequality and domination that challenged the universalistic claims of formal democracy and the market economy. But the immanent critique neither dismissed the norms it uncovered as mere mystifications nor reduced the political institutions legitimated by them to epiphenomenal forms of economic relations. The consequences of the turn to historical materialism for Marx's class theory and for his analysis of civil society, the state, and ideology, were both momentous and disastrous. The concept of *mode of production* replaces *civil society* as the object of critique, and the concept of civil society is alternately dehistoricized to refer to all "civilized" societies and/or understood as "bourgeois," that is, identified fully with capitalist production and exchange relations when referring to modernity.[51] As the correlate of the forces/relations model of production the concept of class is projected backward as the motor of all history and presented as the key to the understanding of relations of domination and struggles for emancipation in all dynamic "historical" societies. As we will see, this approach vitiated Marx's original insight into what was peculiar about class and precluded an investigation of nonclass forms of domination, stratification, and differentiation.[52]

Marx's identification of civil society with the capitalist mode of production has consequences for the concept of critique and the theory of ideology. The method of analysis internal to the theory of historical materialism is presented as science. Accordingly, critique loses its primacy and ideology, its truth content. Having identified production as the fundamental activity through which the world is constituted, Marx extended the concepts of *mode of production* and *division of labor* to account for all institutional forms, "in the last instance." The introduction of the base/superstructure model according to which the state, law, and ideology are mere epiphenomenal expressions of the mode of production serves to dissolve the rich opposition of state and civil society discussed earlier. The state, law, civil liberties, universality appear as ideological expressions of bourgeois property relations serving to protect capitalist interests rather than guaranteeing individuality, personhood, citizenship, and the like. The truth of the citizen is now the bourgeois, *tout court*.

The fundamental character of ideology, then, is that it is pure illusion. Understood in terms of the division of labor (mental labor), ideology is the illusion of consciousness that it is independent of the social conditions in which it emerges.[53] Devoid of truth content, ideology is either a distorted conception of history (history of politics, law, science, morality, ideas) or a complete abstraction from it.[54] Accordingly, the "critique" of ideology cannot take the form of revealing its true normative principles or of demonstrating the internal contradictions of its assumptions. (It is worth noting here that, having embraced the idea of a scientific theory of society and economy and having exonerated the natural sciences from the status of ideology, the one set of "bourgeois" theory not criticized as ideology in this theoretical approach is political economy!) Critique of ideology is reduced to the vitriolic criticism of its illusory pretensions. Serving the ruling classes by veiling their specific interests in the guise of universality, ideology comprises politics, law, philosophy, ethics, and so on.[55] "Real relations" between individuals are now comprehended by Marx as relations of *production*. Being a mental product that is illusory, being false consciousness, ideology is not subjected to an immanent critique; instead, Marx rejects its claims and *counterposes to it* the science of modes of production or historical materialism. This science, modeled on a positivistic understanding of the natural sciences, according to Marx, proceeds empirically to bring out the connection of the social and political structure of society with production. It is thus presented as the positive substitute for ideology. This "hard-nosed" realism is accompanied by the assumption that the proletariat is a universal class and thus needs no ideology. It requires only scientific theory—Marxism. It should come as no surprise that the models of communism associated with this theory are either romantic/utopian (the Renaissance ideal of the well-rounded individual freed from the division of labor in *The German Ideology*) or statist/authoritarian.

The positivistic bias of the science of historical materialism has been pointed out by many.[56] To be sure, the structuralist reading of historical materialism heralds the theory as a break with the "anthropological" and "empiricistic" problematic informing the earlier works and their substitution with a science of social relations.[57] For structuralists, philosophy enters into the theory only as the metatheoretical explication of the scientific/structural mode of analysis (theory of theoretical practice). I would argue, however, that the extension of the concept of *mode of production* as the key to the analysis of history by no means indicates the transcendence of the philosophy of praxis. Rather, it rests on a notion of "man" that privileges his material production above all other forms of activity as the determining motor force in history and civil society. Moreover, the exorcism of man as subject leads not to a more scientific analysis but rather to his replacement with a reified subject—the autonomous movement of structures.[58] The structuralist interpretation conceives societal reality as a (false) totality, viewing it only as object, as a finished result consisting of objective structures (sociologism). Indeed, the drawbacks of the structuralist interpretation parallel those of the methodological approach of historical materialism itself: The dehistoricization of the concept of civil society, together with the base/superstructure model, precludes a critical analysis of the historically specific, form-giving, but also *fetishistic* categories of capitalist production relations. Moreover, by conceptualizing the "scientific" theory of the "mature" Marx as historical materialism, the structuralist approach is blinded to the shift in methodology (mode of critique) and in the object of analysis that distinguishes the second critique of political economy (*Capital*) from historical materialism.

The defetishizing critique

Marx's overextension of the concepts of mode of production and, as we will see, class through the forces/relations dialectic applied to all of history is, however, no longer characteristic of the mature critique of political economy. Here the stage theory of historical evolution is replaced by an analysis of social formations that distinguishes between *logic* and *historical genesis*. More important, the dialectic is taken out of history and located within an analysis of the systemic and developmental dynamics of capitalism.[59] A new form of critique emerges in the later texts that is to be distinguished both from the immanent critique of the state and the unmasking and transcendent critiques of political economy in 1844. For the concept of fetishism, linked to the developmental theory (a new form of science) of capitalism, introduces a conception of ideology that requires a mode of critique that goes far beyond the thrust of the 1844 texts. At the same time, the concept of civil society is rehistoricized but never regains the richness of the earlier works, remaining identified with its depth structure—capitalist production relations. Accordingly, the tensions and antinomies that inform Marx's writings as a whole take on a specific form in the late works that delimits the problems besetting the class theory as well as the attempted solutions to these problems.

To be sure, many of Marx's statements regarding his own work contradict the above assertions. One would be hard pressed to find a distinction between historical materialism and the critique of political economy in the published prefaces to the 1859 *Contribution to the Critique of Political Economy* and to volume 1 of *Capital*. The primacy of material production, the base/superstructure model, the extension of the forces/relations contradiction to all of history, the deterministic theory of revolution and the evolutionistic stage theory of societal development, all reappear in the context of Marx's reflections on his own path of intellectual development toward scientific theorizing. Moreover, the notion of "necessity" attached to historical development and the concept of science reappears in regard to the "natural laws" of capitalist reproduction and the inevitability of not yet fully industrialized societies having to follow the path of the most advanced capitalist country, England.[60]

Nevertheless, we do not have to make Marx's self-understanding our own. Indeed, we can partly base our argument for the transcendence of the theory of historical materialism on Marx himself by reference to the methodological introduction to the *Grundrisse* (unpublished during Marx's life). Here Marx distinguishes between historical genesis and systemic analysis with reference to the difference between the emergence in history of the capitalist system that cannot be analyzed through the categories of that system and the systemic logic itself, which presupposes the historical presence of capitalism.[61] He states that, in order to construct a theoretical system of concepts adequate to the present dynamics of the capitalist system, one must be guided by their articulation (*Gliederung*) in *modern civil society*.[62] More important is Marx's rejection of historical analyses that proceed from a concept of *labor in general* to establish the common importance to all societies of economics (or the mode of production). Such an approach would miss the essential differences between social formations by imposing categories of the present system analysis onto the past.[63] With this Marx implicitly distinguishes his late works from political economy, from his own earlier theory of historical materialism, and, I would add, from the structuralist interpretation.

The distinction between logic and genesis implies that the dialectic (forces/relations, abstract/concrete, essence/appearance) is no longer projected onto all of history but is seen as the logic only of capitalism. The limitation of the dialectic to the internal dynamics of capitalism is based on the presupposition that only there is activity socialized so as to render it systematic, fetishistic, calculable, or rationalized. For the first time the economy emerges as a systemic totality whose reproductive logic is fundamental to the reproduction of social relations; individuals become subordinated to the economy. The socialization of society (*Vergesellschaftung*) is, as Lukacs noted, a uniquely capitalist phenomenon that expresses its systemic character insofar as it integrates production and exchange in society as a whole and reduces individual actors to their representative roles (character masks) of the basic system categories.[64] Correspondingly, the theory of alienation as the separation of individual and species development is historicized and can no longer play the role of a philosophy of history. Marx now identifies production for the sake of production (rather than for the satisfaction of needs) as the systematic cause for the separation of the development of species capacities from the enrichment of the abilities and needs of individuals.[65] In addition, with the restriction of the concept of labor-in-general to capitalist society (abstract labor), the evolutionist theory of historical materialism loses its basis and is abandoned.

The claim still could be made that the analysis in *Capital* is nothing other than a science of the structure of the capitalist mode of production.[66] But I want to argue that the method of *Capital* as well as the relation between system and class posited there by Marx cannot be comprehended without the recognition that, in addition to its status as a (social) science, it is also a *critique with specific philosophical presuppositions*. Moreover, insofar as the methods of science, critique, and philosophy are not united in a smooth whole but conflict with one another, only a critical rather than a justificatory analysis of these texts could clarify the problematic status of the class analysis to be found there.[67]

Insofar as there is a "scientific" moment to *Capital*, it must refer to the theory of capitalist development and crisis tendencies as well as to the mode of presentation (*Darstellung*) or unfolding of the concept of capital.[68]

Thus the Marxian theory is scientific in the sense that any social theory can be said to be so, that is, insofar as it attempts to account for the systematic and lawlike characteristics of its object domain. But "science" here must not be understood in the positivistic sense or as pure theoretical practice—rather, the Hegelian concept of *Wissenschaft* is more apt. In fact, the systematicity of the system disclosed in *Capital* (or the notion of a decentered totality), whose internal logic structures the dialectical unfolding of the categories and their "agents," is precisely the notion of science that is operative in Hegel's *Logic*. The influence of this work permeates the movement of *Capital* as a whole, with the major difference that Marx's analysis does not pretend to be presuppositionless. Instead, Marx presupposes both the categories of political economy and the historical presence of the capitalist system of production. It is worth noting in this context that the difference between understanding the scientific object of *Capital* as a structure and understanding it as a system is more than terminological. For the analysis that unearths a *structure* whose categories—mode of production, forces and relations of production—can be used to analyze precapitalist societies *conflicts* with the approach that unfolds the *system* logic unique to one social formation, capitalism, the first society to appear historically whose socioeconomic relations form a totality.

The charge of historicism can be made to the latter understanding. It can immediately be dispensed with when one observes that the theoretical unfolding of the logic of capitalist development is also a *critique*. This is possible only if the centrality of the concept of fetishism is recognized in the late works. Indeed, the concept of fetishism takes over the function that the concept of alienation had in 1844, both explaining the nontransparency of social relations and affording a critical thrust to the theory of value. The dialectical unfolding of the categories in *Capital*, which involved moving from the contradiction between use and exchange value, the twofold character of labor, commodity fetishism, up through the contradiction of living and dead labor (the capital fetish) and the ghost walks of "Madame la Terre" and "Monsieur le Capital" is rooted in the theory of fetishism.[69]

In addition, the centrality of the concept of fetishism to the late works implies a new concept of ideology that breaks with the version in the theory of historical materialism. As part and parcel of fetishized reality, as the theory that reproduces and reaffirms the commodity and capital fetishes, political economy is the ideology par excellence subjected to critique. Ideology, however, can no longer be understood in the sense of the earlier theory—as mere illusion—but rather is seen as the necessary and correct expression of a *false* reality. Its *defetishizing critique* can thus be identified neither with the muckraking activity of historical materialism nor with the norm critique of Marx's earlier writings. But neither is it similar to the unmasking critique of the presuppositions of political economy of the *Manuscripts*. Instead, the new critique takes the form of a theory that unfolds the logic of development of capitalist production as a crisis theory in order to account for the necessity of its ideological appearance in political economy and empirical consciousness, as well as to accomplish, through its very articulation, a defetishization of the frozen categories.[70] The categories of political economy form the basis of the critique because political economy exemplifies the fetishistic modes of experience within capitalism directly: its categories allow comprehension of economic activity and actors only under the form of the object and not as social activity. The very labor theory of value not only serves to articulate the structure of the capitalist mode of production but also is the expression of a fetishistic logic that, for Marx, must be abolished. The thrust of the critique is the overthrow of a system that reduces social relations to the absurdity of calculable value relations between things, commodities.

Far from seeking to develop a closed structural system radically sealed off from the given, the critique of political economy is thus directed at abolishing theoretically its own fetishistic object—the nomological capitalist system—and undermining the historically present conditions of its own possibility as theory. The dynamic of defetishization operative on the theoretical level is indeed referential and has a political thrust. It is aimed at affecting the practice of those whose activity and consciousness are frozen in the fetishized relations of capitalist production —the workers. This means that the philosophy of praxis still informs the late works, although its categories (objectification, alienation) operate in a new way. On the one hand, abundant descriptions of the alienation of labor may be found in these texts that are reminiscent of the descriptions in the earlier 1844 critique of political economy. Far from repeating, however, the attempt of the *Manuscripts* to grasp this alienation directly, by placing it conceptually within a philosophy of history, Marx does not reintroduce alienation *as a category* in *Capital*. Rather, the critical character of the undertaking resides in the presupposition of alienation as a historical *experience* and the construction of a theory that, instead of reproducing this experience in concepts, delves beneath the level of experience to constitute the logic of its overthrow. The experience of alienation by the wage worker reduced to selling his labor power as a commodity, foregoing all control over his activity and product, and subject to the despotism of the capitalist in the factory, is a basic aspect of the capitalist mode of production that allows for the construction of a theoretical system as an antisystem, an inverted system, a critique.[71]

Nevertheless, the political project implied by the praxis philosophical presuppositions still informing the late works raises a number of difficulties. Is the critique of fetishism geared toward the unfolding of a positive theory of development as a crisis theory whose function it is to point to breaks in the system that could indicate objective possibilities for praxis and point to the path the worker must follow in breaking through fetishism—as has been maintained by Lukacs? Or is the function of the totalizing analysis in *Capital* neither to arrive at a positive theory of a structure nor to indicate the path that the potential revolutionary subject must follow but rather to develop an antisystem that theoretically dissolves its object with no claims of mediating between itself and the praxis of its addressees? [72] The former approach still recognizes a scientific moment to *Capital*; the latter rejects it entirely. *We are, in effect, confronting a three-pronged opposition among critique, science, and philosophy inherent in Marx's texts themselves.*

There is a fruitful ambiguity in *Capital* between an approach geared to critique and defetishization and one geared toward developing a positive theory of capitalist development as a more refined political economy able to determine the laws of motion and the crisis tendencies of the system. Neither of these approaches is fully consistent with, or adequately related to, a theory of revolutionary praxis. For one must ask on what basis one can claim that the logic of *Capital*, even if interpreted as fetishistic, is able to identify in one and the same analysis the class whose activity is most systematically reduced to the functions required by capital and the class that will be able to constitute itself through a practical process of enlightenment as *the* revolutionary subject. The groundlessness of this assumption will be discussed in chapter 6. Let me indicate here the relation between the antinomic methodologies of the late works and the concept of civil society informing these texts.

It is undeniable that the late works provided a far more penetrating analysis of the developmental tendencies and contradictions of the capitalist mode of production than anything to be found in the earlier writings. Nevertheless, this gain is accompanied by a fundamental drawback: the reduction of "civil society" to the capitalist mode of production in an even more emphatic form than earlier. Insofar as *Capital* presents the dynamics of production, reproduction, and the transformation of capitalism solely through the critique of political economy, cultural, and juridical subsystems receive only passing comment. In fact, Marx goes so far as to state that capital itself *creates* civil society.[73] Although past history is freed from the tyranny of the dialectic of production, it returns in the analysis of civil society with a vengeance. The base/superstructure model receives a curious transformation such that the sphere of circulation appears as the ideological surface appearance of production relations whose developmental logic increasingly gives the lie to its original presupposition—simple commodity exchange. Both the legal and political forms of modern society and the norms underlying them now appear as the necessary expressions of the sphere of circulation—of exchange relations. The original Hegelian model of civil society integrated through needs and property relations now appears as the juridical reflection of the sphere of circulation in which "free" and "equal" buyers and sellers exchange their commodities for equivalents. The normative principles and institutional supports of civil society are reduced to their ideological content and basis: production relations.[74]

It is this reduction of civil society to the dynamics of the mode of production that is the source of the tension between the critical, philosophical, and systemic moments of Marx's mature work. The separation of system logic from the historical genesis of the system serves to demonstrate the specific historicity of capitalism vis-à-vis the past and the future. But the vision of the future is a contradictory one due to the unresolved tensions in the analysis. On the one hand, the developmental theory of accumulation (which is not an antisystem) implies a model of communism that would preserve the productivist logic of capitalism in a more rationalized form, namely, central planning.[75] On the other hand, the critique of political economy corresponds to a normative model of the future as a community/society of freely associated individuals freed from the structural/functional differentiation that imposed a hierarchy of class relations (workers' control as a productivist and institutionless antimodern utopia). But the latter becomes extremely tenuous given the reduction of civil society and its normative principles and institutional articulation to the status of epiphenomena of bourgeois relations. Social integration through values, norms, noninstrumental motivations is collapsed into system integration (the reproductive logic of socioeconomic relations) with the result that Marx is left with no way to immanently ground a model of the future that could point beyond the economic logic of the present.[76]

The greatest danger, however, in assuming that noneconomic, social norms and institutions have their genesis or "truth" in economic relations lies in the correlative tendency in those who adhere to that assumption to reject the universalistic principles of formal democracy as merely bourgeois and to press for the abolition of civil society altogether. The destruction of the capitalist system seems to require the destruction of civil society (including its legal/institutional underpinnings) as the precondition for the realization of "substantive" freedom and equality. The error in such reasoning lies in the belief that the *formality* of the norms/law is the basis for their lack of substantive realization, instead of understanding that their ideological character lies in their not being formal enough.[77] In other words, the drawback of "bourgeois" society and politics is the presupposition that capitalist property/production relations is the necessary precondition for individuality, freedom, democracy, and so on. The tragedy of modern civil society lies in the attempt to universalize and formalize its norms on the limited basis of capitalism. To reduce these principles even further to the economic basis of civil society is only to bring a logical fallacy to its height of absurdity.

In effect, what this approach implies is a shift from a critique of such fetishism to a reproduction of its logic. The loss of a basis immanent in the present for a Marxist politics and ethics would be less disturbing if the logic of development of the capitalist system were not simultaneously presented as the logic (objective possibility) of its overthrow. For once communism is grounded only in the internal, crisis-ridden, developmental, fetishistic logic of capitalism, the question of values and institutions can no longer be posed. If the universalistic values generated by the earlier immanent critique of civil society are retained, as they are by Marx, they must become transcendent and arbitrary. Moreover, the theory of development derived from the critique of political economy becomes overburdened with the task of accounting for the move from present to future. The reduction of the political, social, normative underpinnings of civil society to the logic of the capitalist mode of production results in a collapse of system logic with present and future history. The critique of political economy is impoverished vis-à-vis the earlier immanent critique of civil society, for it can maintain a relation to praxis that is only deterministic or arbitrary. It is therefore not entirely without foundation that centrally planned statist societies reject, in Marx's name, formally democratic structures as well as an independent civil society as bourgeois. One could say that, although no amount of civil liberties, voluntary associations, or public spaces could, without the abolition of capitalism, ever equal socialism, in the spirit of Marxian theory, even if not according to its formal logic, no (civil) society could be called socialist without them.

It will be my task in the following chapters to see whether the class theory can serve as a successful mediation between the scientific, critical, and philosophical presuppositions in Marx's corpus. It is my thesis that the antinomies in Marx's work derive from the analysis of modern civil society that reduces civil, political, juridical, normative, cultural moments to secondary aspects of the alleged anatomy of that society— its political economy. *And the most important means by which the reduction of civil to bourgeois society is accomplished is nothing other than the specific Marxian concept of class as the correlate of production relations.* I intend to trace the parameters of the class concept in relation to the shifts in the analysis of civil society discussed above. I will argue that, despite the rehistoricization of the forces/relations dialectic in the critique of political economy, the presupposition that the internal dynamics of at least capitalist society can be grasped through a critique of production forms and comprehended as class relations rests on the productivist logic that distorts the Marxian perception of modern civil society.

A double liability inheres in any analysis that presents class relations as the universal basis of domination and emancipation in modern society. On the one hand, such a class theory precludes the recognition of fundamental forms of domination that cannot be fit into the structure of class relations or seen as their instruments. On the other hand, it obscures the complex character of the *social sphere* that emerged with the state/society distinction by viewing conflicting interests, the structure of needs, and the legal underpinnings of this sphere as the surface expression of relations of production, as class relations. Marx's most important insight in the analysis of civil society was that the problem of democracy and freedom could not be solved without resolution of the social question. The class theory was a grand effort to synthesize into a "dialectical" whole the workers' movement, the struggle for political democracy, and a systemic analysis of capitalist reproduction. But Marx's tendency to reduce political interaction to the instrumentality of class relations, and civil society to capitalism, led him to dissolve the political into the social question. The assumption of unimpeded growth and potential abundance also excused Marx (wrongly) from confronting fundamental political questions of choice.

The models of communism flowing from Marxian class theory resolve into three alternative visions: apolitical, statist, or technocratic. For an analysis that viewed the multiplicity of interest groups, voluntary associations, and publics of modern civil society as particularistic fragmentation resulting from capitalist class relations, the future society could only be seen as fully socialized, resolving antagonisms between individual and society, universal and particular, in transparent social relations organized through conscious rational planning. Because we now know that this is a dangerous myth, predicated upon the destruction of that very heterogeneity that heralded the onset of modernity, we must return to the analysis of civil society with the advantage of hindsight. The Marxian critique of capitalist class relations remains fundamental to any reassessment of civil society that seeks to avoid apology. In order to pose the project of a socialist civil society, however, the parameters of civil society and the formally democratic state must be reassessed. Marx's insight into the contradictory institutionalization of civil society remains the crucial starting point. My purpose in reconstructing the class theory is to show that despite the inadequacy of Marx's solutions, and, to some extent, presuppositions, the problem Marx confronted is still in many ways our own. Only an immanent critique of the last dogma of Marxism, the class concept, could pave the way for a solution.

Chapter 2

The Philosophical Presuppositions
of the Class Theory

Class versus order: the step beyond Hegel

Marx's class theory begins with the "discovery" of the proletariat as both the problem and the solution to the tensions of modern civil society. He was, however, as he himself admits, certainly not the first to recognize that the reproduction of civil society depended on the formation of a social class excluded from both the general welfare and the political life of that society—the class of wage workers.[1] Theorists representing all sides of the political spectrum had already discovered the plight of the working masses in modern society. Political liberals like John Locke, despite his celebrated notions of the individual and his rights in civil society, reflected seventeenth-century (English) bourgeois prejudice with statements to the effect that although the "human beings of the labouring class were a commodity out of which riches and dominion might be derived . . . the labouring class was rightly subject to, but without full membership in, the state." [2] Reactionary German romantics focused on the misery of the working man, and one of the "fathers of sociology," Lorenz von Stein, elaborated an empirical analysis of the situation of the working class and the means to better its lot.[3] French socialists pointed to the same problem, advocating measures that ranged from Fourier's utopian communities to Louis Blanc's social workshops. And somewhere in between there was Saint-Simon, the advocate of the rational development of science and technology by an elite of engineers who would guide the Industrial Revolution toward happiness and satisfaction for all.[4] What distinguishes Marx from these thinkers is his integration of philosophy and sociology into the framework of a class theory that leads him to consider the proletariat as a unique class, able to solve both its own problems and those of civil society as a whole.

The link between a sociology of class oppression and a philosophically grounded theory of revolution derives from Marx's critical appropriation of Hegel's theory of civil society. As previously indicated, Marx sought to extract the "rational kernel" of Hegel's theory of civil society (the principles of autonomy and justice) from its mystical shell (the theory of the state) and to find in the framework of civil society a dynamic that might point to its realization. Hegel had already determined the nature of the problem inherited by Marx: the concept of civil society as a system of needs, of isolated individuals confronting one another solely in terms of antagonistic interests dictated by market relations. Marx's critique of Hegel demonstrates that the concept of the modern state as a viable ethical community is a myth. Moreover, his analysis of civil society contends that corporate organization as a mechanism of social integration goes against the rational impulse of civil society. Finally, he insists that the police, the judiciary, the bureaucratic administration "are not deputies of civil society itself in and through whom it administers its own general interest, but representatives of the state for the administration of the state over and against civil society." [5]

There was, however, an additional mode of integration and structuration of civil society to which Hegel pointed as an antidote to atomization—its internal *stratification*. Hegel seems to have understood the nature of modern, as opposed to premodern, stratification when he argued against the determination of individual class status according to birth, rank, or heredity.[6] Instead, he maintained that the system of needs, work, education, and property—in short, individual merit and skill—are the fundamental determinants of the individual's position in civil society. He refers, however, to the stratification of civil society as an *estate (Stand)* system, limiting the number of estates to three legally and politically articulated groups defined according to a particular mode of consciousness and esprit de corps: agriculture, business, and bureaucracy.[7] Estates, for Hegel, are thus not merely economic groupings but totalities with specific modes of consciousness that serve to integrate the individual into communal structures and to assure his social standing as a member of a socially and politically recognized group. Accordingly, Hegel defends a constitutional political system based on an assembly of estates. Arguing that the Stande of civil society are already communities, Hegel assures their political relevance by basing election to the legislature not on atomized individual electors but on Stand membership and representation.

Hegel advocates an estate system of stratification in order to secure a communal life for the "son of civil society," wrenched from the family and facing the political state alone. Membership in a legally constituted estate provides social standing, recognition, and direct participation in communal life for the individual, thereby protecting particularity and firmly rooting political activity in civil life. The defense of estates is also, however, an attempt to avoid a system of stratification based solely on economic standing and individual self-interest. Such a system, typical (according to Hegel) of formal democracy and direct individual suffrage, can only result in the degradation of political life to the caprice and self-interest of the private individual. From an antidemocratic standpoint, Hegel thus anticipates Marx's critique of formal democracy in *On the Jewish Question*. For both, the central issue is *stratification*:

The circles of association in civil society are already communities. To picture these communities as once more breaking up into a mere conglomeration of individuals as soon as they enter the field of politics . . . is eo ipso to hold civil and political life apart from one another and as it were to hang the latter in the air, because its basis could then only be the abstract individuality of caprice and opinion. . . . So-called "theories" of this kind involve the idea that the classes (*Stande*) of civil society and the Estates (*Stande*) which are the "classes" given a political significance stand wide apart from each other. But the German language, by calling them both *Stande* has still maintained the unity which in any case they actually possessed in former times.[8]

Far from being ignorant of the nature of modern class stratification, Hegel's theory of estates is a conscious effort to avoid its consequences.

Indeed, Hegel's analysis of poverty as a socioeconomic condition, artificially (that is, socially) produced with the reproduction of civil society itself, illustrates this point. Poverty to Hegel is not an incidental by-product of civil society but is inherent in the very processes through which production and needs are expanded, resulting in wealth and extravagance for the propertied and want, destitution, and poverty for the propertyless. It is no accident that Hegel reserves the term *class* (*Klasse*) (as opposed to *estate* (*Stand*)) to refer solely to the one group in civil society that, lacking property, is reduced to poverty and is thereby unable to attain standing within the estates or corporations deemed so essential to the stability of civil society.[9] As a purely socioeconomic stratum without legal or political identity, the poor constitute for Hegel a *class*, not an *estate*, symbolizing precisely the type of stratification that Hegel wants to prevent. It is worth quoting the relevant passage in full:

When civil society is in a state of unimpeded activity, it is expanding internally in population and industry. The amassing of wealth is intensified by generalizing a) the linkage of men by their needs, and b) the methods of preparing and distributing the means to satisfy these needs because it is from this double process of generalization that the largest profits are derived. That is one side of the picture. The other side is the subdivision and restriction of particular jobs. This results in the dependence and distress of the *class* tied to work of that sort, and these again entail inability to feel and enjoy the broader freedoms and especially the intellectual benefits of civil society.[10]

This class of working poor, a direct product of the economic successes of civil society, has both objective and subjective features, according to Hegel: Objectively, it is poor, without property or skills, without membership in a corporation or estate, and tied to manual labor. Subjectively, it develops the needs common to civil society, but in the absence of the means to satisfy these needs it loses its self-respect, sense of right and wrong, honesty, and becomes an *atomized rabble (Pöbel) with no allegiance to the society whose benefits it is denied.*[11] Indeed, Hegel goes so far as to state that, as such, poverty appears as the wrong done to a particular class by society as a whole.[12]

Most important for our analysis, poverty understood as a *class* systematically produced by the internal relations of civil society constitutes the one fundamental threat to civil society that Hegel's system of mediations admittedly could not solve. Neither private charity nor public welfare is adequate to the problem, although both alleviate economic distress, because they violate the principle of civil society—"the feeling of individual independence and self-respect in its individual members," which come from either skilled labor or property.[13] On the other hand, although colonization and public curbs on industry are suggested by Hegel as measures the state could adopt to alleviate poverty, they too are by no means deemed sufficient. For the problem of the *Pöbel* is not simply its poverty but its existence as a *class of individuals that cannot be integrated into the mediating institutions of civil society* (estate structure) *but claims the rights of this society.*[14] Thus we have the existence of a class of day workers, unemployed individuals, and beggars excluded from the central institutions that mediate between civil society and the state by embedding individuals in a normative, moral social order (sittlichkeit). The very achievement of the modern order: subjective freedom of the individual, formal legality and institutionalized morality are threatened by the poor. The Pöbel thus symbolizes for Hegel the greatest threat to civil society and its unresolvable problem. "It hence becomes apparent that despite an excess of wealth civil society is not rich enough, i.e. its own resources are insufficient to check excessive poverty *and* the creation of a penurious rabble (Pöbel).[15]

Despite his recognition that civil society creates its own internal threat in the form of a class, class analysis remains peripheral to Hegel's theory of civil society because he insists that estates are its dominant mode of stratification. The significance of Marx's critique of these mediating institutions for the class analysis of civil society can now be clarified, for clearly Hegel's combination of the political and legal status of precapitalist estates with the mobility, centrality of economic criteria (labor, property), and absence of restrictions of birth and heredity characteristic of class stratification is extremely tenuous. By demonstrating that political estates and corporations contradict precisely the unique features of civil society that Hegel himself recognized—abstract right, private property, reciprocity, and exchange relations of the system of need—Marx shows that socioeconomic distinctions, that is, class relations, rather than estate distinctions constitute the differentia specifica of stratification of modern civil society.

Marx argues that, although the estates and corporations in feudal society had a political significance, with the emergence of absolute monarchy and hence of a distinct political state these institutions were radically transformed and retained only a social rather than a political meaning. The transition to modern society "changed the differences of estate of civil society into mere *social* differences, into differences of civil life (*Privatleben*) which are without significance in political life. With that the separation of political and civil society was complete.[16] Therefore, the fleeting organization of civil society into corporations attests not to its political impulse but to *social inequalities* devoid of political meaning in the old sense. Thus the separation of state and civil society entails not merely the distinction of the private and the political but also the intrusion of the social in the form solely of socioeconomic inequalities and their organization into interest groups within civil society. The social moment of civil society, misconstrued by Hegel as political, refers to both the integration of individuals through the bourgeois form of alienable property into social relations of exchange and their *stratification* according to the nonpolitical criteria of money and education.

The privatization of life in civil society entails the reduction of social relations and institutionalized morality or norms to instrumental rationality guided by the sole norm of efficiency. Like Hegel, Marx recognized that the utilitarian version of market society (a disembedded, deinstitutionalized system of needs) would mean the loss of ethical life in the Greek sense. For Marx, of course, this meant the absence of legitimate normatively regulated social interaction based on free association. But unlike Hegel, Marx believed that the very differentiation of state and civil society caused the reduction of the social to economic relations.

Thus, in the first instance, "class" becomes for Marx a *sociological* category describing the relations of inequality and exclusion inherent in the very separation of civil society and the state, which Hegel simultaneously discovered and denied. The differences of property, education, skill, and money express *socioeconomic inequalities* of isolated individuals whose interest groups can by no means be understood as political corporations that enable them to transcend their particularity. Accordingly, *Marx's concept of class is a historically specific category, rooted in the separation of civil society and the state, that distinguishes modern from premodern forms of stratification.*[17]

As the expression of the separation of the state (abstract political community) and civil society (depoliticized, privatized, abstract individuality), however, the concept of class serves as a critique not only of Hegel's theory of estates but also of its opposite—the claim characteristic of natural law theory that freedom and equality are established within the framework of a formally democratic state because it has abolished estate privileges. The formally democratic state bases its claim to universality and legitimacy on the fact that it recognizes only independent legal persons and accords no privileges or recognition to particular groups. The legislature is presented as the elected representative of sovereign individuals considered, from the standpoint of the constitution, to be free and equal. The concept of class as the expression of systematically reproduced social and economic inequalities and exclusion accordingly plays the critical role of demonstrating the fact that one cannot get at the stratification of civil society by looking at its political articulation (mode of representation). Indeed, the stratification of civil society into socioeconomic classes reveals that key relations of domination take a *nonpolitical* (nonjuridical) form in modern society. Nevertheless, Marx regards the substitution of class for estate stratification as a *historical advance,*[18] for the transformation of political estates into socioeconomic classes rests on the emergence *within political life* of the principle of universality, that is, the right of all individuals to participate in sovereignty and to be regarded as persons regardless of differences of rank or birth. Estates, or politically and legally constituted status groups, are by definition particularistic and antidemocratic insofar as they attach to differences between individuals (their work, property, social status, interests, etc.), distinctions in rights and privileges within political life itself. Accordingly, any attempt to reintroduce estate or corporate structures into modern civil society can be only an illusory defense of particularity that undermines the universalistic morality inherent in concepts of freedom, personhood, and citizenship.[19]

The two remaining features of civil society discovered by Hegel—property relations and the Pöbel—now move to the center of Marx's own class analysis. In a sense, Marx generalizes the situation of the Pöbel (which is peripheral to Hegel)—namely, its presence as an estateless conglomeration of privatized individuals—into the characteristic position of all individuality in civil society as a whole. All individuals in modern civil society are shown to be uprooted, privatized, without "standing," estateless. Insofar as this is so, we must act unethically. Thus, what renders the position of the Pöbel unique cannot be its lack of estate or its status as a class but must be its lack of property. And, indeed, the possession or nonpossession of property and the freedom from or the necessity to perform wage labor become for Marx the determining factors of his class analysis of civil society. The peripheral concept of the Pöbel is thus transformed in Marx's hands into the sociologically identifiable class of wage workers, central to the economic reproduction of civil society but excluded from its benefits, not because it is not an estate but because it does not possess property. Not estates but property relations and the system of abstract rights that guarantees them constitute for Marx the central principle of stratification of modern civil society. In fact, the exclusion of the propertyless from the right to vote reveals that formally democratic states were once quite conscious of their own internal limitation. The concept of class, then, rooted in the separation of the formally democratic state and civil society, enables Marx to criticize modern society in the name of its own claim to legitimacy, its universalistic values. Before he proceeds to seriously examine the opposition of wage labor and property and the structure of class domination, however, Marx gives the concept of class a curious twist, attaching to it a philosophical significance distinct from and, as we shall see, contradictory to its sociological meaning.

The crucial step is made when Marx asserts that class, in the form of the proletariat, carries within itself the solution to the problems of civil society. Because it is a *universal class*, the proletariat is potentially the main protagonist of a radical revolution that can realize "true human emancipation." The philosophical significance of the concept of universal class and its function within the framework of Marx's analysis become clear in the context of his critique of political revolutions. According to Marx, the revolutions that constituted the modern democratic state as distinct from civil society were merely political and hence partial, insofar as only a

part of civil society emancipates itself and attains general domination; . . . a definite class proceeding from its particular situation, undertakes the general emancipation of society. This class emancipates the whole of society but only provided the whole of society is in the same situation as this class, e.g., possesses money and education or can acquire them at will.[20]

In the political revolution that overthrew absolutism, one estate, the third, was able to liberate itself only by abolishing all estates and by creating a political realm that in principle is *universalistic*; but because this revolution did not abolish the efficacy of systematic socioeconomic distinctions in *civil life*, it only confirmed the particular interests of classes and revealed private property as the content of political emancipation. The philosophical problem facing the critic of partial political revolution is, thus, to locate the particularity of a subject (for Marx, a particular class) *within* civil society able to make a universal revolution that abolishes all classes, private property, and the conflictual structure of particular interest.

The uniqueness of the proletariat as a class "in but not of civil society," a class essential to the framework of modern production relations but denied property, personhood, and citizenship, is that it has no particular interest to affirm in maintaining the civil society that rejects it. Because of the general nature of its oppression, because of its radical chains, Marx maintains that the proletariat is a universal class,

which has a universal character by its universal suffering and claims no *particular right* because no *particular wrong*, but wrong in general is perpetrated against it; . . . a sphere which cannot emancipate itself without emancipating itself from all other spheres of society; which, in a word, is the complete loss of man and hence can win itself only through the complete *rewinning* of man.[21]

In short, because the oppression of the proletariat does not take on a direct political form (it is not an estate), struggles against its oppression must transcend political revolutions by revolutionizing everyday life. The "particularity" of the proletariat that sets it apart from other classes is thus its universal claim to human emancipation grounded in the total character of its alienation and dehumanization in civil society.

Two problems become evident regarding this early derivation of the proletariat as a universal class. The first is Marx's obvious failure to envision the inclusion of the proletariat in civil society or the state through its own struggles for civil, social, and political rights and its development of quite particular interests and organizations for their realization *within* modern civil society. In this case, surely, the continued domination of the class by property and its exclusion from effective power remain, but such would not privilege its associations or struggles with the attribute of universality as opposed to other groups struggling for rights and powers. The critique of civil society and the state would still be valid, but the exclusive radical status accorded the proletariat by virtue of its radical exclusion would have to be revised. Moreover, even if the proletariat succeeded in abolishing the *class* structure of domination, what precludes the emergence in postrevolutionary society of new forms of stratification and domination? Clearly, we are thinking of the new mode of domination exercised in the name of the proletariat in the so-called socialist societies,[22] but we speak not only with the advantage of hindsight. Given Marx's understanding of the "bourgeois" revolution as the revolution of an estate that abolishes all estates but nevertheless institutes a new mode of domination on the basis of class, he should have seen the possibility for a similar process regarding class revolutions. In our estimation, the philosophical presupposition that leads Marx to equate the abolition of class domination with the end of domination altogether is the unfortunate combination of Hegel's notion of the "negation of the negation" with the concept of "universal class" to arrive at the absolute character of proletarian revolution. In effect, the universality and emancipatory role of the proletariat are logically and not sociologically derived. From the start, and by definition, the proletariat is identified as the radical negation of the society that negates it—it need only recognize itself and act in order to liberate humanity. But this argument reveals only the needs of philosophy, not those of the class itself.

This brings us to the second difficulty. Even if one accepts the necessity of the self-abolition of the proletariat (the abolition of wage labor and class stratification) as a precondition for its liberation, this cannot be equated with the telos for the creation of a free society based on the democratization of all spheres of life. By changing the function of the concept of universal class from that of mediating the separation of civil society and the state (Hegel's bureaucracy) to that of abolishing this dualism, Marx assumes but does not demonstrate that the alleged absence of particular interests of the proletariat within civil society precludes the emergence of such interests once its repoliticization has taken place. Indeed, at first glance, Marx's conception of the universality of the proletariat seems quite deficient when compared with Hegel's universal estate. After all, Hegel utilized criteria like education, custom, condition of life, self-image, accountability, and internal controls in his treatment of bureaucracy. Marx's assertion that no stratum could mediate between particular and general interests within the framework of civil society is well founded, but his projection of universality onto the proletariat is less so. For the question remains: What makes the revolution of this class—even if one grants (as we do not) its negative universality (absence of particular interests)—more than merely a revolt of the oppressed *against* oppression; that is, what makes it a positive revolution *for* the emancipation of humanity? Why should this oppressed class be able to realize the demands of Reason—the norms and values and needs of the species as a whole, uncovered by critique? Why should the weapon of critique grip these particular masses? The necessity of critique to find an addressee, a material force to whose praxis it can relate, is clear. "It is not enough for thought to strive for realization, reality must itself strive towards thought." [23] But from the other side: How can critique claim to relate to the praxis of the proletariat so that this class can incorporate critique into its own action and attempt to realize its imperatives?

Interest versus need: the criteria of radicality

That Marx was aware of these questions is evidenced by his effort to give the concept of universal class a positive grounding that moves beyond the logic of negativity thus far discussed. He introduces two criteria, which are to provide the positive basis of the claimed radical universality of the proletariat as a class: the category of radical need and the concept of labor as objectification. Together they constitute the key categories linking the philosophy of praxis to the concept of class. The thrust of Marx's critique of civil society was to connect the objectified universalistic values inherent in but only partially realized by modern institutions to the praxis of individuals striving for emancipation. Theory (or philosophy turned critique), if it is to gain practical significance, must be able to identify and inform the activity of its addressees. Accordingly, in the essay that "discovers" the proletariat, Marx points to the category of *need* as the central mediation between theory and praxis: "Theory can be realized in a people only as it is the realization of the needs of that people. . . . only a revolution of radical needs can be a radical revolution." [24] Moreover, from the earliest writings through *Capital*, Marx consistently associated the revolutionary thrust of the proletariat with its potential to develop radical needs.

Two central tenets of Marx's theories of need and labor can be traced back to Hegel: the idea that the multiplication and differentiation of needs in history are the means through which individuals emerge from the animal world of natural necessity to become many-sided and self-determining; and the notion that work has a liberating moment insofar as it creates the condition of possibility of expansion and satisfaction of needs through the humanization of nature. [25] But whereas this orientation enabled Hegel to reject Rousseau's argument that the fewer needs one has the more independent one is both of nature and of the control of others, his analysis of the "system of needs" nevertheless appears to confirm Rousseau's fears regarding societal development. [26] Hegel had to admit that in the empirical context of civil society the imperatives of particular need satisfaction led to the subjugation of abstractly autonomous individuals to the external and naturelike laws of the market. He also recognized that the concrete activity of the laboring classes tends to deform and impoverish the members of that class, turning work and the satisfaction of needs into one-sided specialization and nonsatisfaction of needs for precisely those on whom the increasingly sophisticated differentiation of the system of needs depends.

It was, above all, Marx's distinction between a *philosophically elaborated theory of need* and the *concept of interest*, the clue to the historically specific system of needs of civil society, that enabled him to move beyond Hegel's dilemma. As opposed to Althusser, who insists that Marx abandoned the concept of civil society and the interrogation of its system of needs with the move to historical materialism, we would maintain that Marx's innovation lay not in abandoning the former concepts but in relating the system of needs described by Hegel to the specificity of the capitalist relations of exchange and production and in distinguishing this system from a philosophically elaborated, evaluative concept of need.[27] The first step was to interpret the antagonistic, instrumentalized system of needs described by Hegel as the sign of a historically specific form of *need alienation* based on the integration of needs into a competitive interest structure. The limitation of the satisfaction of needs to effective market demand is only the most obvious sign of this problematic. The fundamental issue is the analysis of the process, unique to civil society, through which needs become structured into the conflicting particular interests of egoistic individuals.

It is no accident that *modern* philosophy and economic theory developed the category of "interest" as a general category of motivation, for this concept most clearly defines the system of needs within modern civil society. The concept of interest associates "rational" calculation (*Zweckrationalitat*) with the articulation of and efforts to satisfy needs. For theorists of civil society from Hobbes to Hegel, interest comes between passions, desires, and their objects to express the way in which the self-responsible but isolated individual must constitute his needs in the absence of societal and communal guarantees of welfare.[28] The infinite expandability of needs and the structuration of needs into the private, calculable interests of the egoistic individual who competes with others to satisfy his self-interest are taken to be natural features of individuality per se. As a motive for action, then, interest logically implies both the opposition between particular and general interest—defined as *self-preference* versus *concern for society*—and the antagonism between particular interests of particular individuals. It is this interest structure that Hegel describes as the system of needs. But though Hegel severs himself from the natural law tradition by historicizing this structure of needs and relating the continuous expansion of needs to its obvious counterpart—the competitive structure of the market—he nevertheless remains within the same problematic by seeking to reconcile particular and general interest (represented by the state) through a series of mediating institutions that preserve rather than abolish the antagonistic interest structure. Like his predecessors, Hegel collapses the concepts of need and interest, identifying free individuality with bourgeois individuality and accepting the system of need of civil society as the unavoidable consequence of the dissolution of traditional, premodern communities.[29]

Far from embracing the problematic of particular/general *interest*, Marx's major advance was to dispense with this formulation of the problem altogether.[30] Instead of opposing general to particular interest as did both his "bourgeois" predecessors and his "Marxist" followers (the state for the former and the party for the latter represent the general interest), Marx considered them to be two sides of the same coin, rooted in the structure of civil society that opposes bourgeois to citizen and posits egoistic subjects as the only conceivable form of individuality. For Marx, "interest" as the exclusive motive for action, whether particular or general, is the expression of the alienation of need specific to capitalism. As such, it is certainly not the fate of modernity but only the fate of one specific social formation. The opposition between bourgeois and citizen, between egoism and particularity of individual, private self-interest and universalistic, moralizing, self-sacrificing "general interest" of the citizen, constitutes a double abstraction and alienation of individual needs inherent in capitalist society. Moreover, here the general interest is not a motive of the individual but proceeds behind the back of the individual.[31] According to Marx, however, those concerned with the *transformation* of capitalist civil society—namely, its communist critics—distance themselves from this problematic

because they alone have discovered that . . . the "general interest" is created by individuals who are defined as "private persons." They know that this contradiction is only a seeming one because one side of it, the so-called "general" is constantly being produced by the other side, private interest, and by no means opposes the latter as an independent force with an independent history.[32]

The significance of the identification of interest relations as an alienated need structure specific to capitalism lies in the implication that the "general interest," even if posited in the form of "class interest," cannot be a motive for class activity pointing beyond capitalism. Only a radical transformation of the system of needs, only the abolition of the interest structure, and not the extension of calculation from private to general interests could free individuals from the alienation of need.

To be sure, Marx's class theory did seek to envisage *motivations* that would lead the proletariat to struggle for emancipation from civil society and its system of need and labor. These motivations, however, were not interests but *radical needs*, that is, needs that constitute a challenge to the capitalist system of needs and provide an impetus to revolutionary praxis.[33] In fact, the argument that the proletariat has no particular right or interest to affirm within civil society is important because it identifies the emergence of radical needs as opposed to interests, and struggles around needs, as the central mediation between a critique geared to emancipation and praxis. The concept of class interest, when it appears in Marx's writings, usually refers to those needs embedded within the market and productive framework of capitalism and not to a motive that transcends this framework.[34] Accordingly, the fact that Marx considered only needs, and theory that relates to needs, to be radical indicates his concern to integrate the universalistic norm of self-determination, stemming from critique, to the revolutionary praxis of a class in a nonauthoritarian manner. For no one, no party or theorist, can claim to have better knowledge of the needs of an individual than the individual himself. On this basis, the principle of self-constitution becomes a fundamental philosophical prerequisite for emancipatory class struggle in Marx's theory. In other words, what the method of immanent norm critique made self-evident was that the revolutionary class, the proletariat, has to be the conscious agent of its own emancipation. For theory to speak to its addressees, the latter must develop the radical needs for the realization of the norms that theory uncovers. A mutual process of enlightenment between the critic and his subjects is presupposed by the theory of radical need: "The educator must himself be educated." [35]

Marx's interrelated theories of need, objectification, and alienation presuppose a philosophical "value concept" of need.[36] *Need* as a category of value refers to the concept of human abundance or enrichment—the free unfolding of the capacities, senses, and activity of the human being evidenced by the expansion and refinement of needs. This theme, associated with the vision of a future communist society, pervades Marx's writings from the earliest works through the *Theories of Surplus Value* and provides the normative standpoint from which Marx formulates and criticizes both the capitalist system of need and alternatives to capitalism that rest on the restriction of needs. "Crude communism," for example, despite the fact that it abolishes private property, is criticized for "extending the category of work to all men and thereby regressing to the unnatural simplicity of the poor and crude man who has few needs." [37] As opposed to the vulgar bourgeois equation of wealth with mere having, as well as to the ascetic, leveling, "antimaterialist" models of a future alternative, the concept of "man rich in needs" is ceaselessly presented by Marx as the fundamental value ushered in with modernity that must be realized in an emancipated society:

It will be seen how in the place of wealth and poverty of political economy come the *rich human being* and the *rich human need.* The rich human being is simultaneously the human being *in need* of a totality of human manifestations of life—the man in whom his own realization exists as inner necessity, as *need.*[38]

Both the concept of "human essence" (species being) that links the predicates of universality, sociality, consciousness, and self-activity to the concept of humanity and the theory of objectification that roots the development of "human essence" (species being) in the active appropriation and formation of social life by historically situated individuals, interacting with one another and nature, are evaluative concepts integrally linked to the value concept of need. If the emancipated individual is a "man rich in needs," a species being replete with many-sided relationships, able to appropriate the wealth of societal development as an individual, the precondition for the emergence of this form of "social individuality" is a historical process in which needs and the possibility for their satisfaction are expanded. The concept of need as a universalistic value and the emergence of radical needs (that is, needs for this kind of wealth) are thus predicated on the argument that needs are generated in a sociohistorical process of objectification. For, if needs were understood as given, biologically, and as expandable only through the "artificial" agency of society against and in violation of pristine nature (Rousseau), there could be no basis for the transformation of need structures that is the prerequisite for an emancipated society.

It is thus no accident that Marx deemed the first historical act to be the creation of *new needs* through the social activity involved in the process of production and objectification.[39] Despite Marx's confusing distinctions between "natural," "physiological," or "necessary" needs and "socially produced" needs, the genesis of need is always a *historically* and *culturally* mediated act. In short, both internal and external nature, needs and their objects, exist for man in the exchange between socialized individuals and symbolically or instrumentally mediated nature. Marx had no concept of survival needs as a group of needs independent of history and culture. Accordingly, the basis of his critique of the capitalist structure of need was not an ascetic or naturalistic standpoint but the universal value of many-sided individuality. The thrust of Marx's critique was not aimed at the emergence of "luxury" or "false" needs but pointed to the *limitation of the development of many-sided needs to particular social strata* and to the reduction of the needs and even the senses of disadvantaged groups to the barest minimum. This is the basis of the concept of alienated needs. When viewed in terms of the constitution and unfolding of human capacities through objectifications, history appears as alienation, for clearly the moment of self-realization concomitant with the concept of objectification cannot be applied to the masses of unfree and limited individuals who have been the human actors of the past. Alienation as a philosophical concept applicable to the past refers to the split, historically ascertainable, between the development of productive capacity, cultural values, and needs for the species as a whole and the impoverishment and one-sided development of the individual. And, from the standpoint of the value concept of need, the tension and antagonism between species and individual development, between cultural wealth and individual impoverishment, are the sign of alienation of needs for past history and, in its most extreme form, for capitalism. It follows from this that the concept of alienation of needs is meaningful only if it is applied to the *totality of the structure of need* of a given society and not to specific groups of needs or their objects.[40] Marx therefore does not attempt to set up a dichotomy of true and false needs within the capitalist system of needs but criticizes this system—the structure of interest—as a whole in terms of the interrelation between the structure of production and the structure of need.

It remains to be seen how the critique of civil society allowed Marx to construe the proletariat as the bearer of the normative predicates of species development (universality, sociality, consciousness, autonomy) and as the class that develops the radical needs for an emancipated society in which individual and species development would come together and alienation would be abolished.

The dualistic concept of labor

The deepening of the critique of civil society through the analysis of alienated labor provides the pivot to Marx's theory of the proletariat as a universal class. On the basis of the *concept of labor*, Marx attempts to move beyond the negative universality associated with the proletariat to the positive determination of its emancipatory potential as a class that develops radical needs. The concept of labor, however, presented in the 1844 Paris *Manuscripts* as the unifying principle and active center of civil society and history, is a dualistic one. The same category—labor—unites the philosophical notion of "objectification" (species activity) with an "economic" referent (productive activity, or work), in the historically specific form of wage labor. In effect, what Marx tried to do in this early critique of political economy was to integrate the two concepts of labor in order to posit the specific life activity of the working class—alienated labor—as the source of its revolutionary potential and its privileged position to press for the realization of species capacities in the future.

The philosophical concept of labor is conceived as a process of *objectification* through which individuals create their needs, abilities, and world. In this sense, labor is the conscious universal life activity through which active, social, and free individuals develop. As such, it is a transhistorical, normative concept—a regulative principle in the Kantian sense—integrally related to the value concept of need. The philosophical concept of labor refers to all human activity on an equal plane. Art, philosophy, religion—in short, all products of human interaction with nature and with one another—are objectifications irreducible to economic relations. Nor can they be taken as expressions of a presupposed, eternally present human subject. As nonalienated species activity, labor is not only the source of the expansion of capacities and needs but also the condition of possibility of freedom, or the transcendence of the circle of natural necessity via creation independent of "natural" need. Indeed, Marx implies that production is specifically human only when it is free from physical need, when objects are formed according to self-given criteria.[41] As such, labor is a vital need for the free human individual. Those who labor in the above sense develop a wealth of needs and abilities that make them into independent social individuals.

But Marx's analysis of alienated labor shows that the activity of the proletarian has just the opposite result: It prevents him from recognizing himself in his product, it separates and atomizes him from his fellows, it turns his free life activity into a forced and deforming means of survival, and it subjugates him to the domination of another—the capitalist.[42] The more the worker works,

the more powerful becomes the alien world of objects which he creates over and against himself, the poorer he himself—his inner world becomes. . . . The more the worker produces . . . the more civilized his object, the more barbarous becomes the worker. . . . It is true that labor produces wonderful things for the rich, but for the worker it produces privation. . . . It produces intelligence—but for the worker, stupidity, cretinism.[43]

Several points flow from this analysis. In order to free themselves from the alienation of their activity and the domination of the capitalist, the class of wage workers cannot simply agitate for reforms (higher wages, benefits, class interests) but must abolish the very conditions of their existence as a class—the wage labor/capital relation. It is not simply the fact of exploitation or loss of the product that oppresses the worker but his very activity: "labour itself, I say, is harmful and pernicious." [44] Clearly, the concept of labor that is operative here is not the philosophical concept of objectification but the historically specific category —wage labor. The "economic" concept of labor—production in general —is taken over from Smith and Ricardo and historicized by Marx to refer solely to the specific form that labor takes within the framework of the capitalist mode of production. In this context, alienation, too, functions as a historically specific category, describing the *experience* of the worker under modern conditions of production. Considered together, then, the dual aspects of the concept of labor provide a normative concept of species activity (which Marx hopes to see actualized in the future society) and an economic category that, when subjected to immanent critique, yields the fundamental relation of the capitalist system.

This, however, also means that the stratification of society through the division of labor, the individuation of its members into socioeconomic classes, is the fundamental flaw of alienated civil society, which must be abolished before free, many-sided individuality can appear. The critique of labor is complemented by a critique of class. In effect, the very fact that one can describe a group of individuals as a socioeconomic class indicates the reduction of individuality to external economic processes. In other words, what political economy and capitalist production presuppose—the integration of the individual into a competitive interest structure and into a class—entails the abstraction not only of the individual's activity but of his needs and personality as well. It means that the individual has become, from the standpoint of capital, a mere worker, a commodity and an instrument of labor equivalent in status to the machines that periodically replace him.[45] Over and over again Marx argues that as a member of a class the individual is rendered banal and abstract. The *commonality of class status* and the *homogeneity of class interests* are inherent features of civil society that violate its own principle of many-sided, free individuals coming together in freely chosen communities:

It follows from all we have been saying up to now that the *communal relation into which the individuals of a class* entered, and which *was determined by their common interest* as against a third party, was always a community to which these individuals belonged only as *average individuals*.[46]

Accordingly, the struggle of the proletariat against its existence as a class is the precondition for its emancipation. On the basis of this sine qua non, however, Marx presumes that the struggle of the workers contains universal human emancipation, because the whole of human servitude is allegedly involved in the relation of workers to production, or the relation of alienated labor to private property.[47] Apart from the new significance given to the concept of labor, however, we have not really gotten beyond the negative determination of the universality of the proletariat. This class is still presented as the total negation of species being whose own self-negation is identified with the reconciliation of individual and species and the abolition of all forms of alienation.

Although the philosophical prerequisites for a radical revolution have been elaborated, Marx has not demonstrated why the proletariat as a class is capable of realizing philosophy. On the one hand, the struggle against wage labor, against class relations, is predicated upon the emergence of a wealth of needs within the life conditions of the proletariat that challenge the interest structure of civil society. On the other hand, Marx's own analysis of the structuration of needs of the proletariat as a working class seems to preclude this possibility and to affirm its dehumanization. In the detailed analysis of the experience of the proletarian in the *Manuscripts*, Marx argues that hand in hand with economic and political alienation of the proletariat goes its impoverishment as a class. This impoverishment, which increases with the development of capitalism, is two-sided. The worker is denied material wealth due to the tendency of capital to force wages to a minimum level. This "objective" impoverishment is accompanied by a loss of "subjective" wealth—namely, the degradation of the individual worker to a mere laboring animal whose needs and senses are reduced to the bodily level of survival.[48] Indeed, the class opposition of capital and labor enables the *bourgeoisie*, not the proletariat, to expand and refine its needs while the worker is turned into an insensible being unable to sustain even its animal needs.

The stratification of need according to class—refined needs for the bourgeois, brutalized needs for the worker—is no mere consequence of the difference of poverty and wealth but is rooted in the fact of wage labor itself. Whereas labor in the philosophical sense is the active, fulfilling process of self-objectification, under the conditions of the division of labor all semblance of self-activity is lost, and labor sustains the life of the worker only by stunting it. Subjected to a process of detailed, repetitive labor, the worker's activity serves to enrich the species at the cost of individual self-development. Thus, *inherent* in the *class position of wage workers* is the wholly negative development of the individual into a worker, denuded of property, culture, and human needs. At the same time, those needs that capitalism does develop and integrate into its system of needs take on the perverted form of private and egoistic self-interests, serving to further isolate and reduce the individual to the calculation and power of the other:

Under private property . . . every person speculates on creating a *new* need in another so as to drive him to fresh sacrifice, to place him in a new dependence and to seduce him into a new mode of enjoyment and therefore economic ruin. Each tries to establish over the other an *alien* power, so as thereby to find satisfaction of his own selfish need.[49]

This rather bleak description of the alienation of need into a competitive interest structure certainly seems to conflict with the assertion that the proletariat is the bearer of species development. How can this brutalized class create a society of freely associated, many-sided individuals, rich in needs and capable of self-organization? An impoverished class cannot accomplish such a task. Only if Marx could point to the enrichment as well as the impoverishment of the proletariat could the claims for the universality of the proletariat stand. One could, of course, argue that, by generalizing the commodity relation, by orienting production to the expansion of value, and by creating a purely class society, capitalism *frees* needs from their embedment in the rigid social hierarchies of the past that allocated needs according to the "quality of person" particular to caste, estate, and so on.[50] Marx often praises capitalism for its "civilizing tendency," that is, for making "production for the sake of production" in the form of "production for profit" its driving principle and thereby breaking through those forms of society in which production is oriented to and limited by the satisfaction of a narrow framework of need. For the first time, individuals are no longer excluded in principle from the wealth of needs; the accidental character of class membership allows for the development of needs of all kinds in the poorest of men and women. In short, by breaking down the "natural" and "traditional" barriers to the expansion of needs, production, and capacities, capitalism universalizes needs within the condition of alienation and creates the condition of possibility for the development of the richness of the individual as an end in itself. In principle, at least, the limitations of precapitalist societies are overcome. Struggles for emancipation can now be made in the name of the internal legitimations of capitalism itself: universality, development, and satisfaction.[51] The fundamental antinomy of the capitalist system of need is, however, the opposition between the development of the highest level of enrichment and expansion of needs and the peak of individual impoverishment. Capitalism thus limits the enrichment and universalization of needs created by itself by imposing a social division of labor that reproduces poverty and alienation for the working class.

Although Marx does point to the development of positive radical needs on the part of the proletariat that challenge the interest structure, he succeeds only on a logical and not on a sociological or empirical level of analysis. In an argument unique to the *Manuscripts*, he adapts the logic of Hegel's "master/slave dialectic" to the condition of the proletariat in order to ground its revolutionary potential in its laboring activity. The dualistic concept of labor serves as the basis for the claim that members of the proletariat, because they work, have the *possibility* of becoming conscious of alienation and of developing the radical need for nonalienated species activity. To be sure, the capitalist's needs are also alienated insofar as they are integrated into the competitive interest structure and expressed through the ever-increasing need for money and one-sided pleasure—recreation.[52] But, whereas the capitalist has both luxury and power to make him feel satisfied within alienation, Marx contends that the worker feels dehumanized, is conscious of his degradation, and therefore strives against it. The need for true species activity thus presumably stems from the consciousness of alienation of labor and the necessity to transcend it.

Moreover, because the worker labors commonly with others of his class, the experience of the worker qua worker enables him to develop a new positive need: "the need for society" over and against the atomized and competitive framework of market relations. "When communist artisans associate with one another, theory propaganda, etc. is their first end. But at the same time as a result of this association, they acquire a new need, the need for Society, and what appears as a means becomes an end." [53] Implicit in this argument is the idea that once the working class becomes conscious of its alienation and forms itself into a self-conscious class, the initial purposes of its association—the defense of interests—is superseded through the development of radical needs (society). For this reason, Marx defends union activity. Indeed, the famous distinction between a class-in-itself (against capital) and a class-for-itself refers to the distinction between interest and need.[54] In other words, a group of individuals constituted as a socioeconomic class by capital—the proletariat—through struggling for its externally determined interests, forms itself into a class-for-itself insofar as it develops new needs for human association, unalienated activity, autonomy, etcetera, which point beyond capitalist relations.

Despite the force of this argument, Marx never really succeeds in demonstrating that the experience of alienated labor leads to the self-constitution of a revolutionary class with radical needs and the potential to develop a new form of social individuality. Moreover, the concept of need is unable to carry the burden Marx tries to place on it. Indeed, the image of man-rich-in-needs, along with the concept of radical need, stands in the place of (a), a practical philosophical reflection on "the good life" or the value choices involved in interpreting and acting upon needs and (b) a social and political theory of democratic association and institutional forms necessary to make the concept of social individuality meaningful. The theory of need can be seen only as a first, insufficient step in this direction. Marx, however, never went farther. He also failed to demonstrate the uniqueness of the needs developed by the working class. The need for society or association, for example, is hardly unique to the proletariat—witness the plethora of voluntary associations in all civil societies for all social strata. And, although the dualistic concept of labor points to the expansion of needs for the species as a whole, it in no way demonstrates that because the proletariat labors it, as a class, can develop the wealth of needs so described. The description of the reduction of needs via alienated labor indicates the opposite. Thus, on the basis of the *philosophical* and *sociological* critique of civil society, the radical potential of the proletariat as a class cannot be grounded. Rather, *the philosophical and sociological moments of the concept of class appear to be antinomic.* The philosophical preconditions for a radical revolution (self-creation through *objectifying* praxis, development of many-sided needs, self-constitution, etc.) come into conflict with the sociological analysis of the class designated as the revolutionary subject. Perhaps Marx privately knew this difficulty, for he states that "It is not a question of what this or that proletariat, or even the whole proletariat, at the moment *regards* as its aim. It is a question of *what the proletariat is,* and what in accordance with this *being,* it will historically be compelled to do." [55] Clearly, this statement contradicts the philosophical presuppositions of the theory of need, for if the proletariat develops radical needs it must know it; if not, who is the privileged observer who understands that proletariat better than itself? We seem to be brought back to the concept of class interest, for the above statement is conceivable only in reference to some imputed class interest of which the class member is not conscious but which the theorist or party claims to know.

The problem, however, lies not so much in the belief in the revolutionary potential of workers as in the concept of *class* itself and the projection of radical needs onto the proletariat *as a class.* As Marx's theory of need implies, only individuals can have needs and be conscious of them. It is therefore meaningless to speak of the radical needs of classes as such—in effect, *a socioeconomic class qua class can have only interests.* This is precisely the violence of class stratification that Marx himself reveals. The attempt to ground the revolutionary potential of the proletariat in its self-constitution as a class with radical needs thus indicates the central antinomy not of civil society but of Marx's class theory: the antinomy between the philosophical and sociological components of the concept of class. To belong to a class is the sign of the domination over the individual of the division of labor, capitalist market forces, and production imperatives that determine the structure of interest. Of course, Marx assumed that the proletariat is a unique class because it can develop not particular interests but radical needs. His class theory of revolution is a theory of the transcendence of the interest structure by communities fused together through struggles around radical needs, that is, through a social movement. In this sense he is the theorist of the workers movement. He never became aware, however, of the logical inconsistency of constructing need as a predicate of class; for "class," as Marx himself shows, is not a community of many-sided individuals rich in needs but only a collection of average individuals, of class members with similar interests. Indeed, by presenting themselves as the guardians of class interests of the proletariat and dispensing with the difficulties involved in the notion of self-constitution around needs, the reformist Social Democrats and the Bolsheviks, with their manipulative, elite party politics, were more consistent in their class politics than Marx.

In our view, Marx's confusion flows from the double collapse of the philosophy of praxis that pointed to the emergence of radical needs as a precondition for a radical revolution, and the *concept* of the proletariat as the bearer of these needs, with the sociological category of the working class, and of both with the structural category of production—wage labor. For the critic of civil society, the philosophically derived proletariat replaced Hegel's universal estate in the function of mediating the antagonisms of particularity in civil society. As a class, the proletariat was to fuse competitive individuals into a conscious community *opposed* to the oppositional structure of civil society. But Marx's critique of the concept of mediation can be turned against him—for the concept of class reproduces internally the fundamental antinomy of universal/particular, freedom/necessity, in the form of an antinomy between a socioeconomic analysis of stratification and a theory of revolution based on the concept of need. This becomes evident as soon as one questions Marx's fundamental premise that an *anticapitalist and/or socialist revolution must be a class revolution.* That the working class might challenge capitalist relations on the basis of class interests indicates little regarding the objective possibility for the development of radical needs pointing to an emancipated society. The two become the same only if we assume in a deterministic manner that a postcapitalist society is by definition an emancipated one. The twentieth century should by now have destroyed this illusion.

Nevertheless, the purpose of our argument is not to affirm the classical Leninist position that the working class can, on its own, develop only a trade union (reformist) consciousness. Like the reformist theorists of the Second International, Leninism resolves the antinomy of Marx's class theory (radical need versus class interest) in favor of the concept of interest. As opposed to this approach, we would argue for the possibility of the emergence of radical needs at the point of production, among other places, but insist that these are not imputable from the outside to average class members who embrace their class status. Radical social movements composed of individuals challenging the reduction of their needs, abilities, and activity to the imperatives of interest relations can emerge in any domain of society. This distinction may appear trivial, but it provides the only orientation that precludes the subordination of individual need to an alleged "general" class interest. In a sense, our approach is the opposite of traditional Marxism. Rather than cling to the dogma of class as revolutionary subject, thereby sacrificing the normative moments of the critique of civil society to the efficiency of interest politics, we attempt to preserve the nonauthoritarian relation of theory and praxis based on the concept of need. The first step in our critique is thus to disassociate the philosophical presuppositions of the theory of radical contestation, derived from the immanent critique of civil society and addressed to self-legislating needs, from the concept of class.

Philosophical presuppositions reconsidered

It is necessary to go a step farther and critically examine the philosophical presuppositions themselves. The demonstration of the antinomy between the philosophical and sociological components of the class theory—that is, the difficulty of linking universal, revolutionary subjectivity to a sociologically identifiable class—does not mean that Marx's sociology is false while his philosophy is unproblematic. This position, typical of praxis philosophers, is untenable. Here we can only point to some of the difficulties involved. The first concerns an illegitimate leap in Marx's philosophical reasoning, which moves from an immanent norm critique of civil society that affirms the universalistic character of its legitimating norms versus the inadequate institutional basis for their realization, to the *unfounded* conclusion that a particular and collective subject must *represent that universality* in its being in order to struggle for its realization. Indeed, Marx's critique of civil society provides no basis for assuming that the addressees of a critique that uncovers and seeks to realize universalistic values must themselves constitute a single, universal, collective, and homogeneous subject. The concept of universal class thus breaks down, not solely due to the internal antinomies of the concept of class but also due to the unfounded concept of universal subject, be it a class, a race, a generation, a sex, a party, or whatever substitute has been found for the proletariat. Moreover, Marx's effort to identify a *true representative* of universality as a *particular group* (a homogeneous subject) violates both his own critique of Hegel's panlogism and the normative principle of free, self-determining, many-sided, and *differentiated* individuality. Certainly, a critique with practical and emancipatory intent must be able to speak to the needs of individuals whose struggles imply the elaboration and realization of the universalistic values inherent in formally democratic institutions. The search for a universal subject, however, projects the ideology of "bourgeois" revolutions onto future struggles. As Marx himself has argued, the self-presentation of a particular class as the general *representative* of society as a whole characterizes the logic of emancipation of the bourgeoisie based on the illusory notion of universal interest.[56] But this logic is the logic of class domination as well: "Only in the name of the general rights of society can a particular class lay claim to general domination." [57] That Marx presumed to have transcended the dilemma of universal/particular interest by attributing universality to a subject on the basis of radical needs indicates the deep tension within his own philosophical presuppositions between an open-ended, future-directed critique and the remnants of a rationalist philosophy that interprets history panlogistically. The concept of universal class and the identification of one historically produced, empirically existent group as the bearer of universality rest on the problematic attempt, derived from Hegel, to present history as positive and rational.[58] The universal class, the subject/object of history, the negation of the negation, are concepts in Marx's thought that imply a return to Hegel's absolute through the substitution, first, of species for *Geist*, second, of the class as the general representative of society for the species.[59] The concept of universal class subjugates the contingencies of historical praxis and the plurality of potential actors to the demands of "reason"—the demands of a logic that seeks to discover its own operations on the level of human praxis. This brings us to the tension at the core of Marxism between a radical critique included within the contingent historical process and a positive conception of historical development presented as the truth of history itself. On the one hand, by being installed within history in the effort to "think history," Marxism is the permanent confrontation to any absolute knowledge. But by positing the existence of a universal subject as the ultimate vindicator of past and bearer of future history, Marxism confuses the real with the rational and closes itself off from the very process of critique it has initiated. The tendency of Marxism to develop a positivist and determinist theory of history thus cannot be attributed solely to the one-sided vulgarizations of Marx's philosophy by his epigones. Nor can it be remedied by an uncritical return to the philosophical dimension of his theory. Instead, it is rooted in the ambiguity of a critical theory that seeks within a historically existent fact—the working class—the principle of constitution of totality and the organization by history itself of its own salvation. Accordingly, the radical nature of Marx's philosophical position, that of a critical thought that finds its roots in human praxis and reveals the openness of a history that is constituted through the activity, needs, and values of human actors, is endangered by the attempt to locate the meaning and resolution of historical development in the determinant existence of a universal subject.

Marx's radical interrogation of history was predicated upon a critique that stressed that the emergence of modern civil society presupposed the dissolution of prior communities whose traditional legitimations and roles fixed and restricted the individual's place in both society and nature. But the *fallacy of representative logic* led Marx implicitly to seal off his own interrogation of present and future history by determining in advance the place and form of subjectivity destined to *represent* universality and transform prehistory into history. Moreover, the erroneous logic of representation permeates and distorts the theory of praxis, or objectification, as well. To conceive of the movement of human history through the concepts of objectification, praxis, and alienation requires neither the concept of a historical subject nor the notion of unbroken, continuous progress. However, once universality in the form of simultaneously immanent and transcendent norms and values is attached to a particular empirical subject as its concrete representative—in this case, the proletariat—the tendency to confuse the life activity of this subject with the universal self-generative activity of the species becomes almost unavoidable. The class theory rests on a twofold logic of representation that designates a class as the bearer of universality and its labor as the representative activity of the self-constituting, objectifying praxis of the species, albeit in a negative form. But the normative concept of objectification, like that of universality, becomes perverted when attached to a particular concrete representative. The transcendental/empirical ambiguity of the concepts of labor and species, when unified by Marx in the form of the self-constitutive labor of the class, leads to the unwarranted limitation of praxis to labor and self-formation to a socioeconomic group.

The dangers implicit in the restriction of the self-constitutive process of the species to the concept of social labor have been drawn out by Jürgen Habermas.[60] In brief, Habermas argues that to narrow the concept of praxis to labor is to implicitly reduce the interest in knowledge and emancipation to an interest in technical control. The social subject whose consciousness derives solely from his laboring activity, whether this is conceived of as direct labor or as the applied labor of the "general intellect" (science), is a subject that knows social life processes through steering and control mechanisms alone.[61] Habermas, however, tries to show that, despite Marx's scientistic self-understanding, the dimension of ideology critique in his theory has as its referent a dynamic of reflection that implies self-formative processes other than the subject/object dialectic of labor.[62] The essence of the argument is that Marx's theory of class struggle and revolutionary praxis, along with the critique of ideology, appropriates dimensions of Hegel's concept of objectification that transcend the restriction of self-formative processes to production. By returning to Hegel and reconstructing the concept of objectification to include "the struggle for recognition," Habermas shows that attempts to ground radical potential in social labor rest on a one-sided interpretation of the famous master/slave section of the *Phenomenology*. Whereas Hegel's analysis does imply superior possibilities on the side of the working slave to develop a degree of self-consciousness through self-recognition in the objects he forms, Hegel nowhere states that through the dialectic of labor alone autonomy or full self-consciousness can be attained.[63] What the working slave attains through objectifying labor is recognition of himself in his object. Yet this is not at all identical with the mutual recognition of two subjects, for it does not entail acknowledgment of the slave's humanity by another self-consciousness. Insofar as the relation between the slave and his production is a subject/object and not a subject/subject relation, the process of recognition and emancipation remains incomplete and cannot be concluded solely through the dialectic of labor.

Accordingly, Habermas retrieves the concept of mutual recognition from Hegel in order to insist that the logic of recognition and the dialectic of labor are *two* dynamics of objectification, irreducible to each other. This implies that the process of emancipation cannot be unfolded solely from the dialectic of labor since a new stage of reflection (critique) is not immediately the result of the labor process. The correlate of the dialogic relation of subject to subject is not technical control but the struggle for recognition. This involves a self-constituting praxis challenging forms of institutional domination. Mutual recognition among free subjects requires that all participate equally in the interactive constitution of meanings, values, need interpretations, and institutions.

Habermas thus interprets Marx's emphasis on institutionalized relations of production—the relations of domination and struggle among social classes—as an indication that in his material investigations he took account of social practice encompassing both labor and interaction.[64] By emphasizing struggles over institutionalized relations of domination as the process in which two potential subjects form and interact, Habermas maintains that Marx adds to the "self-generative" act of social labor the "self-formative" process mediated by the interaction of class subjects in regard to relations of oppression and emancipation.

This reconstruction of the philosophical presuppositions of Marx's class theory is doubly instructive. By restoring to the concept of praxis the dimension of critical reflective enlightenment, Habermas rescues the antiauthoritarian moments of Marx's theory of revolution and need. Nevertheless, praxis-philosophical presuppositions of the concept of class are reconstructed *without* asking why this praxis is restricted to the formation of *class* subjects. Though one can develop a twofold theory of objectification (work and interaction) from the analysis of production and struggles over power relations, the fact remains that Marx limits praxis and conflict to classes defined vis-à-vis relations of production. Presumably the recognition that both struggle and social labor constitute self-formative processes avoids the productivist bias of the philosophy of labor because it separates the process of reflection and generation of consciousness from the instrumental transformation of nature. But since Habermas does not question the dogmatic restriction of self-formative praxis to the struggle between socioeconomic classes around relations of production, the productivist bias is not thereby abandoned. In fact, Habermas himself defines class struggles in terms of categories of production: "The conflict is always about the organization of the appropriation of socially created products, while the conflicting parties are determined by their position in the process of production, that is as classes." [65] The argument that this dynamic points to the constitution of a revolutionary class makes limited sense only if one presupposes the collapse between civil society and the economy, namely, the identification of institutional relations of domination as simply relations of production. If, however, social relations of domination are not limited to production relations, if the state, the family, culture, education, etcetera, also produce and reproduce relations of domination, then the exclusive link between praxis and class subjectivity breaks down. Unless the various spheres of social life are reduced to mere epiphenomena of economic relations, the notion of critical revolutionary praxis involved in struggle against institutionalized forms of domination and legitimating ideologies must point to the possible emergence of a plurality of radical social movements and groups whose needs and struggles point to a new form of society. Indeed, Habermas's own insistence on the distinction between labor and interaction provides the much needed philosophical basis for the possibility of looking to other spheres of social life for the emergence of radical protest that could be as important as the protest of the working class. Thus Habermas's reflection on the theory of class struggle does indeed uncover a missing philosophical component of the concept of praxis, lost in Marx's insistence on the identification of praxis with labor. But the broadening of the notion of self-formation through the dynamics of interaction and struggle for recognition, instead of grounding the concept of class subjectivity, renders adherence to the class theory of revolution arbitrary and dogmatic. The examination of the philosophical presuppositions of revolutionary and emancipatory praxis leads not to the identification of a single class subject but to a much needed indeterminancy regarding the addressees of the critique of civil society.

It should by now be apparent that the thrust of our analysis of the relation between philosophy and the class theory is to argue that philosophy, be it the philosophy of labor or the philosophy of praxis in the broader sense of Habermas, cannot serve to ground the revolutionary subjectivity of a class. The antinomy between the philosophical presuppositions of a radical revolution of radical needs and the concept of class was never resolved or even recognized by Marx. Within the framework of the theory of historical materialism, however, and in the "mature" critique of political economy, Marx attempted to provide the class theory of revolution with a historical and systematic basis in addition to philosophy. We will therefore turn to the analysis of these efforts in order to see if the concept of class, when placed within either a theory of historical development or a theory of capitalist reproduction, escapes the antinomies previously discussed.

Chapter 3

Class and History: The Evolutionist
Version of the Theory

*From philosophy to science: the dehistoricization
of the categories*

The classic reformulation of the concept of class from the standpoint
of the theory of historical materialism was written by Marx to Joseph
Weydemeyer in 1852:

As to myself, no credit is due me for discovering either the existence of
classes in modern society or the struggle between them. Long before me,
bourgeois historians had described the historical development of this class
struggle and bourgeois economists, the economic anatomy of the classes.
What I did that was new was to demonstrate: 1) that the existence of classes
is merely linked to *particular historical phases in the development of production,* 2) that class struggle necessarily leads to the dictatorship of the proletariat, and 3) that this dictatorship itself only constitutes the transition
to the abolition of all classes and to a classless society.[1]

It will be my task in this chapter to analyze this formulation and to
unfold the fundamental antinomic structure of the concept of class
it implies. In short, I will attempt to present the best-known model of
the class theory, the one that corresponds to the evolutionist theory
of history. In propounding the theory of historical materialism, Marx
hoped to ground his class theory (above all, the revolutionary potential
of the proletariat) in the scientific analysis of the logic of history—
that is, in production relations. But, far from closing the gap between
the philosophical and sociological components of his class concept, the
theory of historical materialism added another and more complex set
of contradictions to a correspondingly reformulated class theory. In this
chapter I will reveal the links between the new class concept, the triumph of determinism over contingency, and an ultimately statist model
of communism.

As is well known, *The German Ideology* is the first text to present its theoretical contribution and method—historical materialism—under the guise of *science*. It is considered by some to be the text that most fully and finally breaks with the eschatological philosophy of history of the earlier works through the formulation of a new method of historical analysis, as well as with the "humanist" conception of "man" through its replacement with the concept of "mode of production" as the theoretical starting point of analysis.[2] "Scientific" economic history writing substitutes for philosophy and critique. But though the theory of historical materialism is unambiguous in its objectivistic and deterministically conceived evolutionary model of history and civil society, *The German Ideology* and the *Theses on Feuerbach*, together with the other historical materialist texts, are by no means as one-sided as the interpreters of Marxism as science would have it.[3] Although Feuerbach and the Young Hegelians are subjected to biting criticism, Marx opposes to them *not only* the science of historical materialism *but also* a philosophy of praxis (albeit no longer in the form of a theory of objectification) that is most clearly articulated in the *Theses on Feuerbach*.[4] Thus the tension among the various components of the class concept between a teleological philosophy of history and an immanent critique of political economy is not resolved but transposed to a new plane. It reappears in the theory of historical materialism as an antinomy between an open-ended theory of revolution (based on concepts of class struggle and praxis) and a deterministic theory of historical development.[5] No reading that suppresses the concepts of praxis in favor of the analysis of modes of production can adequately comprehend the antinomy between the two that is *symptomatic* of the theory as a whole.

Marx assumed that he had transcended the ahistorical position of political economy and the abstract speculative standpoint of philosophy with the development of the "science" of historical materialism. But instead of further historicizing the theory of alienation and class on the basis of a more adequate critique of political economy (an alternative taken up in *Capital*), Marx absolutized the very political economic standpoint he had earlier criticized as economistic by extending the categories of production to past and future history.[6] He places "history" at the center of the discussion, replacing the static conception of *homo economicus* as well as the speculative philosophy of self-consciousness with a consideration of the "actual activities" that constitute the movement and development of social formations—production. Accordingly, history cannot be understood through philosophy or through the specifics of capitalist relations but must be approached through an analysis of the distinct *modes of production* through which men produce their means of subsistence, needs, consciousness, and social relations. *Labor*, then, becomes the activity par excellence that constitutes history. But the concept of labor is now reduced to the one-sided economic notion of *production* (labor in general), next to which the broad philosophical concept of objectification (and alienation) plays at most a subordinate role. Labor, in the sense of production, thus replaces objectification and the historically specific concept of wage labor as the unifier of history and civil society.[7]

The materialist approach to history presumes to proceed empirically and scientifically from "real premises"—real individuals and the material conditions of their lives. Although Marx does presuppose that production as a historical act encompasses, in addition to the transformation of nature, the development of new needs, social relations, forms of consciousness, and so on, the subject/object dialectic is essentially a productivistic one in which the level of the division of labor and development of the productive forces determines the other modes of social life.[8] The centrality of production to historical development is stated quite explicitly by Marx:

Thus it is quite obvious that from the start there exists a materialist connection of men with one another, which is determined by their needs and mode of production, and which is as old as men themselves. This connection is ever taking on new forms, and thus presents a "history" irrespective of the existence of any political or religious nonsense which would especially hold men together.[9]

On the basis of this "materialist premise," the tenets of the theory of historical materialism can be stated quite briefly. Every philosophical problem, Marx argues, can be resolved into an empirical fact, for production is the foundation of the whole sensuous world.[10] The driving force of history is the conflict between forces and relations of production. The forms of connection between men, and their social relations, change through their constant relation to and clash with the forces of production. The contradiction of wage labor and capital, therefore, is relativized into just one form of the more general contradiction between forces and relations of production that determines the dynamics of each historical period. Each society stands on the shoulders of the preceding one, but no prior society is fully transformed until its productive forces have been expanded as far as possible within the existing frame-work.[11] History, thus, moves dialectically, developing according to the objective logic of contradiction between forces and relations of pro-duction, *of which class antagonisms are the expression.* This movement proceeds inexorably to a stage (capitalism) in which the immense de-velopment of the forces of production leads to the final abolition of domination (through class struggle) and of the fetters hampering the further growth of the productive forces. Thus, under communism, only class domination, as the basic fetter to growth, disappears; the develop-ment of the forces of production, the core of history, continues under the aegis of rational planning.[12]

The concept of civil society undergoes changes that conform to the new theory of history. On the one hand, and for the first time, the term *bürgerliche Gesellschaft* is used to refer to all civilized societies in history. As such, it "embraces the whole material intercourse of individ-uals within a definite stage of development of the productive force." [13] On the other hand, and also for the first time, the term *bürgerliche Gesellschaft* is reserved for modern society but is now understood as bourgeois (capitalist) rather than simply as civil society. Bürgerliche Gesellschaft, within the framework of historical materialism, is wholly identified with its "anatomy," the (capitalist) mode of production and the division of labor. These are seen as the fundamental structures through which men are individuated and all their relations—legal, po-litical, cultural—turned into social relations.[14]

The consequences for the class theory of the reduction of the concept of civil society to bourgeois property and production relations will be-come clear further on. We are first interested in identifying its basis. What appears as a contradiction between the transhistorical and his-torically specific concepts of civil society becomes internally consistent as soon as one grasps that it is through the reduction of "civil society" to "mode of production" that Marx was able to generalize the dialectic of forces/relations of production (the anatomy of civil society writ large) to all of history. Both concepts of civil society here rest on the materialist premise that labor as production is the activity unifying history and society. Both modern bourgeois society and history as the history of civil society (or the evolution of modes of production), given the absolute primacy of production, are resolvable into a base (mode of production)/superstructure (politics law, culture) model. Accord-ingly, the difference between historical materialism and Marx's earlier analyses is not the abandonment of the category of civil society (Althusser) but the projection of its alleged "depth structure" (mode of production, base/superstructure model) to all of history.

The reduction of all modes of activity to epiphenomenal expressions of production relations is clearly expressed by Marx:

> This conception of history thus relies on expounding the real process of production—starting from the material production of life itself—and comprehending the form of intercourse connected with and created by this mode of production, i.e. civil society in its various stages, as the basis of all history; . . . and also explaining how all the different theoretical products and forms of consciousness, religion, philosophy, morality, etc., etc., arise from it and tracing the process of their formation to that basis.[15]

The nonreductionist concept of civil society is replaced by a new synthesis of political economy with evolutionism that collapses *civil society* with the *economy*, and *history* with *economic development*. The similarity between this doctrine and the enlightenment theories of progress and evolution cannot be dismissed lightly.[16] Clearly Marx's attempt to historicize political economy has resulted in the universalization of its productivist logic to all of history, for to constitute history and society along the single parameter of "mode of production" is to impose the political economic postulate of an autonomous economy, dubious even for the nineteenth century, onto the past, present, and future. All social formations are leveled to the same grid of time—the time of production—that imposes an evolutionary logic of progress on both their genesis and their decline. All are evaluated according to the same criterion—developmental productive forces, the value to which all else is subordinated. Thus the theory of historical materialism was able to transpose "critique," "civil society," and "alienation" into "science," "mode of production," and "division of labor" only on the basis of a productivist anthropology whose scientific guise is far more ideological than anything to be found in the earlier writings.

Nevertheless, as Habermas and Wellmer have pointed out, there is apparently a deep-seated contradiction between the conception of history as the evolutionary unfolding of the objective contradiction between forces and relations of production and that of history as constituted through class struggle.[17] Marx repeatedly refers to the motor of history, indeed, to history making itself, as class struggle. In effect, the concept of praxis as revolutionary activity, as class struggle, and the evolutionary deterministic model of historical development are two poles of an antinomy held together in an uneasy combination through the concept of class. Classes form as active self-constituted subjects precisely in the context of confrontation with other classes. They are *also* determined, limited, and indeed opposed, due to the objective structure of production. But if praxis is no longer identical with objectifying labor, what assures the link between economic contradictions and the self-constitution of conflicting groups struggling for emancipation? [18]

Assuredly, within the theory of historical materialism, it is the link between the concept of production and the concept of class that gives Marx the illusion of a consistent theory of history and an unproblematic class theory. Marx is able to state, within the same text, that the basis of all history is the development of the productive forces and that revolution is the driving force of history, because he has collapsed production categories with the sociological category of class and imposed both onto all social formations.[19] Having equated production relations with class relations, Marx sees no contradiction in attributing, first to the former, then to the latter, the source of development. But this implies a concept of class quite different from the one thus far discussed.

The class theory: from critique to dogma

The fundamental change in the concept of class within the theory of historical materialism is its *dehistoricization*. Just as the productivist rationality of capitalism is projected onto past history as its internal developmental logic, just as the concept of civil society loses its historicity, so too the concept of class is denuded of historical specificity and generalized as the category expressing fundamental struggles and confrontations for all history. This is the significance of the famous beginning of the *Communist Manifesto*:

The history of all hitherto existing society is the history of class struggles. Free man and slave, patrician and plebeian, lord and serf, guildmaster and journeyman, in a word, oppressor and oppressed, stood in constant opposition to one another, carried on an uninterrupted, now hidden, now open fight, a fight that each time ended, either in a revolutionary re-constitution of society at large or in the common ruin of the contending classes.[20]

To be sure, Marx states in the same text that precapitalist societies were characterized by a complicated arrangement of orders: patricians, knights, plebeians, and slaves in Rome; lords, vassals, serfs, and guild-masters in the Middle Ages. Yet all these entities are nevertheless referred to or understood as classes. Clearly, the concept of class no longer expresses a stratification principle unique to capitalist society (socioeconomic relations of domination based on the formal separation of the state from civil society and the emergence of the market as a self-regulating distinct sphere that allows for the formation of social identity of opposed socioeconomic groupings). Nor can class struggle be conceived of as a synonym for social movements whose struggles are the motor to history in a "nonproductivist" sense—that of democratization of society and state.

One could of course argue that the concept of class in the theory of historical materialism simply refers to unspecified groups related to the structure of society with conflicting needs and interests bound up with one another in a complicated relation of domination and dependence. The content of the concept of class, however, is *not* diluted to the extent that it becomes a mere empty terminological synonym for social relations of oppression—this would be unobjectionable, if uninformative. Indeed, even if such were the case, it is questionable whether the struggles of oppressed groups against domination can be seen as the fundamental dynamic of societal change and historical development. It is certainly not the case that the slave, the plebeian, the journeyman, or the serf ever waged a successful struggle in the sense of wresting power from dominant groups and becoming the new ruling class in a transformed social structure. Moreover, it is meaningless to equate the Greek citizen, the Roman patrician, and the feudal lord with one another through the category of class.[21] To do so would only undermine the very purpose of historical investigation into the specificity of social and political relations of particular social formations. Thus, even in this innocuous form, it is misleading to construe history as the history of class struggle.

For Marx, however, the concept of class retains its socioeconomic determination and is projected backward (along with the concept of mode of production) as the motor of all history and the key to the understanding of relations of domination and struggle for emancipation in dynamic societies. Accordingly, all societies are leveled to the same plane of production relations and are fraught with the same kind of internal antagonisms. Relations of domination are reduced to productions relations and comprehended as class antagonisms. The apparent opposition between the *evolutionary* forces/relations model and the *revolutionary* theory of class struggles is resolved by attributing to the revolutionary classes the role of *representing* progress in the further development of the forces of production. In all past history, however, this development of productive forces has taken place spontaneously, not consciously, so that the coherence of history forms behind the backs of individuals as an objective logic, a cunning of reason, that turns the revolutionary activity of classes into the vehicle of history's internal progression. The illusion of revolutionary praxis as the dynamic of history is thus rescinded by Marx as soon as he creates it, for class struggles of the past, whatever their conscious intent or articulated interests, have meaning to Marx only insofar as they express the conflict between forces and relations of production and lead to the further development of the productive forces.[22] They do not, in other words, lead to emancipation. Indeed, the theory of historical materialism goes so far as to identify the self-activity of individuals and classes with the development of the productive forces themselves.

In effect, what the generalization of the class concept to all history accomplishes, then, is the blocking of an analysis of the specificity of either precapitalist or capitalist societies. For the imposition of both these concepts, *class* and *mode of production*, onto all social formations entails the universalization and naturalization of the specific capitalist features of a distinct economic/social space between the private (family) and the public (state). The extraction from aspects of capitalist reproduction of an anarchic and contradictory economic logic of development and its projection onto history lead to the development of the pseudologic of the forces/relations model and the systematic inability to perceive noneconomic forms of domination or social relations. Because the relations among the various groups designated as classes (patricians, lords, serfs, citizens, slaves, artisans, etc.) are vastly different, as are the political, social, cultural, and economic structures of the societies they belong to, the concepts of class and mode of production necessarily become abstract and distorting when generalized beyond capitalism to the past. Thus the antinomy between the deterministic model of historical evolution and history as (in part contingent) class struggle or praxis is only apparent; through the workings of the representative logic, the transhistorical *concept of class* encompasses both poles of the opposition. The contending classes correspond to and derive their interests from the conceptual pair of forces and relations of production. Productive forces are embodied, personified, represented by the potentially revolutionary classes; property or control over the means of production and the social product is personified by the ruling class.

Accordingly, both the idea of history as the history of class struggle and the forces/relations model rest on a single panlogism; their unity is assured when class becomes the embodiment of production relations.

As Georg Lukacs pointed out, however, the dialectic of forces/relations, indeed, the theory of historical materialism itself, cannot be applied to precapitalist societies, for their economic life did not yet possess that independence or internal structure that the theory presupposes.[23] According to Lukacs, historical materialism could provide self-knowledge to reified capitalist society, but it could not do so for the past where religion, politics, and myth penetrated "economics," where, to use Karl Polanyi's phrase, the economy was embedded in other relations.[24] It is "vulgar Marxism" to apply historical materialism to all of history. A similar error is castigated by Marx in the case of "vulgar economics": "it mistook purely historical categories, moreover categories relevant only to capitalist society, for eternally valid ones."[25] Lukacs's criticism, however, stopped at the door of class theory because his purpose was to relativize and thereby save the theory of historical materialism for the analysis of capitalist society.

The class concept itself has been developed from certain features of capitalism, however, and has been illegitimately raised to the status of a pure scientific category applicable to all societies. Indeed, the very concept of class takes its content or meaning from the analysis of the bourgeoisie, the first *class* for whom production and property acquire primary importance vis-à-vis both its position of power and its legitimating ideology. As C. Castoriadis has brilliantly argued,

> to define a concept of class valid for all socio-historical formations by reference to the relations of production is tantamount to stating that the type of relation which all other classes in history maintain to these productive relations is identical to that which the bourgeoisie maintains. This is outrageously false, because the bourgeoisie is the first class by which the relation to production emerges as fundamental, the class whose major concern is production, the class that defines itself as essentially concerned with production, the class that defines men's acts and their relations by reference to production.[26]

Moreover, the bourgeoisie does not form a class as the mere reflex of a given level of productive forces but, as Marx himself often states, becomes a class only insofar as its members transform their given socio-historical situation (as owners of specific forms of productive forces—merchants, bankers, industrialists, etc.) and impose their logic of production onto society as a whole, subordinating everything to the principle of production for its own sake, or capital accumulation. One thus discovers in Marx's own historical accounts of the emergence of the bourgeoisie as a class an ambiguity between conceiving this class as determined fully by the productive forces it represents (private property) and conceiving it as the creator of these forces.[27]

The class concept that emerges from historical materialism refers to the objective relation to society's productive relations, independent of the thought or initiative of members of the class itself. But it is clear that production relations (of a certain kind) gain primary importance only by virtue of the gradual self-constitution of the bourgeoisie as the capitalist class and the creation of new socioeconomic relations unimaginable in prior societies. The bourgeoisie has a historical role precisely because it was not fully determined by production relations. Rather, through a new signification—the primacy of production—and through a new activity—the subordination of most aspects of life and the destruction of all traditional obstacles to the principle of accumulation—the extremely disparate strata composing the bourgeoisie (from thirteenth-century merchants to modern bankers and industrialists) became the capitalist class and imposed its model of development, of modernization, on society and the working class.

Accordingly, despite his objectivistic theoretical formulation of the concept of class, Marx's actual discussion of the birth of the bourgeoisie does not reduce it to the reflex of production relations or technological change. The recognition of the importance of the medieval city and its internal organization as well as the discussion of primitive accumulation, two crucial moments in the formation of the bourgeoisie that escapes the forces/relations model, reveal Marx's flexibility in historical class analysis. The formation and internal organization of the city, its supersession of individual family economy, and the creation of public political and economic spaces described in *The German Ideology* refer to activity by nascent "bourgeois" strata that far exceeded their "relation to the means of production." [28] This refers, obliquely, to be sure, to the democratization of social and political life—a struggle born with modernity itself, and quite distinct from capitalist development. The process of primitive accumulation, correspondingly, which led in the long run to the emergence of a working class crucial to the development of the wage labor/capital relation and to the capitalist class itself, took place independently of the technical development of productive forces and of the bourgeoisie itself (landed aristocrats and not bourgeois entrepreneurs instigated this process).[29] Indeed, Marx's account of the gradual emergence of the bourgeoisie as a class belies the mechanical conception of classes as passive representatives of productive forces.[30] The bourgeoisie constitutes itself as a class through its creative activity, through the development of new relations and the subordination of all social relations to its productive principle, and finally through its revolutionary struggle with other strata. Indeed, there is no Marxian concept of class without class struggle: "The separate individuals form a class only insofar as they have to carry on a common battle against another class; in other respects they are on hostile terms with each other as competitors." [31] The activity of a social stratum cannot, then, be predicted from an analysis of forces and relations of production.

Nevertheless, despite the space given to the process of self-constitution of classes through struggle (revolutionary praxis), the emphasis on production relations remains fundamental to the historical materialist *concept* of class. The lines of opposition and the interests involved, as well as the "objective possibility" of successful class formation, are determined by production relations. The "object" under investigation, the bourgeoisie, is not allowed to remain unique but becomes one of many manifestations of the *concept* of class. Because Marx's interest was, first, in revealing what classes are in general and, second, in pointing to the uniqueness of the proletariat in particular, the specificities of the bourgeoisie are treated as mere reference points for a universal concept of class that can be integrated into a systematic theory of historical development.

We have already argued that the bourgeoisie is the first *class* insofar as it raises production relations to the supreme level of significance and forms itself through the projection of its form of activity and ideological conception of this activity onto society as a whole. Indeed, the "independence" of the economic and the primacy of economic relations have meaning only in regard to the signification, typical of laissez-faire ideology, that economic relations are indeed free from such things as political and religious qualifications. Yet Marx's argument that the bourgeoisie replaces the complicated class antagonisms of feudal society with simplified class conflicts between itself and the proletariat, that it substitutes naked direct exploitation and self-interest for the political and religious *illusions* of the past, thereby revealing the *truth* of past history—that "man is at last compelled to face with sober senses his real conditions of life and his relations with his kind"—reveals that his *concept* of class is nothing other than an abstraction from certain aspects of a reality the bourgeoisie itself created for the first time.[32] The tendency of capitalism to reduce signification and political, social, and ideological forms to the expression of economic interests, the fetishistic dynamic of capitalist social relations discovered by Marx in his later works, is here generalized into the truth of social relations of all history.[33]

The problems involved in the dehistoricization of the categories are not restricted to their application to past history; they penetrate the historical materialist class analysis of capitalism. As is well known, the *Communist Manifesto* sings the praise of the capitalist class because it develops the forces of production and thereby creates the possibility for a new society that could break with the cycle of want, deprivation, domination, and alienation in past history. Besides homogenizing and simplifying class antagonisms, besides expanding the productive forces, the bourgeoisie "creates a world after its own image" by drawing all nations into "civilization" through the medium of the world market.[34] The subjugation of nature's forces by man—the development of the forces that slumbered in the lap of social labor—is accompanied by a process of *universalization* and internationalization of capitalist class relations overcoming national boundaries and local differences.[35] For Marx, this process of *homogenization universalization,* and *development* is the positive expression of the civilizing tendency of capital against the prejudiced and "barbaric" particularisms of noncapitalist peoples and countries:

National differences and antagonisms between peoples are daily more and more vanishing, owing to the development of the bourgeoisie, to freedom of commerce, to the world market, to uniformity in the mode of production and in the conditions of life corresponding thereto. The supremacy of the proletariat will cause them to vanish still faster.[36]

The success of the bourgeoisie allows for the development of world history, albeit only as one history with one fundamental logic: the development of the forces of production and the reduction of barriers, local and national and cultural, to economic "progress." Marx thus embraces the key ideological tenet of capitalism, namely, the idea that capitalist development is the only possible one for the present; alternatives must wait for the future.

The interests and fate of social classes are accordingly deduced from the logical model of production relations. In short, all social strata that are neither bourgeois nor proletarian are either doomed to disappear or consigned to historical and political irrelevance. Clearly, Marx's intent is not to provide a comprehensive picture of social stratification in bourgeois society. Rather, the concern is to relate classes to potential political activity, focusing on the allegedly dynamic classes and the logic of their development. It is obvious that the two-class model derives from the forces/relations dichotomy and that the interests, possible combinations, and political orientations of social groups are completely collapsed with those imputed from production relations. Marx simply equates categories of "capital" with "bourgeoisie," "wage labor" with "proletariat." [37] As yet there is no distinction between the system logic of capitalism and either its genesis or the variety of historical forms it can take.[38] The limitation of history to one mode of development with a single dialectical logic is complemented by the collapse of logic and history within bourgeois society. The praxis of class struggle whose outcome and form is predicted in advance is nothing other than the personification of conflicting production relations. The concept of class struggle or revolutionary praxis does not break through the one-dimensional subject/object dynamic of the philosophy of history based on the concept of labor as objectification but results in an even stronger determinism and objectivism. History and development are simply collapsed with one another. In the framework of historical materialism, history and struggle can bring no surprises; nothing really new can be created because the class concept already reveals where history is going and what forms of social relations will predominate in the future.

This becomes clear as soon as one investigates the formation and grounding of the proletariat as the revolutionary class on the basis of historical materialism. Indeed, the whole thrust of the latter is to provide a *scientific* analysis for the objective formation of a potentially revolutionary class (and the natural historical development of communism) based on the transformation of the structure of production initiated by capital. The bourgeoisie, according to Marx, has forged the weapons that will be used against it—the massive productive forces that outstrip bourgeois property relations—as well as the men to wield these weapons—the working class. Moreover, it is the bourgeoisie that creates the common-objective class conditions for workers by subjecting them all to the machine and destroying the individual character of proletarian labor.

The advance of industry, whose involuntary promoter is the bourgeoisie, replaces the isolation of the labourers, due to competition, by their revolutionary combination, due to association. The development of Modern Industry, therefore, cuts from under its feet the very foundation on which the bourgeoisie produces and appropriates products. What the bourgeoisie, therefore, produces, above all, is its own grave-diggers. Its fall and the victory of the proletariat are equally inevitable.[39]

Finally, the bourgeoisie demonstrates its own inadequacy as a ruling class because it cannot even guarantee the physical existence of its workers and reduces them to pauperism. From this "objective" standpoint, then, the homogenization, dehumanization, immiserization, and leveling of the proletariat (bemoaned in the 1844 *Manuscripts*) become, through a cunning of reason, the very features that assure unity of interest and possibility of success for the class representing the new productive forces of the future.

The most significant preparation by capital for the proletarian future, however, is the transformation of the mode of production into a *social* process resulting in a collective social product. Through the development of modern industry the bourgeoisie masses workers together in the factory, thereby increasing the productivity of *social* labor. But capital thus creates its own fundamental contradiction between private property and social or collective production, for the development of industry socializes the productive forces, abolishing the unity of private property and individual labor that furnished the ideological justification for property in the first place.[40] The argument in the *Manifesto* seeks to show that the proletariat is the legitimate heir of capitalist society and the future organizer of production on a new basis because it *represents* the new socialized productive forces, indeed, because it *is* the most collectivized productive force. Thus Marx contends that when capital is converted into common property it is not the personal property of individuals that is transformed into social property but only the social character of property that is changed; it loses its class character.[41]

According to this model, the proletariat receives moral affirmation, is ascribed its historical role, not because it labors per se but because it is objectively the class that carries the socialized forces of production. It is the progressive side of the contradiction between social power and private appropriation, between forces and relations of production. Indeed, Marx goes so far as to argue that the bourgeoisie even creates the universality of the proletariat insofar as it universalizes its mode of production through the world market, creating the preconditions for the emergence of a world historical revolutionary subject.[42] Accordingly, the proletariat is designated the universal revolutionary class not only because it has no particular interests to affirm or because it bears all the burdens of society without the benefits but because it foreshadows a new mode of production and individuality crucial for the future society. The negative turns into its opposite; the reduction of individuals to the level of mere workers—their homogenization, depredation, universalization, loss of individuality and particularity—becomes the positive objective basis for their historical mission. In one stroke, the *necessity* of *capitalist* development is affirmed as is the subordination of the workers to the capitalist logic—their time will come, but only in the future.

The theory of revolution: radical rupture or more of the same?

The historical materialist theory of revolution presumed to unite the analysis of development, modernization, evolution, change, social movements, and political action in a grand synthesis through the medium of the class theory. This synthesis was not only tenuous, however; it also had political implications (statism) that contravened the intentions of its author. For, far from allowing Marx to articulate the emancipatory thrust of *the* social movement of his time, far from enabling him to address the creativity and historicity of social action, it enclosed the political and social meaning of the workers' movement in a dialectical logic of contradiction and production that was able to grant meaning to collective action only from the standpoint of the future—a future already preconceived by the theory itself.[43] Indeed, the same faulty generalization regarding the concept of class occurs for the concept of revolution; it is derived from a class model of the French Revolution universalized into the definition of revolution *tout court* and imposed as a goal on the workers' movement.[44]

There is no doubt that the French Revolution of 1789, together with the subsequent restoration, reaction, and reemergence of domination and oppression, profoundly impressed Marx and served as the model for his theories of history and revolution. The adoption of the revolutionaries' claim that history can be made, that historical creation involves a radical break with the past and with tradition, that society can be created anew, was reconciled with the conviction that revolution is the result of an irresistible force (that is, it is historically necessary), through the interpretation of class struggle as the expression of the contradiction between forces and relations of production. But the conceptualization of the French Revolution as a revolution of the bourgeois class rests on the fallacious application of the forces/relations model of historical development to a complicated historical event that does not lend itself to universalization.[45] Marx's view of this event reads as follows:

the means of production and of exchange, on whose foundation the bourgeoisie built itself up, were generated in feudal society. At a certain stage in the development of these means of production and exchange, the conditions under which feudal society produced and exchanged became no longer compatible with the already developed productive forces, they became so many fetters. They had to be burst asunder; they were burst asunder. Into their place stepped free competition, accompanied by a social and political constitution adapted to it and by the economical and political sway of the bourgeois class.[46]

The absurdity of this reconstruction of class revolution, totally collapsed with the pseudologic of production relations, is hardly exhausted by the blatant omission of absolutism as a social formation intervening between feudalism and the revolution that allegedly instituted free competition, political democracy, and the political sway of the bourgeoisie.[47] The logicization of history under the sign of "dialectical revolution," through the attribution of a class status to radical movements and a "historical content"—the development of productive forces—to revolution itself, constituted a reduction and neutralization of history and revolution to the antagonistic relations of the single field of capitalist production magnetized by political economy.[48]

In order to fit the logical model, the complex event called the French Revolution is made transparent and necessary through the medium of class theory. It is presumed to be a "bourgeois" revolution waged by the class representative of progressive productive forces developed in the womb of the old society. As bearer of the developing productive forces, the bourgeoisie is dubbed a progressive class *an sich*. It succeeds by presenting its particular class interests as the universal interest of society, by transforming the ideal of freedom, equality, fraternity into forms adequate to capitalist supremacy—free labor, private property, formal democracy—only after it has established its hegemony. The next step for Marx's theory of revolution was to argue that every class aiming at domination, including the proletariat, must, like the bourgeoisie, present its interest as the general interest of society and strive to conquer political power on this basis.

Unfortunately, however, this class model of revolution rests on illusions of historical macrosubjectivity, bad social history, and the collapse of genesis and structure. The fact that the postrevolutionary organization of power did not derive simply from the activity of the entrepreneurial bourgeoisie is ignored. Moreover, it is only after a long period of development, begun at the close of the Middle Ages and lasting at least until the middle of the nineteenth century, that the bourgeoisie emerges as the capitalist class and imposes capitalist relations of production on all of society. Accordingly, the French Revolution was not a class revolution in the Marxian sense but rather a struggle partly in the name of universalistic values, partly in the name of a plethora of particular interests of a variety of social strata, whose initial outcome was not the political power of the bourgeoisie but the usurpation of power by the military (Napoleon), the restoration of aristocracy. Merely because the revolution ultimately cleared the path for the socioeconomic development of capitalism, one cannot project a teleology onto the strata making the revolution and presume that the ideals for which they fought were veils for the interest of the rising bourgeoisie. To understand the French Revolution as bourgeois is to view the universal values, the struggles over the signification and nature of society, as the veiled representative of bourgeois interest and to see the rebelling social groups as mere pawns, unconscious agents of bourgeois domination.

The arbitrariness of this analysis is reflected in Marx's tendency to assimilate the logic of proletarian revolution to the model unfolded for the bourgeoisie. Just as the latter emerged from the womb of feudalism representing progressive productive forces, "A similar movement is going on before our eyes." [49] The proletariat also emerges from the womb of a society that it, as the new productive force, will transform. It too becomes conscious of material interests against a third party; it too organizes itself on the basis of its objective position in production and gradually advances politically until it makes a revolution enabling it to become the new ruling class.

The "real" process of class struggle and proletarian revolution, according to Marx, goes through the following stages. First, the proletariat forms "more compact bodies" and organizations, but as yet these bodies (left unspecified) are the consequence of the union of the bourgeoisie and not its own active union. Gradually, the proletariat's *interests* and conditions of life are equalized as machinery obliterates qualitative differences in labor and reduces wages. The workers begin then to form organizations (unions) against the bourgeoisie, but still for such reasons as keeping up their wages. The real fruit of the workers' struggles are, for Marx, the permanent associations they found, which *centralize* local struggles into a national struggle between classes. Finally, because every class struggle is a political struggle, the self-organization of the proletariat into a class is accompanied by its organization into a political party.[50] The parallel to Marx's model of bourgeois class formation is now complete.

Contrary to the above, however, Marx insists that the nature of the class movement of the proletariat and the future outcome of its struggles are *radically different* from that of the bourgeoisie and from all classes in past history. Unlike the previous movements, the proletarian movement is the *self-conscious* movement of the *majority*. Although its struggle with the bourgeoisie must take place initially on a national level, it is inherently *international*. Although it, like the bourgeoisie, must seize political power by taking over the state, the interests it represents are *truly universal*. Accordingly, when the proletariat takes over the state, it *abolishes class relations*, insofar as "class rule in general ceases to be the form in which society is organized, that is to say, as soon as it is no longer necessary to represent a particular interest as general." [51] Moreover, the proletariat, unlike the bourgeoisie, allegedly *abolishes its own mode of production* rather than imposing it on the rest of society.

In a curious statement in *The German Ideology*, Marx argues for the radical break with past history as follows:

In all previous revolutions the mode of activity always remained unchanged and it was only a question of a different distribution of this activity—a new distribution of labor to other persons, whilst the communist revolution is directed against the hitherto existing *mode of labor*, does away with *labour*, and abolishes the rules of all classes with the classes themselves.[52]

What the above must mean is that, insofar as all forms of property are abolished—the division of labor, the subjugation of a class of individuals to the productive tasks they perform, and the contradictory logic of past (pre)history—the conflict of forces and relations of production and class struggle is radically transcended with the proletarian revolution. Since the proletarian struggle allegedly does not affirm the particular interests of a class, since it opposes the division of labor, and above all since it abolishes the subjugation of individuals to the material powers of their own creation, it institutes a radical break with past history. Correspondingly, communist society, like the proletarian class itself, is projected as the absolute other, the absolute negation of the past and the beginning of real history. The proletariat completes the process of dispelling political and religious illusions initiated by the bourgeoisie by dispelling material mystifications and creating illusionless, transparent social relations for the first time.[53] In short, the accidental form created by capitalism of the world historical cooperation of individuals, namely the division of labor and corresponding increase in the social productive power of the whole, will, with the unique class revolution of the proletariat, turn into the conscious rational control and mastery of these powers.

Of course, on closer inspection, it turns out that precisely the characteristics that allegedly distinguish the proletariat from other classes—universality, homogeneity, sociality, transparency—are, on the one hand, myths and, on the other, are derived from precisely that (bourgeois) logic of production to which the proletariat is said to be radically opposed. For according to the theory the condition of possibility for proletarian universality, its ultimate goal, and its progressive nature lie in the further development of the forces of production initiated by the bourgeoisie. Indeed, the very object to be appropriated by the revolutionary class is

the productive forces which have been developed to a totality and which only exist within a universal intercourse. Even from this aspect alone, therefore, this *appropriation must have a universal class corresponding to the productive forces and the intercourse.* The appropriation of these forces is nothing more than the development of the individual capacities corresponding to the material instruments of production. . . . Only the proletarians of the present day who are completely shut off from all self-activity are in a position to achieve a complete and no longer restricted self-activity which *consists in the appropriation of a totality of productive forces* and the development of a totality of capacities entailed by this.[54]

Despite the attempt to depict the proletariat and postcapitalist society as radically different from the past, despite the effort to transcend the economistic and ahistorical standpoint of political economy, the class theory of historical materialism absolutizes the capitalist tendency to reduce social relations to production relations. Consequently, the class theory is never able to break with the "mirror of production," and, like the capitalist society he opposes, the logic of Marx's argument reduces the liberation of human potential to the liberation of the productive forces.[55] The phantasm of the science of history that understands prehistory as composed of stepping-stones on a dialectical route to capitalism (the privileged moment of prehistorical development because it generates consciousness of production) turns against Marx when he tries to scientifically ground a radically different future. Just as the symbolic wealth of precapitalist societies is utterly lost in the arrogance of a theory that sees everything in the image of its own time, so too the future alternative becomes an impoverished one when conceptualized in terms of the reproductive logic of capitalism. It is ironic that the proletariat is assigned by Marx the identical essence to which bourgeois society attempted to reduce it—labor power. Defined in the universal according to the universality of labor power and based on the rationalist representative logic typical of "bourgeois" consciousness, the class of proletarians must, to be consistent, assume the task begun by the bourgeoisie—the finality of production and its rationalization.[56]

Consequently, and most importantly, the historical materialist concept of class itself encloses the activity and struggles of workers into a model that remains that of the bourgeoisie. The bourgeois class is defined not only by the ownership of the means of production but by the very goal of production. Thus, to impose the concept of class on the workers is to confine working-class struggle to antagonism at the level of the relation to the means of production but not to break the finality of capitalist forms of productivity. Indeed, one could maintain that the conjunction of the workers' movement and Marxism turns out to be a misfortune rather than a dialectical blessing. Insofar as Marxism succeeded in becoming the ideology of working-class struggles (which preceded Marxism historically), the resultant rationalization of the workers' movement and its revolt and the acceptance of the status of class enclosed it within the general rationality of the capitalist version of an industrial order.[57] To the extent that workers' movements interiorized communist ideology, their politics were reduced to whatever activity prepared the way for the accession to power and the attainment of class consciousness preserved by the party. Movements that do not correspond to this goal are considered either reformist (trade unionism, etc.) or unserious (pre- and post-Marxist utopian discourse and all non-Marxist libertarian movements). On the other hand, to the extent that workers' movements were not identical with Marxism, they could not be perceived from the Marxist standpoint. The rich history of workers' struggles against capitalist productivist rationality, the creative forms of organization and demands that express radical needs for new modes of life, new values, and an alternative present—that is, an alternative model of industrialization (as well as the struggles of nonworkers for

emancipation) remain closed to the class theory of historical materialism or comprehensible only as errors deviating from the real historical
mission of the proletariat.[58] Since the workers are ascribed their revolutionary task from the start, nothing really happens in the history of
their struggles. Historical materialism does not have the means to think
the history or historicity of the workers' movement because its own
criterion of intelligibility blinds it to whatever escapes its logic—it can
find only itself in history.[59]

Statism and the abolition of politics: the ruling-class model

Much of the recent neo/post-Marxist literature has recognized the absence of an adequate theory of the state or of politics in Marx's oeuvre,
and there have been various Marxist attempts, for the most part unsatisfactory, to fill the gap.[60] The base/superstructure model, according
to which the state, law, and ideology are conceived as determined ("in
the last instance") by the mode of production, is certainly the source
of this deficiency, for it implies that political power and domination
represent something else: the social relations of domination of the only
sphere with real weight in the historical materialist framework, the
economy. I wish to take this argument a step further and analyze the
links between the base/superstructure model, the dissolution of the rich
opposition between state and civil society, a statist logic of revolution and the future communist society.

To the historical materialist the state is seen, according to the parameters of the class theory, as a superstructure inhabited by a parasitic
body of officials under the control of the ruling class. The concept of
ruling class thus replaces Hegel's bureaucracy, estates, and corporations
as the single mediation between a reduced concept of civil society
(bourgeois society/mode of production) and the superstructural state.
Political power is reduced to the socioeconomic imperatives of class
domination and the state to a mere instrument of the ruling class—its
form of organization.[61] But this is not all. As the famous passage in
The German Ideology asserts, the class that is the ruling *material* force
of society, the class that has the means of production at its disposal, is
also the ruling intellectual force of society. Its ideas are the ruling ideas,
its culture displaces traditional culture, and it or its agents take hold
of the state and rule in the interests of the class.[62] Assuredly, this image
of class rule fits only the requirements of the theory, according to which
the dominant class must represent its particular interests as universal

and conquer political power to create an illusory community that appears as the neutral representative of the nation as a whole but is in fact the instrument ensuring the class's solidarity and hegemony.[63] In short, the centralization of the means of production in the hands of the bourgeoisie must, for Marx, be accompanied by a political centralization that allows for the emergence of its unified class interest.

It is this reduction of the state to a mere power instrument of the ruling class that precludes the investigation of the internal dynamics of the political sphere and the nature of the power of those who occupy its ranks. The meagerness of Marxist analyses of the state can thus be attributed to an overextended and overburdened class concept. Although Marx does point to situations in which the bourgeoisie does not rule politically (Bonapartism) even though capitalist relations predominate, these situations are seen as an extraordinary deviation from the paradigm of class rule.[64] Indeed, we would have to agree with C. Wright Mills that "ruling class" is a badly loaded phrase because it implies that an economic class rules politically, thereby reducing the institutions, members, and logic of the state to the status of an instrument in the hands of the dominant class, denying autonomy to the political order and its agents.[65]

In addition to serving as the mediation between civil society and the state, between the economic and political power of the dominant capitalist class, the concept of "ruling class" serves another function: the foreshadowing of the model of proletarian revolution that has the takeover of the state and the establishment of its own dictatorship as a fundamental component. The generalization of the model of bourgeois class formation pervades the goal of proletarian rule and the means to achieve this goal—the formation of a political party and the takeover of the state. The ascribed vocation of the working class—development of class consciousness, formation of a party, state power—not only conforms to the development of the bourgeoisie but is based on an internal logic of representation/substitution that hypostatizes the being of class. The representability of the class, the rationalistic imputation of interests to it from the productive forces, calls for the principle of the party, itself an instance claiming to selflessly represent the common interests of the class. Bolshevism is consistent with this version of class theory: "The immediate aim of the communists is . . . : formation of the proletariat into a class, overthrow of the bourgeois supremacy, conquest of political power by the proletariat." [66] The state becomes simply the means through which the proletariat universalizes its interests on the political plane. The science that uncovers the goal of the workers' movement closes the gap between the theory of revolution and the theory of historical development.

This extreme form of the class theory leads to a vision of the future society that explicitly justifies the *strengthening* rather than the dissolution of the state. Indeed, the antinomy between the evolutionary and revolutionary theories of history reappears in the theory of historical materialism in the form of two contradictory models of communism —one statist, the other antistatist. On the one hand, the transition to communism is reduced to the dynamic of forces and relations of production of which class struggle is the reflex—the necessary condition for communism being the further development of the productive forces. The vehicle for this task is the revolutionary party of the proletariat, which must conquer political power and strengthen the state by continuing the process initiated by capitalism of concentration and centralization of capital:

The proletariat will use its political supremacy to wrest, by degrees, all capital from the bourgeoisie, to centralize all instruments of production in the hands of the state, i.e. of the proletariat organized as the ruling class, and to increase the totality of productive forces as rapidly as possible.[67]

The first stage of communism will accordingly entail a dictatorship of the proletariat based on its domination and extension of the state apparatus as the sole organizer of production, distribution, credit, communications, transport, and so on.[68] Civil society, obviously, is to be abolished. Here the expansion of the productive forces is clearly related to the development of the centralized state apparatus. Far from abolishing labor, the communist state imposes it on everyone, extending factories and industrial armies even to agriculture.[69] The abolition of private property in the means of production and of all classes in the name of the general interest implies the dissolution of all mediating instances between state and society. Thus an explicit, dictatorial statism, at least for the "first stage" of communism, flows directly from the class theory.

On the other hand, Marx assumed that, with the development of the forces of production, class distinctions would eventually disappear and the state would be transformed into a vast association of the whole nation; it would wither away. In a vision that is both utopian and normative, Marx describes communism as the society in which individual and community are reconciled, the division of labor and classes and the state abolished:

In communist society, where nobody has one exclusive sphere of activity but each can become accomplished in any branch he wishes, society regulates the general production and thus makes it possible for me to do one thing today and another tomorrow, to hunt in the morning, fish in the afternoon, rear cattle in the evening, criticize after dinner, just as I have a mind, without ever becoming hunter, fisherman, shepherd, or critic.[70]

This transcendence of the division of labor is possible only on the basis of community. Counterposing the concept of community to the state, Marx argues that only within a community of freely associated individuals could the common interest of society, previously snatched away from society's members and made an object of government activity, be returned to society as its own concern.[71] Thus the value of free, many-sided individuality organized in free associative communities has primacy over the idea of collective state planning of production.

This model of communism is, however, not only vague and ungrounded in the analysis of civil society, it is essentially antimodern. Moreover, it is associated with another concept of community that is quite ominous in its implications. Prior to the theory of historical materialism, Marx had argued that to belong to a class is to have one's personal development determined by conditions external and independent of the individual. He spoke of the subsumption of individuals under the class—a fact that allows for the development of common interests but is based on the leveling of individuality.[72] The theory of historical materialism, however, maintains that the revolutionary *class of proletarians is a community* of concrete, differentiated individuals capable of abolishing the previous form of subsumption of individuals under classes on the basis of universal interest and socialized production.[73] The implication is that, insofar as the class interests of the proletariat are truly universal, there can be no conflict between individual and class (community), between particular and general interest, between need and interest. The subsumption of productive forces under the conscious control of the producers abolishes the externality of alienating class conditions, rendering social and material relations completely transparent. This is possible because the class community is a sociality; the socialized production it performs and the collectivized productive forces it represents become the model of organization of a communist society in which classes are abolished because everyone has become a producer (associated producer!). In short, because the proletariate is allegedly already a fully social entity, because its labor is directly collective, denuded of any individual character or properties, the tension between the abstract egoistic "bourgeois" individual and the abstract political community dissolves in communist society without the aid of political institutions.

Thus, in his enthusiasm to combat the privatization and atomization of civil society, Marx went to the opposite extreme with the concept of a class community. The private and the political are subject to the tyranny of their dissolution into the socialized communist community of the class in which social relations and production become the model of sociation par excellence. But this pseudoemancipatory ideal with its fetish of social relations only does violence to individuality by ignoring its difference from the social and communal and dissolving it into the collectivity. As Weber argued, the concept of class as a community is a myth—in its proletarian garb, it can only lead once more to the sacrifice of the individual to an illusory community.[74] In the theory of historical materialism the socialized productive forces and their class representatives have as their corollary the state as the representative of the collectivized individuals in the classless society. Far from preserving the positive aspects of bourgeois individuality in a new synthesis or a new relation of individual and community, the society of associated producers, of "social individuals," levels both in the image of a reunified base and superstructure.

Indeed, what the withering away of the state entails is the dissolution not of the administrative organs but of politics itself.[75] The instrumentalist/representative concept of politics, together with the presupposition that political domination is class domination, both expresses the inability of historical materialists to develop a meaningful concept of politics and explains the statist conclusions they must reach. The *Communist Manifesto* concludes by singing the praise of the destruction of politics:

When . . . class distinctions have disappeared, and all production has been concentrated in the hands of a vast association of the whole nation, the public power will lose its political character. Political power, properly so called, is merely the organized power of one class for oppressing another.[76]

The state, accordingly, remains as the administrative instance of society; what withers away is political interaction. Small wonder that this

Saint-Simonian image serves as a perfect substitution of the technocratic ideology of interest-free total administration for the so-called
communist states. Indeed, Marx, against all his intentions, provides the
basis for the antidemocratic single-party state penetrating all of civil
society when he argues that civil liberties and democratic forms in
bourgeois society are mere reflections of capitalist market relations that
communism can well do without.

Unfortunately, the relegation of politics to the dustbin of history not
only does not extirpate (theoretically) domination but precludes the only
means by which statist domination could be guarded against—the
creation of institutions in an independent civil society allowing for the
participation of individuals in the choice of adequate norms, goals, and
institutions for social life. When confronted with the "social problem"
of expanding needs and economic domination, Marx assumed that
abundance, productivity, and good administration could be a solution
guaranteeing individual satisfaction. He assumed that the resolution of
the irrational organization of bourgeois society lay in the homogeneous,
transparent, socialized, and universalistic proletariat, which would create a future society in its own image. Accordingly, the need for political institutions, for space for reflection on values, norms, and need
interpretation (politics in the classic sense of the word), for the articulation of mechanisms allowing for compromise between interests, was
deemed unnecessary.[77] In short, the class theory of historical materialism assumed the problem of "ends" to be solved. Revolution is just a
matter of "means."

By viewing capitalist modernization/industrialization as a necessary
stage in historical development, by positing the state as the object of
class struggle and the future subject of modernization under the aegis
of the proletariat, the class theory of historical materialism, despite
Marx's intentions, represented the logic of capitalist productivism. It
could not articulate the historicity of the social movement of the working class, oriented toward a different model of industrialization subordinated at the very least to the value of social justice and often also
to democracy, for its message was that the workers must wait. They
must wait until the capitalist mode of production "fully matured," until
industrialization was carried out by and under capital.

The young Marx was able to develop a normative concept of politics
(an interactive model of direct participatory democracy) and a tentative
critique of the state on the basis of the immanent critique of the

state/civil society duality. I have argued that the theory of historical materialism, with its emphasis on the concept of mode of production, blurs this distinction between state and society by reducing the state to the form of organization of the bourgeoisie, to a capitalist state, and by reducing civil society to its "base" production relations—through the vehicle of the class theory. Accordingly, the political (law, parliaments, interest articulation, and compromise structures) as opposed to the administrative aspect of the state and the social (associations, norm articulation) as opposed to the systemic/economic moments of civil society are either not addressed or dismissed as epiphenomenal.

With the reduction of the concept of civil society to its base, the bulk of Marx's theory from historical materialism to the critique of political economy transmits the following message: Insofar as the political state is a class state, in an emancipated society public power must lose its political character, production must be in the hands of associated producers, and the sole legitimate function of the state must be the administration of things. In short, Marx's tendency was to reduce political relations to epiphenomena of production relations, to identify politics with class domination, to locate the genesis of bourgeois political norms in the automatic reflection of economic processes, and to assume that relations of domination must be class relations. Politics is merely the ideological representation signifying conflicts and power relations of the sphere of production. The lack of room for a public space between and embedding state and economy in Marx's analysis of modern society is accordingly complemented by its absence in his image of communism. Although Marx personally clung to the value of democracy, he could no longer ground the norms and values he embraced in an immanent critique of modern civil society once it was identified with particularism—with bourgeois ideology. Indeed, the collapse of historical genesis and societal structure (generalization of the forces/relations model to the dialectic of history), of evolution and history, of political revolution and social movements, of development and change, in a single teleological theory prevented Marx from addressing the issues of the genesis of social norms, political legitimacy, interpretation of needs, self-interpretations and projects of social movements in anything but the most cursory manner. The logical culmination of his class theory within the theory of historical materialism was either an explicitly statist or a subtly technocratic utopia based on the completed socialization of society and the emergence of the "social individual," the associated producers whose immediate, direct, transparent sociality does away with the necessity for political mediations as well as for formal legal guarantees. In the telos of this theory, freedom tends to be sacrificed to abundance.[78] It remains to be seen whether Marx's break with the theory of historical materialism allows him to reconstruct a more convincing and less dangerous class concept.

Chapter 4

The Historical Writings

History or historical materialism?

I on the contrary, demonstrate how class struggle in France created the circumstances and relations that made it possible for a grotesque mediocrity to play a hero's part.[1]

At first glance, Marx's historical writings appear to be freed from the extreme determinism and panlogism of the doctrine of historical materialism.[2] Their importance to us is not the historical information they provide but their status as examples of class analyses of revolutionary current events. Here, if nowhere else, we should expect to find the clearest expression of the interrelation between praxis and "objective" structures, between political action and economic conditions, and between the "subjective" and the "objective" factors in an empirically informed sociological class analysis. Indeed, the complexity of events and the immersion in present history lent a flexibility to Marx's writing. Here he confronts the active struggles of several social strata other than the bourgeoisie and proletariat, as well as the role of a state over which the "natural" ruling class has obviously relinquished control. The 1848 revolution and the 1870 Paris Commune called for an analysis of political forms and ideological motivations that could not be derived from economic interests imputed from forces and relations of production. Moreover, they required an interrogation of a historical process that ran counter to the evolutionary model of historical materialism.

To be sure, the brilliance of Marx's insights into the diversity of cultural, traditional, and symbolic factors involved in concrete political activity is, in the end, covered over by the reimposition of the logic of historical materialism and its concomitant class theory on the heterogeneity of historical events. Indeed, insofar as Marx's self-conception of his historical writings is concerned, they represent an example of the use of the materialist conception oriented to

tracing political conflicts back to the struggles between the interests of the social classes and fractions of classes encountered as the result of economic development, and to show[ing] the particular political parties as the more or less accurate political expression of these same classes and fractions of classes.[3]

Yet this effort never quite succeeds. Contrary to Marx's own one-sided self-interpretation, there is a fundamental ambiguity in his historical writings—the unrecognized and unresolved tension between an open-ended, nondogmatic, critical sociology of class, at work in the *process of analysis* itself, and the superimposition of the *interpretive schema* of the closed, totalizing, and leveling logic of historical materialism. This ambiguity, moreover, is the source of the richness of the historical writings and their continued importance, for they provide examples of the role that class analysis could play when freed from an overambitious and ultimately sterile theory of history.

In effect, we find Marx reasoning against himself in the historical writings, refuting de facto but reaffirming de jure the class theory formulated prior to the historical investigations. His terse criticism of the work of Hugo and Proudhon on Napoleon's coup d'état reveals an ambiguity in his approach that can be turned against his own theoretical analysis.[4] Whereas Hugo's work is dismissed for treating the coup d'état *voluntaristically* as the unexpected and inexplicable violent act of a single individual, Proudhon is attacked for the opposite error of presenting the coup as *determined* by antecedent historical development, that is, for objectivism. But the concept of class itself internalizes and reproduces the tension between voluntarism and objectivism or determinism. Marx's class analysis of political struggles hovers between a rich investigation into traditions and politics of France in relation to social strata and an attempt to conjure away ambiguity through an unaltered theoretical model. On the one hand, the forces/relations model does not determine directly the analysis of the role of classes or the relations of class and politics; sociology and structure are not collapsed. On the other hand, Marx remains theoretically blind to his own discoveries because the ultimate meaning of historical events and the objective possibilities for historical actors are derived not from their own trajectory but from the prefabricated class theory.

The historical writings hint at a notion of political struggle and of history quite different from that of historical materialism.[5] Tradition, repetition, myth, a nonreductionist understanding of symbols and ideology, political and revolutionary action not determined by imputed economic interests but motivated by a multitude of meanings, needs, and motifs coming discontinuously from the past—all these appear as the components of historical activity that belie the historical materialist model of progress and evolution and the collapse of logic and genesis. Indeed, the genesis and dynamics of "bourgeois society" seem no longer to be attributable to the progressive logic of forces and relations of production, expressed in self-conscious, interest-oriented class struggles. A distinction is made, for example, between the revolutionary social upheavals of the French Revolution of 1789, which required heroism, sacrifice, terror, civil war, resuscitation of past traditions and art forms, and the "sober reality" of bourgeois society that emerged after the struggles subsided.[6] Just as Cromwell and the English borrowed passions, speech, and illusions from the past to accomplish their revolution, so too the eighteenth-century French resuscitated Roman costumes and phrases to glorify their struggles and generate revolutionary enthusiasm. It was these myths and borrowed traditions and not simply the (false) universality of bourgeois class interests that moved people to historical action (in conjunction, of course, with interpreted needs) and allowed for the creation of the necessary conditions for the emergence of a new social structure. In the theory of historical materialism, revolutionary praxis as the source of historical creation either derives its logic and content from the contradictions of the forces and relations of production or appears as inexplicable spontaneous voluntaristic activity. Here, however, Marx seems to understand that, far from emerging from a void or from the simple recognition of class interest, radical ruptures are motivated by a plethora of needs, values, traditions, utopian aspirations, etcetera, that resurge from a never completely dead past to form new combinations and take on new meanings.

Moreover, as the revolutions of 1848 and 1870 show, even by the mid-nineteenth century capitalism had not accomplished the homogeneity or transparency or simplicity of class relations and politics alluded to in the *Communist Manifesto*. The revival of old dates, names, edicts from the past, and the multiplicity of factions, parties, and social strata reveal that the structure and dynamic of bourgeois society are far from straightforward. Despite the absorption in the production of wealth and in the peaceful competitive struggle, conflicts are not based simply on opposed economic interests clear to all but are occluded, complex, and multidimensional. Marx summarizes this alternative conception of history succinctly enough to merit quotation:

Men make their own history, but they do not make it just as they please; they do not make it under circumstances chosen by themselves, but under circumstances directly encountered, given, and transmitted from the past. *The tradition of all the dead generations weighs like a nightmare on the brain of the living. And just when they seem engaged in revolutionizing themselves and things, in creating something that has never yet existed,* precisely in such periods of revolutionary crisis *they anxiously conjure up the spirits of the past* to their service and borrow from their names, battle cries, and costumes in order to present the new scene of world history in this time-honored disguise and this borrowed language. Thus Luther donned the mask of the Apostle Paul, the Revolution of 1789 to 1814 draped itself alternately as the Roman Republic and the Roman Empire, and the Revolution of 1848 knew nothing better to do than to parody, now 1789, now the revolutionary tradition of 1793 to 1795.[7]

No historical materialist could consistently embrace such a view of historical development because it stresses repetition over evolution, radical creative activity over objective contradictions, and the role of symbols, illusions, and tradition over rational calculation or the unconscious logic of interest conflicts. Indeed, one could even conclude that there is space here for historical actors who neither are nor could become classes.

But what Marx gives and concedes with one hand, he takes away with the other. This brilliant insight into the importance of symbols and traditions of the past in addition to needs, interests, and ideas in motivating historical activity (as well as the role of continuity and discontinuity) is immediately diluted by Marx's explanation of why such recurrence, such borrowing, takes place. In short, he argues that it is because earlier revolutions (as opposed to the future proletarian revolution) needed to deceive themselves regarding the limits of their content—they needed to disguise particularity and narrow interest with glorious names and high-sounding phrases to create the necessary illusion of universal emancipation and to generate enthusiasm. "Earlier revolutions required recollections of past world history in order to drug themselves concerning their own content."[8] Thus, bourgeois revolutions, according to Marx, storm quickly to success, occur in short-lived ecstasy, quickly reach their zenith, and then subside, the poetry of the past replaced by sober calculations, the limits of capitalist relations triumphing over the universalistic claims of liberty, equality, fraternity.

But it is not the standpoint of the sober reality of bourgeois society and clear-cut interest-oriented action that allows Marx to refer to the role of symbols and tradition in bourgeois revolutions as *self-deception* or as the *illusions* necessary for the genesis yet not for the internal processes of bourgeois society. Clearly, the whole thrust of Marx's historical writings is to demystify the *ceaselessly recurring* illusions, myths, and traditions still weighing heavily on the brains of the actors *within* modern civil society and occluding their class relations and interests. Rather, the reference point is the ideal of a truly universal proletarian revolution made soberly and uniquely in the name of a class interest that indeed for the first time represents the interests of all of society and therefore does not need to draw its poetry from the past:

The social revolution of the nineteenth century cannot draw its poetry from the past, but only from the future. It cannot begin with itself before it has stripped off all superstition in regard to the past. Earlier revolutions required recollections of past world history in order to drug themselves concerning their own content. In order to arrive at its own content, the revolution of the nineteenth century must let the dead bury their dead. There the phrase went beyond the content; here, the content goes beyond the phrase.[9]

A truly radical break with the past, a really emancipatory revolution ending the cycle of want, deprivation, oppression, and irrationalism, is one that requires no illusions to veil the interest of the revolutionary class because this interest is universal, because its goals can become transparent, and because it can move people rationally without recourse to superstition! According to Marx, then, self-criticism, self-understanding rather than self-deception, motivates the class revolution of the proletariat:

On the other hand, proletarian revolutions, like those of the nineteenth century, criticize themselves constantly, interrupt themselves continually in their own course, come back to the apparently accomplished in order to begin it afresh . . . recoil ever and anon from the indefinite prodigiousness of their own aims, until a situation has been created which makes all turning back impossible, and the conditions themselves cry out: Hic Rhodus, hic salta! Here is the rose, here dance! [10]

This image of proletarian revolution, presented as the key to the social revolutions on the agenda of the nineteenth century and to the critical analysis of bourgeois revolutions, reveals the ultimate intrusion of the preformulated class theory of historical materialism. For, given the admittedly narrow role of the proletariat in the revolutions of 1848 and 1870, given his explanation of the failure of two nineteenth-century revolutions on the basis of the objective immaturity of both bourgeois society and the industrial proletariat, Marx certainly could not derive the image of rational, illusionless, interest-guided revolutionary activity from the actual activity of the scarcely existing industrial proletariat. Nevertheless, it is from this theoretical standpoint that Marx evaluates the historical events to whose complexity and irreducibility his own work constantly attests. It is this juxtaposition of two models of revolutionary and political activity, one guided by an open-ended analysis of the complex mixture of needs, tradition, and symbols, the other by rational calculation of class interest, that penetrates the entire class analysis of political activity in Marx's historical writings.

Confronted with a situation in which social strata other than the bourgeoisie and proletariat play a dominant role, and in which the relation between civil society and the state could not be understood through the ruling-class model, Marx tried to present the underlying social relations and interest conflicts among the various classes as the key to political intrigue. At the same time, his own analysis demonstrated that political interaction and its ideological forms are explained not by the logic of interests but rather through a "misunderstanding" by the very actors of this logic.[11] The five classes Marx discusses—the petty bourgeoisie, the peasantry, the proletariat, the bourgeoisie, and the Lumpenproletariat—are already familiar to us from his other writings. Their political roles, however, come as a surprise.[12] For the proletariat and the bourgeoisie occupy the center of the political stage in this "revolution of the nineteenth century" only temporarily, whereas the "middle classes" and their representatives, doomed to insignificance in the *Manifesto*, appear to be the arbiters of the ultimate fate of the revolution and of France.

Interest, illusion, and the five-class schema

Only the role of the petty bourgeoisie approximates the expectations regarding "class" stemming from historical materialism. In the *Communist Manifesto*, Marx had referred to the petty bourgeoisie as an intermediate class whose mode of appropriation places them between capital and labor and subjects them to the constant fear of being hurled down into the proletariat.[13] Because the petty bourgeoisie's mode of production and form of property are anachronistic and peripheral to capitalism, its position in any class struggle between capitalists and proletarians must be external and ambiguous. Its class interest, accordingly, is simply to maintain the status quo and prevent the capitalist progress that spells its doom. Unable to represent their class interest as the interest of society, however, representatives of the petty bourgeoisie are doomed to formulate reactionary or utopian political illusions. In short, this class and its representatives are condemned by their very class interest to illusion. (We shall see that illusion is hardly unique to the petty bourgeoisie.)

The trajectory of the role of this class in the 1848 events seems to confirm the above. The petty bourgeoisie through their representatives start out as democratic republicans, following the lead of the proletariat in fighting for a parliamentary republic.[14] Marx argues that precisely because the petty bourgeoisie is a transition class between capital and labor it believes that it stands above class antagonisms and envisages the real contest as between the indivisible people and their oppressors. Democracy is its natural rallying cry, the myth of the people, the nation, its necessary illusion.

But the democrat, because he represents the petty Bourgeoisie, that is, a transition class, in which the interests of the two classes are simultaneously mutually blunted, imagines himself elevated above class antagonism, generally. The democrats concede that a privileged class confronts them, but they, along with all the rest of the nation, form the *people*. What they represent is the *people's rights*; what interests them is the *people's interests*. Accordingly, when a struggle is impending, they do not need to examine the interests and positions of the different classes. They do not need to weigh their own resources too critically. They have merely to give the signal and the *people*, with all its inexhaustible resources, will fall upon the oppressors.[15]

Nevertheless, once the February republic is declared, the objective situation of the petty bourgeoisie asserts itself—bankruptcies and threats by the wholesale dealer and the banker reveal that universal suffrage alone does not possess the magic of resolution the petty bourgeoisie attributed to it.[16] The class switches sides, and illusion takes over. Instead of turning against the capitalist class and recognizing its real enemy in the capitalist system, the petty bourgeoisie turns against the proletariat, attacking its communist ideology as the source undermining its own property. Thus, after the June days, this class finds itself alone, without the force to wring concessions from bourgeois allies and unable to preserve a revolutionary attitude.

The (to Marx) absurd trajectory of the role of the petty bourgeoisie is completed when its representatives form the Social Democratic party and appropriate the name Montagne to defend the principles of republicanism against the royalists in the legislative assembly.[17] In a scornful critique of its democratic representatives, Marx argues that the fixation on "people's rights" and "people's interests," the symbolic representation of its own democratic ideals as the ideal of the "indivisible people," is symptomatic of the position of the petty bourgeoisie that prevents it from grasping the reactionary character of its particular class interest in relation to the other classes. Given this weakness, the superficial alliances first with the proletariat and then with the bourgeoisie naturally resulted in the manipulation and defeat of the petty bourgeoisie and its representatives.

What is interesting in this analysis is the conflation of historical materialist dogmatism with critical insight into the class character of the petty bourgeois. On the one hand, everything the petty bourgeoisie does and everything that happens to it come as no surprise to Marx because his class theory has already predicted the limits of this class. On the other hand, its specific and important role in political events provides an occasion for Marx to reflect creatively on the relation between a social class and its appointed representatives. Despite his scornful evaluation of petty bourgeois ideology, Marx grasps the importance of the symbolic power of apparently dead tradition in guiding the action of social classes, evidenced in this case by the selection of the name of Montagne by the representatives of the petty bourgeoisie. It is clear that the adherence to a democratic ideal on the part of this class is deducible *not* from its class interests or from its class character but from the fact of its being a *French* middle class and having the tradition of the French Revolution in its historical past as a source of its ideology and dreams. In other words, an elective affinity rather than a causal relation exists between democracy and the French petty bourgeoisie—a relation that is not generalizable to this class in other historical contexts.

More important, however, is the assessment of the relation between the petty bourgeoisie and its own representatives and the generalizations Marx makes regarding this phenomenon. In the first place, he insists that, unlike the politics of estates, the representatives of a social class need not themselves be members of that class or even embrace its socioeconomic interests.

Just as little must one imagine that the democratic representatives are indeed all shopkeepers or enthusiastic champions of shopkeepers. According to their education and their individual position they may be as far apart as heaven from earth. What makes them representatives of the petty bourgeoisie is the fact that in their minds they do not get beyond the limits which the latter do not get beyond in life, that they are consequently driven, theoretically, to the same problems and solutions to which the material interest and social position drive the latter practically. This is, in general, the relationship between the *political* and *literary representatives* of a class and the class they represent.[18]

This distance between a social class and its representatives allows for a gap between *economic interest* and *political interaction* or, rather, reveals that the two must be mediated through symbols, traditions, and so on. Indeed, it is precisely the belief in their republican ideal that leads the democratic representatives of the petty bourgeoisie to foil the interests of the class itself through a premature call to arms based on the illusion that the "people" would rally against the threat to the constitution posed by Louis Bonaparte.[19]

Here representation does not mean (as it does to the historical materialist) the direct political expression of economic interests; here the state is not just the epiphenomenal arena for the clash of the interests and classes of another sphere—civil society. Rather, a far more subtle relationship or affinity between significations and a particular social stratum is unfolded. Marx moves back and forth between an analysis of socioeconomic conditions and an interrogation of the "social imagination"—that is, the significations or representations (Marx would say "ideology") created or resuscitated by social groups.[20] The point is that Marx could not be satisfied with the former alone. Thus representation and representative politics are critically related to social classes in a way that avoids the reductionism of historical materialism; the one is not derived from the other. The fact that Marx derides the symbols motivating the petty bourgeoisie as illusory and the fact that he claims that material interests drive the class to the same positions that its representatives unfold theoretically do not detract from this insight into modern political life. For one could turn Marx's analysis against himself and argue that the political figures are representatives of the class not because they suffer from the same limits that derive from its material situation but because they express meanings and motifs that speak to the tradition and aspirations of members of the social class in question, despite their material interests. In other words, precisely because the meanings, values, or ideals motivating action exceed economic interest, representative politics in its modern form requires a double analysis. Certainly, socioeconomic class relations and interests have to be investigated in terms of their own logic, given the structural depoliticization of civil society and the claims of the modern state to represent and unify the interests of civil society. But the "social imagination" must also be analyzed independently in terms of the historical specificity and traditions of the various groups and of society as a whole, and only afterwards can the relation between the two (class and representation) be investigated. One could in fact argue that Marx himself suffers from illusion regarding even the class interest of the petty bourgeoisie insofar as he insists that the proletariat is the force that really could serve its interests. As he himself shows, the interest of the petty bourgeoisie is above all to retain its small property whereas that of the proletariat is to abolish property. With this type of assertion (i.e., that the proletariat is the natural leader of the petty bourgeoisie in revolutionary struggles), the insights into the relations of elective affinity between social classes and political representation are once more reduced to the logic, or rather the illogic, of class interest. Dogmatic class theory supplants critical sociology. But as soon as one turns to an examination of the other crucial middle and transitional class, the peasantry, one sees that this logic once again breaks down in the actual analysis and explains nothing.

Like the petty bourgeoisie, the peasantry, in the class theory of historical materialism, is destined to become economically marginal and eventually to disappear in the face of capitalist development of agriculture. Nevertheless, since the smallholding peasants constituted the great majority of the French people, the events leading to universal suffrage placed them in the position of arbiters of the fate of France.[21] It is indeed worth noting that, although Marx claims that peasantry is anachronistic from the standpoint of the historical materialist model of development, he recognizes that this class first comes into existence through the revolution that gave birth to bourgeois society in its pure form in France! More important, Marx argues that it was the Napoleonic state that consolidated the peasant form of property in France. In this case, then, a *political* force upheld and assured the conditions for the emergence of a *socioeconomic form of property* and a *social class*, rather than merely expressing juridically the prior existence of economic relations.[22]

Marx's attitude toward the peasantry is a curious mixture of condescension, disgust, and optimism. Referred to as the class that represents "barbarism in civilization," as an asocial and uncultivated group that produces in relation to nature rather than in intercourse with society, as a group without science, talent, or a wealth of social relationships, the peasantry is seen more as a *mass* than a class.[23]

The socioeconomic development of the nineteenth century is, however, according to Marx, in the process of dissolving the anachronistic peasant form of property. Like the petty bourgeoisie, property becomes the peasant's fundamental illusion because the independent and private character of property is being undermined; into the place abandoned by the feudal lord steps the urban usurer, mortgages replace feudal obligations, and bourgeois capital takes over from aristocratic landed property to deprive the peasant of his real ownership.[24] But this is not all. The progressive indebtedness of the peasantry leads to the wholesale expropriation, pauperization, and proletarianization of this class, subjecting it even further to the same exploiter as the proletariat, albeit in a different form.[25] Insofar as Marx takes the development of capitalist relations in agriculture to spell the demise of peasant property, he correspondingly deduces that the interests of the peasantry are no longer in accord with those of the bourgeoisie. The urban proletariat, whose task is the overthrow of capital, accordingly becomes the natural ally and leader of the peasantry.[26]

This curious analysis of the "real" class interest of a nonexistent and simultaneously disappearing class parallels Marx's analysis of the petty bourgeoisie. Instead of stating the obvious, that the *particular* interest of these classes qua classes is and must be to preserve their form of property, Marx insists that their true, long-term interest is identical with that of the proletariat, given the opposition of both to capital. He thinks he finds support for this argument in the struggles of those "revolutionized" peasants who strike out beyond the conditions of their existence and act independently, fighting for local control against the centralized government, for their own schoolmasters against priests, for their own mayors against the prefects, and against oppression by their own offspring, the army.[27] But as Marx himself notes, the evidences of revolutionary solidarity of interest with the proletariat are sporadic at best.

Although Marx does his best to argue for the dissolution of the objective basis for the peasant utopia (small property, glory of the army, dreams of empire, etc.), he nevertheless states that the final expression of political influence of the peasantry is a "hallucinatory" politics haunted by the ghosts and spirits of the past.[28] Illusion must triumph over interest. The brilliant analysis of the affinity of the peasant to Bonapartist representations is based on the insight that because, after all, the peasantry cannot form a class it must find an external representative to act for it. Its class condition, however, no more explains its Bonapartism than did that of the petty bourgeoisie its relation to democracy—only an analysis of French tradition could accomplish that task.

In short, having identified the objective economic conditions of peasant life, Marx had to move once more to the domain of the "social imaginary" to understand the political orientations and roles of this class. Thus the class analysis of the peasantry, when freed from its tie to the developmental logic of historical materialism, allows Marx to unearth the affinity between a specific type of representative politics and a unique social stratum—the *French* peasantry.[29] The actual political activity of the French peasantry requires a sophisticated knowledge of French tradition to be comprehensible. And, as Marx himself demonstrates, it was above all the tradition of Napoleon I that secured peasant property, glorified the peasant in uniform, ennobled the desire for land through the concepts of nation, patriotism, and empire, and, through a strong centralized government, provided that security which economic activity of the smallholder could never produce.[30] Combined with the above sociological analysis of the conditions of everyday life of the peasant, we have here Marxian class analysis at its best.

Accordingly, the response of the peasantry to the burdens of taxation and the threats of expropriation was to strive to resurrect the tradition by voting another Napoleon into the highest political office— the presidency. The fact that Bonaparte only paid lip service to the interests of the peasantry, the fact that he imposed hated and regressive taxes on this stratum, betraying its interests, is, in some sense, irrelevant. For the consistent conformity to the *imagination* of the peasantry secured their allegiance and acceptance when the real coup d'état came on December 2, 1851. Moreover, the events of 1870–71 reveal the force of social imagination over class interest, for even after twenty years of taxation under the new emperor the rebellion of the Paris Commune was, it should not be forgotten, crushed by peasants in uniform.

Marx's failure to reconcile the historical activity of the peasantry with the role assigned to it by the theory is far more interesting than the theory itself. The argument that the Bonapartist dynasty represents not the revolutionary but the conservative peasant, not the enlightenment, judgment, or future of the peasant but his superstition, prejudice, and past, does not come to grips with the problem. For the real point is that Bonapartism represents and unifies the aspirations and imagination of masses of individuals threatened by "enlightenment," "progress," and the revolutionary future advocated by Marxism.

The role of the army confirms the above:

> The army was the point d'honneur of the small-holding peasants, it was they themselves transformed into heroes, defending their possessions against the other world, glorifying their recently won nationhood, plundering and revolutionizing the world. The uniform was their own state dress, war was their poetry: the small-holding, extended and rounded off in imagination, was their fatherland, and patriotism the ideal form of the sense of property.[31]

To be sure, the rise of Louis Bonaparte should not be interpreted as a historical example of the self-constitution of the peasantry into a class. The peasant base of Bonapartism was fragmented, their representative, a manipulator of symbols, not a defender of peasant interests. Nevertheless, the real import of this relation is that the peasantry, although only a class-in-itself, plays a vital political historical role— another sign that within bourgeois society, political action is not reducible to class relations. Doomed to impotence by the class theory of historical materialism, this (class) nonclass is able through a political intermediary to have a major role in determining the direction of French politics. Instead of taking up the challenge that his own insight poses to his theory, Marx, as already indicated, attributes the political importance of the peasantry to a transitional stage in capitalist development. The model of historical materialism is never questioned; instead, history itself is seen as anomalous. It is no accident that Marxist ideologists are always ready to blame a "derailed history" rather than to examine their tenets when a discrepancy arises between history and theory.

The position regarding the "middle classes" would be perhaps comprehensible had Marx been able to confirm his class theory through the analysis of the proletariat and the bourgeoisie in his historical writings. As we shall see, however, in neither case does political action correspond to class interest.

What of the proletariat, the class destined to make the social revolution of the nineteenth century and to accomplish the emancipation of humanity? Although the Paris proletariat is seen as the radicalizing force of the first period of the 1848 revolution, pushing the initial aim of limited electoral reform to the declaration of universal suffrage, although it initiates in June the "first great clash between the two opposing classes of modern society," it nevertheless always seems to be too immature and underdeveloped to achieve success.[32] It always acts (reacts) prematurely. Even by 1870, apparently, the "objective conditions" are too unripe, the industrial proletariat too unformed, for it to carry out its historical mission.

The "objective immaturity" of this class was, according to Marx, based on the immaturity of the French bourgeoisie. Because modern industry was far from shaping all property relations, and because the industrial bourgeoisie had only begun to attain political power, the proletariat had to remain limited.[33] Despite the limits of its immediate interests, its illusions, and the narrow objective possibilities for its constitution as a universal class, Marx insists that the proletariat's premature emergence on the scene served a crucial purpose—the dissolution of illusions for society at large and the unmasking of its class structure. Marx sees, for example, the merit of universal suffrage urged by the proletariat not in the temporary embodiment of the norms of freedom, democracy, and political participation but in the unchaining of the class struggle and in the condition of possibility both for the disillusionment of the middle classes and for the unmasking of the class rule of the bourgeoisie.[34] The same holds true for the June defeat of the Paris proletariat. Provoked by the bourgeois republicans of the National Assembly period into insurrection due to the attack on the right to work and on the national ateliers,[35] the proletarian revolt was to Marx the key event revealing the repressive nature of bourgeois society: "By making its burial place the birthplace of the bourgeois republic, the proletariat compelled the latter to come out forthwith in its pure form as the state whose admitted object is to perpetuate the rule of capital, the slavery of labor." [36] With the vicious repressions of June and the trajectory of events thereafter, the bourgeoisie allegedly lost its moral influence by revealing that the Assembly represented only itself, consolidated not with but against the will of the people. Accordingly, despite its immediate, narrow, empirical historical role, Marx concludes that the proletariat emerges as the natural vanguard of all classes in the revolt against the rule of capital—a lesson allegedly learned after the June defeat.[37]

It seems as if the extreme gap between historical being and the logical expectations regarding the proletariat prevents Marx from perceiving in this class anything other than his own constructs. It remains the logical concept of a force that is the dissolution of illusions, immediately social and historical, that accomplishes the destiny of humanity through the abolition of all tradition. With this rather stark and disturbing image, Marx takes back all of the richness of his analysis of the social imagination.

The only creative moment in the analysis of the proletariat is, I would argue, the assessment of its symbolic meaning to the bourgeoisie and the dynamics this meaning imposes on the process of bourgeois class formation—for, as Marx observes, despite the defeat of the proletariat in June, the fears it inspired remained to haunt the bourgeoisie. It was this fear that presented obstacles to the bourgeoisie's own class constitution and, in the long run, constrained it to relinquish its political supremacy. Let us follow Marx's analysis of this class in order to see to what degree it corresponds to historical materialist expectations.

The bourgeoisie is presented as a class consisting of various factions, each based on a particular form of property with corresponding antagonistic particular interests. The various factions are organized in opposing political parties, although the nature of political representation can neither be deduced from the particular interests of the factions nor understood in abstraction from French history. And yet the analysis of the conflicts of the various sections of the bourgeoisie (the royalist financiers and industrialists, the republican intellectuals)[38] remains a striking example of Marx's ability to nondogmatically relate history and sociology and to unfold the interplay of tradition and interest in a nonreductionist manner. For, opposed to the one-sided view (the view of the contenders themselves) that pure principles and moral standpoints were at work here (or, on the other hand, pure interest), Marx reveals the affinity between a mode of property, class interest, and the various political, symbolic alternatives that tradition has made available. Here we find Marxian class analysis at its best:

What kept the two factions apart, therefore, was . . . two different kinds of property. . . . That at the same time old memories, personal enmities, fears and hopes, prejudices and illusions, sympathies and antipathies, convictions, articles of faith and principles bound them to one or the other royal house, who denies this? [39]

Thus the relation between class interests and political representations comprises both moments of societal life: social structure and historical tradition. Whereas the adherence to one or the other political position depends on the association between interest and potential political power, from the standpoint of the individual it is tradition and principle that appear as the motive of his political orientations.[40]

The royalist leanings of the two factions, then, reveal the same phenomena of political representation based on symbols and myths characteristic of the middle classes; the politics of the bourgeoisie, too, is enmeshed in illusion.

The source of these illusions is not, however, as in the former cases, to be found in the character of the bourgeoisie as a class; rather, it exists in the image of the threat posed to it by the proletariat. Despite the effective defeat of the proletariat as a real power, this class represents to the bourgeoisie the symbol of its own illegitimacy and a challenge to the limited form in which it seeks to realize the "so-called bourgeois liberties." It is this symbolic threat that prevents the full constitution of the bourgeoisie as a class—that is, its political self-constitution as the ruling class. As is well known, Marx viewed formal democracy and a parliamentary republic as the most adequate form for the class rule of the bourgeoisie because it enables the various factions of the class to unite and place the rule of the class rather than of a faction on the order of the day.[41] But the difficulty facing even this united political representative of the French bourgeoisie was that, whereas the republican form based on universal suffrage makes its class rule complete, it undermines its social foundation for it must confront other classes without the mediation and concealment afforded by the crown. Not parliamentary rule in general but parliamentary rule in France appears impossible for the French bourgeoisie, given its concrete historical situation—a situation of class struggle and seeming absence of secure control over the proletariat. "It was a feeling of weakness that caused them to recoil from the pure conditions of their own class rule and to yearn for the former more incomplete, more undeveloped, and precisely on that account less dangerous form of rule." [42] Accordingly, the bourgeois yearn for monarchy and strive to undermine their own republic, for with the monarchy they could present the illusion of an independent state power separately confronting bourgeois society rather than of a state instrument used for the purposes of class repression.

In effect, the symbolic proletarian threat is responsible for the fundamental contradictions in the class rule of the bourgeoisie because it forced the bourgeoisie to use the republican government to crush the June rebellion, revealing the class bias of the democratic state. The contradiction between the social and the political rule of the French bourgeoisie is expressed in the constitution of the republic that creates, on the one hand, a sovereign and an indissoluble national assembly based on universal suffrage and, on the other, a president de jure responsible to the assembly but de facto having an independent double power base deriving also from universal suffrage and from control of the executive.[43] On the one hand, the "true organ" of bourgeois class rule, the parliament, could function adequately only if it simplified the state machinery and allowed civil society and public opinion to create organs of its own, independent of government power. In other words, for the political supremacy of the bourgeoisie to work, assurances were necessary for the processes of opinion formation and the constitution of representatives of the various bourgeois factions. On the other hand, given the seeming weakness of the French bourgeoisie and its need to control rebellious classes, the intensification of the repressive measures and the direction of resources and personnel of the state power (the executive) in order to maintain a war against public opinion and to crush independent movements were unavoidable. "Thus the French bourgeoisie was compelled by its class position to annihilate, on the one hand, the vital conditions of all parliamentary power and therefore, likewise, of its own, to render irresistible, on the other hand, the executive power hostile to it." [44]

That Marx has here unfolded the dialectic between formal democracy and bureaucracy typical of modern capitalist society and not unique to France should be clear to anyone who has read Max Weber. Because Marx assumes that normally the bourgeoisie should rule through parliament, he must assess the nonrule of the French bourgeoisie and its development of the executive as a peculiar historical deviation rather than an indication of structural features of political relations of domination in a capitalist society. He argues that political domination is the necessary condition for the unity of the bourgeoisie as a class; that, for it to be a class, it must be a ruling class. But his analysis of Bonapartism reveals that capitalism can function quite well without the direct political rule of the capitalist class. Once again, the reader is shown that a structure of domination can exist in which classes dominant in the sphere of production do not necessarily exercise political power. The argument that the French bourgeoisie is unable to accomplish its class rule because it cannot present its interests as universal, that it resuscitates past myths to dissimulate the contingency of the present, of course does not lead Marx to draw the conclusion that perhaps socioeconomic domination needn't require personification in a unified ruling class.[45] If one dispenses with the dogmatism of the class theory, one can translate the foregoing analysis as follows: In the face of threats (real or imaginary) to its social supremacy, the bourgeoisie turns against the republican form of government, opting for a structure of state power that can assure the conditions of capitalist production without running the risks inherent in formal democracy. Such a formulation accounts for the political choices of the bourgeoisie while reopening the question of the relation between structures of domination and social classes.

Class and state revisited

Indeed, despite his interpretation of Bonapartism as the failure of the bourgeoisie to rule as a class, the existence of the Second Empire provides an occasion for a renewed reflection by Marx on the relation of class and state. The question immediately becomes: If the bourgeoisie does not rule as a class with the state as its instrument, what is the role of the state, and what is the status of those who wield its power and occupy its offices? Bonapartism, in short, is a form of state/civil society relation that is not mediated by a class that rules. On the one hand, Marx never deviates from the assessment that the state with its bureaucratic officials, army, and so on, is a parasitic body and an instrument of class repression. He repeatedly declares that with the progress of events during the 1848 revolution the state is increasingly revealed as a class state, as the "joint stock company" of bourgeois supremacy. On the other hand, and simultaneously, the entire analysis of the state in this period serves to show that, far from being a tool in the hands of the capitalist class, or a mere epiphenomenon of the forces/relations dynamic, the state both precedes and exceeds bourgeois class control. As previously stated, this is evidenced by the very existence of the executive power:

This executive power with its enormous bureaucratic and military organization, with its ingenious state machinery, embracing wide strata, with a host of officials, numbering half a million, besides an army of another half million, this appalling parasitic body, which enmeshes the body of French society like a net and chokes all its pores, sprang up in the days of the absolute monarchy, with the decay of the feudal system which it helped to hasten. The seignorial privileges of the landowners and towns became transformed into so many attributes of the state power . . . of a state authority whose work is divided and centralized as in a factory. The first French Revolution, with its task of breaking all separate local, territorial, urban and provincial powers in order to create the civil unity of the nation, was bound to develop what the absolute monarchy had begun: centralization. . . . Napoleon perfected this state machinery. The Legitimist Monarchy and the July Monarchy added nothing but a greater division of labor. . . . Every *common* interest was straightway severed from society, counterposed to it as a higher *general* interest, snatched from the activity of society's members themselves and made an object of governmental activity. . . . All revolutions perfected this state machine instead of smashing it.[46]

One finds, almost word for word, an identical assessment of the genesis, parasitic nature, and continuous expansion of an originally noncapitalist state twenty years later in Marx's analysis of the Paris Commune.[47] Viewed always as a superstructure and an instrument of domination, the state nevertheless in these analyses seems to follow its own logic of development.

Marx's analysis of the structure of state power under Louis Bonaparte presents the reader with a fascinating combination of real insight and dogmatism. For the first time Marx does not present the actual possessors of state power as mere puppets manipulated by the bourgeoisie as the true dominant class. Indeed, the dominant class in civil society is no longer the link or mediation between political and economic spheres, for the state power is not only independent of it *but often acts against its interests.*[48] Moreover, Marx confronts, albeit briefly, the bureaucratic elements occupying the posts in the state machinery. Aware that the bureaucracy is not an estate in the Hegelian sense but unable to fit this stratum into the class analysis of civil society, Marx refers to it as an "artificial caste," recruited from the surplus populations of the various classes of civil society and maintained through the taxes imposed on, above all, the peasantry. Here, then, is an exciting opening in the class analysis that points to a *historically new* (neither estate nor class) principle of stratification, which coexists and competes with class. "Artificial caste" is Marx's way of admitting that he cannot account for the bureaucracy in his class theory; that there is a structure of domination and stratification that escapes the very concept of class but is wholly modern.

This opening, however, never comes to fruition in a new theory. Indeed, after having described the independence of the state from the class structure of civil society, Marx insists that this autonomy is mere semblance, that the state power is, after all, contingent upon and representative of the socioeconomic classes. The Bonapartist state encompasses the class for which Marx had the least pity—the Lumpen-proletariat, "which, in all big towns form a mass strictly differentiated from the industrial proletariat, a recruiting ground for thieves and criminals of all kinds, living on the crumbs of society, people without a definite trade, vagabonds." [49] It is this class whose actual domination was brought about with the coup of Bonaparte. With one blow, then, the structural significance of the bureaucracy, regardless of who occupies the posts, is obscured.

According to Marx, however, the class that Bonapartism *represents* politically is the peasantry. "And yet the state power is not suspended in mid-air. Bonaparte represents a class, and the most numerous class of French society at that, the small-holding peasant." [50] The Bonapartist state represents the peasantry not only ideologically but structurally. Its own existence as a power over society as a whole is, according to Marx, rooted in the existence of the small-holding peasant mass. From the side of the peasants themselves, the independent executive matches their own inability to represent themselves and to form into a class. "The political influence of the small-holding peasant, therefore, finds its final expression in the executive power subordinating society to itself." [51] From the standpoint of the necessary conditions for the existence of a bureaucratic apparatus, Marx maintains that the division of land into a multitude of smallholdings, initiated by Napoleon I, provides the indispensable basis, the material conditions, for an all-powerful bureaucratic executive power:

By its very nature, small-holding property forms a suitable basis for an all-powerful and innumerable bureaucracy. It creates a uniform level of relationships and persons over the whole surface of the land. Hence it also permits of uniform action from a supreme center on all points of this uniform mass. It annihilates the aristocratic intermediate grades between the mass of the people and the state power. On all sides, therefore, it calls forth the direct interference of this state power and the interposition of its immediate organs.[52]

Finally, Marx goes so far as to argue that, with the progressive undermining of small-holding property, the state structure erected upon it will collapse.[53] Clearly, Marx was absolutely wrong, as the extreme counterexample of Stalinism with its destruction of peasant property and enormously exaggerated state power reveals. Although the insight into the leveling tendency of authoritarian bureaucratic state power remains valid, the attempt to ground it in a form of property and to relate it to a class in civil society that the state supposedly represents was merely a clever avoidance of a problem that challenged the application of the class theory to historical experience. It explains only the adherence of the peasantry to the Bonapartist government, not the nature or dynamic of the state itself.

The analysis of the state twenty years later in *The Civil War in France* fares no better. Recapitulating his analysis of Bonapartism in a few pages, he maintains that the state power, which had grown so independent of society, was in fact only the last degraded form of the class rule of the bourgeoisie![54] The importance of the analysis of the Paris Commune, for our purposes, is the articulation of a model of communist society in which the state and civil society are reintegrated in a manner counter to the statism explicit in historical materialism. The most significant change vis-à-vis the *Communist Manifesto* is the argument that the working class cannot simply lay hold of the ready-made state machinery and use it for its own purposes.[55] The Paris Commune represented a radical alternative to the bourgeois state because it involved the abolition of the repressive state machinery and the development of a countermodel of participatory democracy. Its key acts (for Marx) were the dismantling of the standing army, the bureaucratic administrative apparatus, the police, and the appointed judiciary and their replacement with a people's militia, an elected working body of counselors, recallable watchmen as protectors of the commune, and elected judges. In short, central government through the state executive, standing above civil society, is replaced by a restructured civil society with its own institutions guaranteeing the participation of citizens in political life. These measures represented not the return to the medieval commune but the subordination of the national central government to society and the self-government of civil society. Thus Marx maintains that the commune realizes the values of the bourgeois revolutions, preserving their positive achievements with the goal of creating truly democratic institutions on a national level.[56]

As soon as Marx begins to discuss the class relations within his idealized model of the commune, however, disturbing implications of this apparently innocent democratic image of emancipation appear. The emancipated society is presented as a society of *producers*, the proletariat as the natural trustees of the interests of the rural producers, embodying the intellectual lead of town over country.[57] Marx states that the emancipation of labor and the abolition of classes would involve the transformation of everyman into a working man.[58] Despite the central role of the Parisian middle classes in the commune, Marx insists that only the working class is capable of social initiative. And once again the problem of the peasantry is solved with reference to the continuing dissolution of peasant property. Thus, despite the historical activity of the various classes, nothing is said about them that was not said twenty years earlier in Marx's analysis of the 1848 events. Finally, even the ideas for which the Communards struggled are discredited with Marx's insistence that the working-class movement has "no ideals to realize, but to set free the elements of the new society with which old collapsing bourgeois society itself is pregnant." [59] Not surprisingly, these elements are seen solely in terms of forces of production.[60] Thus, even in his most antistatist writing, even where he claims that the future society cannot take over the bourgeois state form, Marx insists that its emancipating class nevertheless must take over bourgeois production in its key characteristics—centralization and concentration—minus private property. This position, although different from that of the *Manifesto* and *The German Ideology*, foreshadows the logic of the argument in *Capital* which, as I shall show, implicitly rather than explicitly calls forth a statist model; for, clearly, the centralization of production would create the need for a strong centralized state (of planners) as well as its own legitimation. Because Marx never directly addresses the question of political and institutional organization in the future society, the tension between the logical implications of his productivist model and his principled evaluative stance becomes all the greater.

The historical writings accordingly do not resolve the antinomies implicit in Marx's class theory but only intensify them. Although the forces/relations model does not determine the role of classes, although these works are the most free from the economism and reductionism of the theory of historical materialism, the class *theory* tends constantly to close off new paths and to prevent Marx from pursuing the insights his sociological class analyses provide. The recognition that tradition, culture, symbols, and myths play an integral role in the political action of individuals is distorted by the rationalistic bias of the class theory according to which action not guided by class interest is illusory. Indeed, the thrust of Marx's historical writings is not to interrogate the complicated interrelation among these factors in historical creation and in social integration but to comprehend them as the absence of class consciousness and explain any "deviations" through an analysis of the limits to class constitution of the various strata of society. Worse, the illusion-guided activity of the classes is denied the status of real historical creation:

passions without truth, truths without passion; heroes without heroic deeds, history without events; development whose sole driving force seems to be the calendar, wearying with constant repetition of the same tensions and relaxations; antagonisms that periodically seem to work themselves up to a climax only to lose their sharpness and fall away without being able to resolve themselves; pretentiously paraded exertions and philistine terror at the danger of the world coming to an end.[61]

Ultimately, the purpose behind such an evaluation is to show that real, conscious, rational historical activity is possible only for the class that acts according to its class interests, and the only class capable of this in the fullest sense is the traditionless, illusionless, idealless proletariat. Though Marx clearly reveals in his historical writings that the concept of class cannot, on its own, account for either political action, all political actors, or the nature of the state, it is that action that is depreciated rather than the class theory that is revised.

If one were to view Marx's writings developmentally, however, one could see that the dual image and analysis in the historical writings foreshadow a more fundamental break with historical materialism in Marx's systematic writings. There the dialectical theory of history is replaced with a nonevolutionary analysis of precapitalist social formations and an elaborate systemic analysis of capitalist reproduction processes. Let us turn to these works and examine the fate of the class concept therein.

Chapter 5

Historical Genesis and Class

Logic and history: past and present

The premise of this chapter is that the "mature" writings of Marx implicitly break with the theory of historical materialism insofar as the historical genesis and reproductive logic of a social system (capitalism) are now distinguished from one another.[1] In the *Grundrisse* and *Capital*, the forces/relations model of the theory of historical materialism is restricted to the internal dynamics of capitalism and reformulated in terms of the wage labor/capital relation. Accordingly, the emphasis shifts from the theory of history to a comprehensive analysis of the logic and limits of one mode of production—capitalism. More important, the "dialectic" is no longer projected onto history as a whole but now appears as the logic only of capitalist society.[2] The implications of this change for the class theory as it relates to the logic and genesis of the capitalist system will be the subject of this and the next chapter.[3]

The limitation of the dialectic to the internal dynamics of capitalism is based on Marx's new presupposition that only with capitalism does the economy emerge as a system that tends to penetrate all aspects of society and to recast social relations in its own image and forms.[4] The "primacy of the economic," the centrality of production, indeed, the base/superstructure model itself, can be applied, it would seem, only to a system whose logic can be articulated in socioeconomic categories because only such a system tends to subordinate and integrate social and political institutions to its own reproductive schema. Accordingly, in the mature writings, capitalism is analyzed through the historically specific categories of the value theory. A distinction (foreign to the theory of historical materialism) is made between the notion of "production in general" and the historically specific form of capitalist production. Indeed, the most striking fact about the late works is that all of the categories that appeared in the earlier writings (division of labor, property, capital, labor, productive forces and relations) are reformulated in categories of the value theory and unfolded through an analysis of the value forms of capital.

The significance of this change is not simply the discovery of the category of surplus value and the logic of exploitation.[5] Rather, the fruit of the analysis of the value forms stamped on the activity and consciousness of all participants is the articulation of the historical specificity of the capitalist mode of production in the very categories employed in its analysis and critique. The "socialization of society" (*Vergesellschaftung*) is, thus, a uniquely capitalist phenomenon in that it implies the integration of production and exchange relations into a whole. On this basis, individual actors can be analyzed as agents reduced to representative roles (character masks) in the basic system categories.

If this interpretation of the critique of political economy holds true, then the objections raised thus far regarding the overburdening and dehistoricization of the concept of class characteristic of the theory of historical materialism implicate only this theory and not the class analysis of capitalism in the later works. In other words, if one were to reformulate the theory of class to correspond to the defetishizing critique of the logic of the wage labor/capital relation unfolded in *Capital*, one could perhaps reconstruct a class theory that avoids the drawbacks of the theory of historical materialism. The critique of political economy endeavors to accomplish a double task: to reconstruct and to deconstruct the logic of the capitalist system through the introduction of the value categories that simultaneously point to the historically specific form of capitalist wealth and to the social relation of domination specific to capitalism. The conceptual distinction between the labor process in general and its capitalist form as a valorization process and the insight that capitalist relations penetrate and structure the technical, material form of the labor process allow Marx to initiate an analysis of the structure of labor and class relations involved. Just what the relation is between the systemic logic of capitalism and class conflict, between logic and history, will be addressed in the next chapter.

The separation of historical genesis and system logic has implications as well for the attitude toward the prehistory of capitalism and a concept of class *not* linked to the logic of capitalist reproduction. Insofar as the former is concerned, the following point might be argued: If the dialectic of forces/relations, and class struggle, no longer accounts for the real movement of *past history*, then the dissolution of noncapitalist forms presupposed by the presence of the capitalist system (but not attributable to it) implies an opening for a discussion of history and change in new terms. On the other hand, the question arises as to the meaning of the concept of class when applied to those social strata whose emergence is presupposed by the distintegration of precapitalist forms (orders, estates) and yet who are prior to the presence (predominance) of the capitalist system. Let us address each of these points separately.

The "historical sections" of the *Grundrisse* and *Capital* must not be understood in terms of a dialectical theory of history. The discussion of precapitalist societies in the *Grundrisse* is not an attempt to unfold a developmental logic of historical stages leading to capitalism. Instead, it must be seen as a sketch of precapitalist social formations that are investigated in order to establish, via comparison, the historical specificity of capitalism. Although Marx groups these societies under the rubric of "modes of production," discussing the property relations and division of labor specific to each, he distinguishes them from capitalism in terms of the noneconomic relation of individual to community that structures production relations.[6] The point of the comparison is to show that only with the emergence of capitalism do production relations achieve primacy. Correspondingly, the discussion of primitive accumulation in *Capital* must be read in light of the primacy of the system logic expounded in the text as a whole. It should be understood as a quasi-transcendental account of the necessary conditions for the emergence of the capitalist system—that is, the development of free wage labor, and capital—rather than as a theory of the transition from feudalism to capitalism.[7] Thus the critical interrogation of the systemic features of the capitalist mode of production has allowed Marx to break both with the eschatological philosophy of history in the early writings and with the productivist and reductionist theory of historical materialism.

As previously stated, the theory of historical materialism relegates capitalism to simply one more stage in the progress of evolution, stressing its continuity with the past and projecting the break with "prehistory" in the future revolutionary constitution of communism. The discussion of precapitalist forms, however, focuses on the radical *differences* between capitalism and the social formations preceding it. *Here the major historical discontinuity is located in the emergence not of socialism but of capitalism.* The key distinction is between the presence in a society based on wage labor of individuals relating merely as workers, separated from the objective conditions of their labor, and those forms in which they relate not as workers but as proprietors.[8] As stated above, however, the crucial terms of differentiation are not "economic" categories but concepts such as community, nature, personal or impersonal dependence, personhood, individuality, society, alienation, and finally, implicitly, class. The focus on these concepts reveals Marx's recognition that specific political and social transformations were necessary preconditions for the emergence of capitalist production and class relations. Instead of accounting for the genesis of capitalism, the continuous development of the productive forces is recognized as a specific feature of capitalist system logic—a logic whose precondition was the dissolution of traditional society. In other words, for the capitalist economy to appear as a system, the traditional restraints and political determinations of economic interaction had to be abolished. Here, at least, Marx is not so far from Max Weber regarding the necessary preconditions for the emergence of capitalism.[9] For both, the capitalist economy is the first self-reproducing economic system, and both had to account for its emergence in terms of those political and cultural transformations that allowed the primacy of the economy to form. Marx's analysis of the genesis of capitalism and of social classes is thus not strictly "economic" but concerned with the preconditions of the emergence of the economy as such.

Foreshadowing his attempt to establish the unique historicity of the capital relation, Marx sets up three general types of social forms in which human productive capacity unfolds, each of which is presented in contradistinction to the only one he analyzes in depth—capitalism:

Relations of personal dependence . . . are the first social forms in which human productive capacity develops only to a slight degree and at isolated points. Personal independence founded on *objective* (*sachlicher*) dependence is the second great form in which a system of general social metabolism, of universal relations, of all-rounded needs and universal capacities is formed for the first time. Free individuality based on the universal development of individuals and on their subordination of their communal, social productivity as their social wealth is the third stage. The second stage creates the conditions for the third.[10]

Let us note immediately that insofar as the first two forms—precapitalist and capitalist societies—are concerned there is no reference to evolution or to a historical dialectic of development; an immanent development is implied only from capitalism to the form that might emerge out of it. The importance of the comparative analysis of precapitalist and capitalist forms is thus not the issue of historical transition but the identification of the unique forms of individuality, society, dependence, and freedom presupposed by the wage labor capital relation. These become, as we shall see, fundamental correlates of modern social classes. In other words, *both the chapter on precapitalist societies and that on primitive accumulation focus on the sociopolitical preconditions for the emergence of the capital relation,* relegating economic factors to the background. The comparative analysis of capitalist and precapitalist societies also entails a rehistoricization of the concept of class, albeit on a somewhat different basis than that of the earlier critique of political economy in 1844.

Although the social formations mentioned by Marx in the *Grundrisse*—pastoral clan communities, antiquity, and Germanic societies—are parallel to those discussed in *The German Ideology,* there are two striking differences in the analyses. First, the formations are no longer placed on an evolutionary continuum through the medium of the concept of division of labor. Second, in the later text, the precapitalist forms of proprietorship are considered to be a number of variations of modes of existence of an "organic relation" between individual and nature mediated through the community, a consideration underplayed in *The German Ideology.* "Property" is not an economic category of distribution as it is in *The German Ideology* but rather implies in each case a relation of the human being to nature and to the community of which he is a part.[11]

What the modern analyst might see as economic factors do not appear as such but rather are embedded in direct sociopolitical relations of domination and/or communal structures. Thus precapitalist societies represent a radical antithesis to capitalism.[12] In short, there are no abstractable "economic" production relations independent of, or determining in the last instance, political forms.

What precapitalist societies have in common (for Marx), therefore, is the relation of working individuals to the objective conditions of their labor (land, nature, etc.) as their property, mediated through communal relations. Other individuals are either coproprietors or independent proprietors integrated into a community in which public property itself appears as a particular (as in Rome or Greece). "In both forms, the individuals relate not as workers but as proprietors, and members of a community, who at the same time work." [13] Thus, unlike capitalist class relations, precapitalist formations do not posit the individual in "dotlike isolation," denuded and reduced to the form of a mere worker. Appropriation and property are not the result of labor but its precondition! Modes of activity are not divisible into pure socioeconomic relations of classes, nor could socioeconomic categories comprehend the forms of interaction among the members of the community. Each individual who labors has an objective mode of existence in his communally mediated ownership of land—he is incidentally and not solely a worker.[14]

The various political forms in which this relation of the individual to nature and to the community is reproduced are, to be sure, only sketchily analyzed by Marx. Indeed, it is astonishing that he was able to distinguish the particularities of the various social formations in the framework of an analysis that is at best a mere outline, a possible guide to research rather than a completed study. Above all Marx's short summary of the precapitalist forms suffices to highlight the uniqueness of capitalism through the medium of contrast. Precapitalist societies differ from capitalism above all because the "economy" is not posited as an independent, self-regulating structure.[15] Correspondingly, work is not subordinated to a project of expanded production of an increasing surplus but has as its aim the sustenance of the individual proprietor and of his family, as well as of the community as a whole. Moreover, the communal form that mediates the relation of individual to nature is not reducible to the concept of mode of production.[16] What needs to be explained is not the unity of active individuals with the inorganic conditions of their labor in the context of a political community but, rather, the separation between the two, posited completely only in the relation of wage labor to capital.[17] Insofar as precapitalist history is no longer understood in terms of an evolution of the division of labor or the productive forces, the explanation of this separation requires an awareness of the political and sociohistorical preconditions of the wage labor capital relation as well as an analysis of its systematic reproduction.

As far as precapitalist societies are concerned, Marx now argues that historical change comes from factors *outside* the social form—population growth, migration, war, etcetera.[18] To be sure, internal change in social relations is significant and is related to these factors, but it cannot be grasped through a dialectical theory of class struggle and economic development *tout court*. Accordingly, the conditions of possibility of change are to be found within the constant tendency to overflow the limits of the communal relations themselves and in the inevitable conflict between communities that regard land and others as its own objective conditions of labor. The most important condition of possible change that Marx notes vis-à-vis the emergence of capitalism is the disassociation between private proprietorship of commune members and the commune itself, for here the situation arises in which the individual can *lose* his property—that is, he can lose the double relation that makes him both a member of the community and a proprietor.[19] It is this loss that constitutes the primary precondition for the wage labor/capital relation and the basis for the emergence of a type of social class unique to capitalism.

The discussion of precapitalist forms and primitive accumulation is based on the distinction between the necessary preconditions for the emergence of the wage labor/capital relation and the systematic reproduction of capitalist social relations once exchange relations and value forms predominate. The chapter on primitive accumulation has as its primary concern the original process whereby wage labor and capital could emerge as a relation of production.[20] This distinction between historical genesis and structural analysis (predicated on the distinction between the *form* of capitalist production and production in general) is, according to Marx, precisely what is lacking in political economy. The blindness of political economists rests on their tendency to see capital as a thing (raw material, instruments of production, etc.) rather than as a social relation (albeit reified) and to eternalize the categories of capitalist production.[21] The focus on the content rather than the form of capitalist production relations, the concern with distribution of goods rather than social relations of production, and the tendency to equate simple commodity exchange with capitalist commodity production compose the fundamental ideological tenets of political economy that serve to justify capitalist class relations.[22] On the one hand, the basis on which capitalist property stands—propertyless workers forced to sell their labor power, means of production in the hands of capital— is conflated with a mythical image of the origin of private property in the labor of the individual. On the other hand, the fact of equivalence exchange in the sphere of circulation is used to legitimate the relation between wage labor and capital in the sphere of production.[23] In short, political economy transposes the insight that an original accumulation of capital had to take place on a noncapitalist basis into a universal condition of capitalist property relations, completely ignoring the fact that capitalist accumulation is predicated upon the systematic destruction of producer/owner property.[24]

The importance of the discussion of precapitalist forms lies precisely in the analysis of the sociological preconditions for the emergence of categories of capitalist production (wage labor, capital, abstract labor, money, commodity, etc.) as forms of life: *dissolution* of the forms of community, proprietorship, and man/nature relations characteristic of the earlier social formations. The striking aspect of this analysis is the implication that, in order for the wage labor/capital relation to emerge, there had to be a process of dissolution of community so that the *social classes* presupposed by the capital relation (i.e., a class of free laborers and a class of "would-be capitalists") could come into existence. Here, indeed, the value categories or production relations are distinguished from their sociological correlates, free labor and capitalists:

A presupposition of *wage labor* and one of the historic preconditions for capital, is *free labour* and the exchange of this free labour for money, in order to reproduce and realize money to consume the use value of labour not for individual consumption but as use value for money. Another presupposition is the separation of free labour from the objective conditions of its realization—from the means of labour and the material for labour. Thus, above all, release of the worker from the soil as his natural workshop.[25]

The chapter on primitive accumulation provides historical examples of this process. What is crucial in this distinction between free labor and wage labor, capitalists and capital, is the point that the two key social classes presupposed by the capital relation are prior to it and are the product of an often violent *political* process rather than the embodiment of production relations.

Social class and the return of contingency

We can now assess the significance of the separation of genesis and system for the concept of class. The discussion of precapitalist social formations and primitive accumulation provides an opening to historical contingency and politics that the rigid determinism of the dialectical theory of history precluded. For the first time in Marx's writing we have a space/time (in logic and in its historical referent) that is neither fully the present nor the past. I am referring to the space/time that is no longer a precapitalist social formation and not yet a capitalist one. That Marxologists use the word "transitional" to describe this space/time indicates their inability to come to grips with a nondialecticized historical period. Marx himself approached this matter far more circumspectly. As stated previously, he does not attempt to give a history of the period that is no longer feudalism nor yet capitalism, although he refers to it in the attempt to analyze the specificity of capitalism. It is in this context that a historically specific concept of class, which is not the character mask, product, or representative of capitalist production relations, attains its significance. The notion of "dissolution," together with the sociological concepts of free laborers and would-be capitalists, implies that prior to the unified reproductive logic of capitalist production, *social classes* freed from rigid political, communal, or naturalistic determinations—that is, *classes as distinct from orders*— had to be present. The concept of social class designates social strata that logically and historically had to precede the establishment of the capital relation as the dominant relation of production. It is only when he analyzes the system logic of capitalism that Marx integrates social classes into the relations of production as correlates (or even worse, as personifications) of the value categories whose interests and dynamic possibilities can be imputed from the latter. Once capitalism establishes itself as a system, Marx assumes that the process of accumulation and reproduction of capital suffices to reproduce the classes it requires. But as far as the historical genesis of the capital relation and modern social classes is concerned, Marx indicates that political processes were central to the development of the new social space, freed from direct political determination, in which social classes could form and identify themselves. Social classes, then, precede the establishment of capitalist value relations while simultaneously replacing the orders and hierarchies of precapitalist society.

The concept of "free labor," for example, signifies a social class presupposed by the category of wage labor but prior to it. As such, free labor entails the following moments: (1) separation of the inorganic conditions of existence from the laborer, the loss of property and the positing of the laborer as a mere worker, a purely subjective capacity confronting the objective conditions of production as alien property; (2) dissolution of the political communal form in and through which its members are proprietors; (3) dissolution of the relation to the earth as the inorganic body and domain of the will of the worker; (4) dissolution of relations in which the worker appears as proprietor of the instruments of production; (5) dissolution of the communality of means of consumption; and (6) dissolution of relations in which workers themselves appear as the conditions of production (slaves).[26] The social class of free laborers, then, is free in a double sense: They are not part of the means of production, nor do the means of production belong to them; they are free from ownership of property.[27] On the one hand, the emergence of free labor is a process of emancipation both of individuals and of productive forces. The master/servant relation (*Herrschaftsverhältnis*) dissolves along with the restriction of societal production to a fixed set of needs, surplus, and use values.[28] The result of this process of dissolution, the emergence of free labor, is thus the emergence of a social class free to sell its labor power on the market to whomever it chooses within the framework of contract relations. Obviously, what is lost in the positing of the individual solely as a *worker* is the relation to nature and communal supports and guarantees of existence characteristic of precapitalist societies.[29] The political definition and restriction of social groups in precapitalist societies are replaced with socioeconomic strata whose political relations will be occluded and fetishized by economic forms.

Though Marx repeatedly contends that the emergence of a class of capitalists or owners of the means of production is part of the same process of dissolution that created the class of free wage laborers, the former class emerges independently of the latter. The primitive accumulation of wealth as private property takes place not on the basis of systematic exploitation of wage labor but prior to it.[30] Thus original capital is only formally capital. It is not capital produced out of itself (as self-expanded value) but accumulation that (whether by force, market manipulation, or labor) can begin to function as capital only when it meets free labor and buys labor power for production. Nevertheless, the original accumulation of capital and the creation of a class of capitalists are part of the same general process of dissolution described in all its brutality by Marx in chapters 26–32 of *Capital*.

The genesis of these two historically new social classes entails more than just a process of dissolution, however. For what distinguishes these classes from precapitalist social strata is not merely the absence of community and proprietorship but the presence of universalized exchange relations that signal the emergence of a new mode of individuality, sociality, and personhood, all of which are presuppposed by the now rehistoricized concept of social class. The critical sociology of class initiated by Marx in his earlier writings (and buried in the dogmatic dissolution of the concept of class in the transhistorical forces/relations model of historical materialism) reappears here, momentarily free from determination and exclusive structuration by production relations. Instead, the historically new, extraeconomic moments of social classes appear in this analysis. In a paragraph describing the dissolution of the relation of the working individual to the objective conditions of labor communally mediated property, Marx states:

> But human beings become individuals only through the process of history. He appears originally as a species being, clan being, herd animal, and in no way whatever as a political animal (city dweller) in the political sense. Exchange itself is a chief means of this individuation.[31]

The isolated individual appearing as a mere worker (class of free laborers) or as an independent private proprietor (class of potential capitalists) is a historical product generated through the universalization of exchange relations and is typical of the mode of reduced individuality that makes up modern social classes. Moreover, the creation of society—of social relations of interdependence in the first instance through exchange relations—goes hand in hand with the creation of isolated individuality. Society and individuality in the modern form are both presupposed by the new social classes.

Whereas in his earlier writings Marx focused on the separation of the state and civil society as the sign of a new social existence for individuals, here the emphasis is on the logic of exchange itself and, later, on the analysis of socialization (*Vergesellschaftung*) in the sphere of production. The structure of private and class interests, of legal personhood and social labor, becomes the ambiguous product of the political process of dissolution of the direct communal relations of personal dependence and their replacement with exchange relations. "Exchange, when mediated by exchange value and money, presupposes the all-sided dependence of producers on one another, together with the total isolation of their private interests from one another as well as a division of social labor." [32] This historically specific division of labor *creates*, according to Marx, the antithesis of private and class interests. At the same time, it (exchange) is predicated upon the simultaneous generation, alienation, and reification (*Versachlichung*) of social relations. For, though individuals produce now only in and for society, they are subsumed under social production that exists outside them insofar as the exchange of all products of labor, all activities, and all wealth occurs privately via the exchange of commodities on the market and not directly through forms of association.[33] Thus, both *society* and *individuality* appear in an abstracted, reified form in which social relations attain an alien power over the individual. The new social classes and, implicitly, the concept of class itself (although Marx never explicitly recognizes this) thus have as their predicates, abstract individuality and sociality.[34]

It is important, however, to note that, whereas the direct relations of personal dependence imprisoned individuals in restrictive social categories (serfs, lords, castes, etc.), the substitution of free market relations entails not the abolition of relations of dependence but their *impersonalization*. In short, the formally and legally free "individual" is now confronted with "society," or social relations of exchange and production that appear as objective impersonal forces restricting and subjugating the isolated individual to a new form of dependency.

Accordingly, the precondition for the wage labor/capital relation is the emergence of the abstract individual denuded of communal ties and restricted needs, integrated into a societal structure of exchange allowing for the interaction between the two new social classes. A double relation of equality and freedom is involved in this structure: equality insofar as each is an exchanger in the same social relation toward the other and insofar as the commodities they exchange count as equivalents; freedom in the double sense that a voluntary transaction without force is involved and insofar as the individual posits his own self-seeking interest as dominant and primary.[35] Finally, the presence of a class of free laborers integrated into universalized market relations entails the emergence of the juridical moment of the Person. Mutual recognition and acceptance of contractual relations, juridically ensured, through which each recognizes the other as proprietor constitute each as a person whose will penetrates his commodity.[36] The familiar characteristics of Hegel's concept of civil society thus reappear, vis-à-vis the presuppositions of the wage labor/capital relation, as moments of social classes whose emergence is part of the universalization of exchange relations.[37] It is worth noting, however, that even at his least dogmatic Marx does not reflect on the elements of civil society— legality, plurality, autonomy, publicity—independently of the process of exchange and the concept of social class.

Indeed, the analysis of capitalist production relations, together with the inquiry into their genesis (historical preconditions), leads Marx to link the attributes of individual equality and liberty to the concept of class. But his critique of the ideological standpoint of political economy vis-à-vis these attributes is geared to the concealment of a new form of domination rather than to the reduction of civil society to economic processes. The section on primitive accumulation in *Capital* documents the historical process through which, against the will of the individuals, the classes of free labor and capital and the system of exchange are formed. And the main body of the texts of both *Capital* and the *Grundrisse* demonstrate how the very realization of equality and freedom posited in exchange proves to be inequality and unfreedom in production involving the wage labor/capital relation. The interrogation of the sphere of production reveals the class relation of domination between the individual persons posited in exchange. "In the exchange between capital and labour, the first act is an exchange, falls entirely within ordinary circulation; the second is a process qualitatively different from exchange, and only by misuse could it have been called any sort of exchange at all. It stands directly opposite exchange; essentially different category." [38] This different category is a relation of domination, a class relation, to which we shall turn in a moment. It remains to be shown through a brief analysis of primitive accumulation that the "accidental" meeting of labor power and would-be capital on the market prior to the full establishment of capitalist relations results not from a gradual evolution of forces and relations of production but from a *political process* that forged the very social classes presupposed by these relations.

In the section on primitive accumulation in *Capital* one can find statements to the effect that the economic structure of capitalism has grown out of that of feudalism. It would be a mistake, however, to construe them along the evolutionist model of the theory of historical materialism, for the point is not that within the womb of feudalism capitalist social relations developed but, rather, that the dissolution of the former set free the elements that later combined to form the latter. In the development of capitalist property and class relations, "it is notorious that conquest, enslavement, robbery, murder, briefly, force, played the great part." [39] Moreover, Marx insists that although money and commodities existed in feudal society they are not in themselves capital but need to be transformed into capital. The history of this transformation, presented ideal-typically through the use of examples from English history, is the history of the expropriation of agricultural producers and their formation into free laborers. The paradigm for this process is the enclosure movement from the fifteenth to the eighteenth centuries. Let us simply note that in addition to the acts of enclosures by market-oriented gentry, *the role of the state is prodigious.*

The spoliation of the churches' property, the fraudulent alienation of the state domains, the robbery of the common lands, the usurpation of feudal and clan property and its transformation into modern private property under circumstances of reckless terrorism were just so many idyllic methods of primitive accumulation. They conquered the field for capitalist agriculture, made the soil part and parcel of capital, and created for the town industries the necessary supply of a "free" and outlawed proletariat.[40]

In addition, the series of legislation by the state against vagabondage, the forcing down of wages, etcetera, witness the *political violence* of the state against the "fathers of the working class," forced against their will into the status of free laborers.[41] The often ignored but extremely important aspect of the role of the political in constituting the class of free laborers, its disciplinary function, is stressed by Marx; for law appears as the main *force* through which the discipline necessary for the wage system was imposed.[42] Marx does maintain that direct political force is no longer necessary to discipline the working class once capitalism establishes itself on its own basis because, he argues, economic force suffices. For the original process of accumulation, however, the state, through its laws, is the main force regulating and disciplining labor.[43] In short, when capitalist relations are being established and the social classes fundamental to capitalism arise, *political power* is fundamental to the constitution of both. Free laborers are indeed a politically created class; they will become an economically reproduced class (according to Marx) only with the self-reproduction of capital out of itself, that is, when value relations predominate and are reproduced as a system—for Marx, both in theory and in reality.

Although capitalists emerge originally as a class independently of the direct exploitation of labor power, as owners of the means of production, their existence is predicated on the presence of a free fund of means of production. Marx's concern with the emergence of this class, however, is not with the genesis of usurer, merchant, or even agricultural capitalist but with the industrial capitalist. Again, the role of the state—colonialism, force, and violence—is crucial, but the condition of possibility for turning accumulated wealth into capital turns out to be free labor. Thus, here too, a social class of future capitalists appears as the precondition for the functioning of capital as a social relation—a social class whose emergence and full development require the presence of another social class as well as the dissolution of traditional forms of interrelation.

What relevant conclusions can be drawn from the above for the class analysis of *Capital?* In the first instance, it is clear that the analysis of the genesis of capitalism has a systematic role in Marx's inquiry insofar as it is posed in terms of the specificity of capitalism as a social relation of production and answered in terms of the genesis of two fundamental social classes.[44] In order to function both as a systematic theory and as a critique, Marx's analysis had to provide the general historical preconditions of capital to clarify the concept of capital as a social relation of production. Second, insofar as the uniqueness of capitalism is presented not simply in terms of the economic structure of the value-producing and value-expanding capital relation but also in terms of the original presence and systematic reproduction of classes, the analysis of the precapitalist forms and the process of primitive accumulation signal the practical/critical intent of the work as a whole: Capitalist reproduction is shown to be the systematic reproduction of wealth as capital, but also of antagonistic relations of domination between classes. The critique of economic categories of political economy is aimed at a process of defetishization that will uncover the social relation of production as a class relation. The distinction between genesis and structure, then, relates to the difference between the genesis of capitalism historically and its self-reproduction as self-expanding value. But it also refers to the distinction between the political genesis of a unique type of social class and the economic reproduction of such classes on the basis of systematic capitalist accumulation. The problematic interrelation of social (class) and economic (value) categories, or the legitimacy of positing social classes as personifications, character masks, of economic categories, can now become the center of our own analysis of Marx's class theory. For the positing of social classes as the historical *presupposition* of the wage labor/capital relation points to a new principle of stratification that is uniquely modern (it is not a system of orders)—socioeconomic principles of the distribution and hierarchization of individuals—but does not preclude consideration of nonsocioeconomic mechanisms of stratification. This distinction allows us to highlight the confusion of the system and class categories in the critical analysis of the system logic of capitalist reproduction that dominates the critique of political economy.

Indeed, I shall attempt to show that Marx forgets his own insights into the role of noneconomic processes in the historical constitution of social formations once he turns to a critique of the process of capitalist reproduction. Marx's recognition that the genesis of the capital relation entailed a *political process*, not only of dissolution but also of constitution of the norms, ideology (personhood, equality, freedom, individuality), modes of being, social classes, and structures of exchange and production of the new social formation, constituted an advance beyond the deterministic, economistic, forces/relations model of evolution of historical materialism. But once Marx turns to the forms of capitalist reproduction, their fetishistic power invades his own analysis, leading him to accept the dissolution of the political and normative moments into economic processes as a fait accompli.

As we will see, the integration of social classes to production relations as the personifications of value categories defetishizes the economic categories at the price of fetishizing social relations of classes. Political, normative, ideological, religious or cultural moments of social life and social action in capitalism are relegated to the periphery on the basis of the assumption that as a system the capitalist mode of production reproduces itself, its social actors, and their necessary motivations out of its own economic logic. Thus the tentative insights into the noneconomic or extraeconomic genesis of capitalism and of modern social classes, the advance beyond both political economy's own productivist myth of this genesis and historical materialist evolutionism, are lost owing to the otherwise important argument that the reproductive system logic must be distinguished from its historical genesis. The political moment in the constitution of classes, economic relations, and individuation is relegated to the distant past of capitalist genesis. It returns, insofar as the capitalist and working classes are concerned, only in the form of instrumental strategic power struggles. The potential critical sociology of class becomes blocked once more in a theory that overburdens the concept of class by integrating it into the system logic of production categories. To be sure, the concept of class now really applies only to capitalist social relations. Contemporary history, however, and, as we shall see, genesis of the future are collapsed with the system logic of reproduction of capitalism through a "redialectized" class concept.

Chapter 6

System and Class: The Subversion
of Emancipation

It should be clear to the contemporary reader of *Capital* that Marx's critique of political economy analyzes and unfolds economic categories in abstraction from cultural, political, and social determinations. But those who argue that this abstraction is simply a methodological device to consider the general system logic of capitalist accumulation in its ideal purity avoid the real issue. Behind the far from innocent methodology is the presupposition that, unlike past social formations, capitalism systematically incorporates a reproductive logic that could be grasped in terms of a historically new phenomenon: a unified, socialized economy. Neither the attempt to present the reproductive logic of the capitalist system nor the choice of political economy as ideology-par-excellence, and hence as the object of critique, is haphazard or simply methodological. Rather, the theoretical reproduction of the logic of capitalism through the critique of the categories of political economy implies that the critic of political economy has inherited its most basic proposition—that the capitalist economy can be analyzed as a self-sufficient, albeit contradictory, system, with its own internal dynamics and reproductive mechanisms. The implications of this assumption for Marx's class theory and the difficulties it poses for the project of immanent critique and the theory of revolution will be the focus of this chapter.

Marx implicitly abandons the theory of historical materialism in his mature critique of political economy by distinguishing between the historical genesis and the system logic of capitalism. With the restriction of the forces/relations dynamic to the internal dialectic of capitalism, the theory of history gives way to a comprehensive analysis of one mode of production: capitalism. One might therefore imagine that a reformulation of the theory of class and class struggle in the context of the logic of the wage labor/capital relation, critically unfolded in *Capital*, could have perhaps led to the recovery of the critical sociology of class hinted at in the early works. The result could have been a theory of both the reproductive logic of class relations and of the objective possibilities of emancipation that avoids the statist conclusions of historical materialism. Perhaps. And indeed, the model of communism presented in the first text to break with evolutionism, the *Grundrisse*,[1] is neither productivist nor statist. Far from generalizing the status of the worker to all of society, or extending the productivist logic of capitalism to the future, the *Grundrisse* model of communism envisages the abolition of the direct labor of the worker and the emancipation of society from the tyranny of labor time. This antiproductivist utopia is derived from reflections on the objective possibilities inherent in the most advanced forms of the capitalist structure of labor. It implies, in short, that on the basis of the application of science to the productive process the potentialities of automation inherent in machine production, once freed from capitalist distortions, would allow for the replacement of direct labor by a combination of machines and highly qualified technical supervisors of the production process as a whole. Their activity, unlike the labor of the proletarian, would be not alienated labor but the fulfilling form of self-objectification that we now know only in science and art.[2] Since neither the labor discipline nor the mobilization of all of society for the development of productive forces would be called for as in the model of historical materialism, the statist utopia of the latter is not to be found here.

At the same time, the possibility of a new enriched mode of individuality is envisioned in the *Grundrisse* not only on the basis of the radically changed structure of labor and the elimination of direct labor but also through the reduction even of scientific labor to a minimum and the increase of free time for all. The free development of individuality as "man rich in needs," relations, and gratifications, would be a concrete possibility in this model of communism.[3] But although this model is certainly preferable to the productivist and explicitly statist version in the *Manifesto*, it suffers from the opposite difficulty: too little politics. As an antiproductivist, antistatist, socioeconomic utopia, it dispenses with politics altogether, offering only an abstract vision of a society in which labor is minimal and needs are gratified.

Even for this one-sided and abstract utopia, however, the question remains: On what basis do *objective possibilities* of machine production within capitalism outlined in the *Grundrisse* become real possibilities informing the demands of groups in motion? And who are to be these groups? Marx, of course, insisted that the proletariat as a class will be the agent of transformation, even if in the long run it must abolish itself as a class. Accordingly, Marx had to demonstrate, through the analysis of the development of the structure of labor in capitalism, the possible emergence in the proletariat of the radical needs necessary to motivate a class struggle *for* such (or any) utopia and against capitalism. And such an analysis—or its beginnings—can only be found in *Capital*, where the critique of the immanent contradictions of capitalist forms imposed on the labor process, and the objective possibilities developed by capital, are presented, according to Marx, scientifically. Unfortunately, however, any effort to ground the concrete possibility of the *Grundrisse* model of communism in *Capital* must fail. This is the case because, as I shall show, the class analysis of capitalist relations inherent in the critical reconstruction of the systemic logic of capitalist reproduction leads to an assessment of the objective possibilities of machine technology, the division of labor, class struggles, and the communist future that directly contradicts those suggested in the *Grundrisse*. Furthermore, if the utopia of the latter is simply apolitical, that of *Capital* is aggressively technocratic, productivist, and, implicitly though not explicitly, statist.

Although the concept of class does not appear as a category in *Capital* (it is not a value category), although here the logic of accumulation is distinguished from the historical genesis of capitalism as well as from dynamics of precapitalist societies, the presuppositions of the class theory of revolution and the implicit integration of class relations into the logic of *Capital* raise serious new questions for all those concerned about Marxian theory and its historical meaning. The problem is no longer the projection onto past history of an essentially capitalist production logic. Rather, it is that of the relation of the system and the critique unfolded in the late works to the empirical present and to the history of the future—a relation that hinges on the concept of class.

Since my concern is the interconnection between the systematic analysis of capitalism and the class theory, I will focus on the unfolding of the wage labor/capital relation, leaving the question of the "real" object of *Capital* to the Marxologists to decide. For whether this object is seen as the concept of capital itself (Helmut Reichelt), as the scientific unfolding of the capitalist mode of production (Louis Althusser), as the explication of the extraction of surplus value and exploitation (Ernst Mandel), or as the phenomenology of forms of appearance of

capitalist relations, it is clear that the actual critique of political economy proceeds through an analysis of the specific forms stamped on production (value forms) and the class relations presupposed by them.
Since the critique of political economy replaces the abstract forces/
relations model with a detailed analysis of the wage labor/capital relation, the reduction of class relations to the reflex of a transhistorical
dynamic of production no longer appears here. The question becomes:
How are the concepts of social class and class struggle related to
the systemic reproduction of the dynamics of the wage labor/capital
relation?

In a sense, the problem can be seen as the opposition between Marx's
critique of the fetishistic categories of political economy (or coherent
system theory) and the attempt to offer a *better* political economy of
capitalism. But even if one gives Marx the benefit of the doubt and
reconstructs his analysis of capitalist reproduction solely in terms of
the former, that is, as a critique aimed at the defetishization of economic categories that employs the theory of value and the concept of
class to reveal the dynamic social relations concealed by production
forms, the difficulties of the project remain unresolved. For, as will become evident, economic categories are successfully defetishized by Marx
through the reification of an originally critical concept—the concept of
class and its twin, the social relations of production.

Let me clarify the issue confronting us. For Marx the wage labor/
capital relation is the central social relation of production within the
capitalist system. The wage labor/capital relation supplies the categories for both the economic (value forms) and sociological (class relations) analyses and is the locus of the link between the two. However,
these categories are value categories—that is, part of the systemic logic
unfolded as the *forms* through which capital reproduces itself. Thus, as
a structural relation of production, analyzed in abstraction from particular capitalist societies, the categories of wage labor and capital are not
identical to the sociological class concepts of capitalists and proletariat;
they are not class concepts. In short, wage labor and capital, and capitalist and proletariat class, are two categorial levels, which must be distinguished insofar as classes are not abstract system categories but
sociological groupings of individuals—a distinction that Marx's categorial framework allows for, or so it seems. The problem is the interrelation between system categories and class concepts. If, on the one
hand, the development, reproduction, and interests of social classes are
derived from the logic of the wage labor/capital relation, itself ap-

pearing as independent of the social classes, then Marx can be accused of a category error—of panlogism.[4] If, on the other hand, class relations are more fully integrated into the logical schema itself—that is, if the value categories and the changing structure of labor are indeed constituted through relations of class struggle and transformed according to these relations—then the concept of class can perhaps function to defetishize seemingly independent economic categories by bringing them back to the social relations of domination between classes. But this could not represent a counterlogic to the system into which classes are so fully integrated. And the temptation to submerge this second alternative in the panlogism of the first was hardly overcome by Marx, as we will see.

Logic and history: the dynamics of present and future

After almost one hundred years of interpreting *Capital*, the second version of the interrelation of class relations and economic categories remains to be interpreted. In any case, the first would immediately land the writer and reader of *Capital* in "historical materialism," albeit a highly Hegelianized version thereof. The most important texts for us are therefore the chapters on the working day, manufacture, and machine production in volume 1 of *Capital*. Unlike the general discussion of accumulation, these texts provide an in-depth analysis of the dynamics of the labor process and the process of class struggle, integrating the latter into the logic of value relations as a constitutive moment. Although one could not call this analysis historical, a historical and sociological dimension (that of contingent class struggle) is constitutive in part of the structural dynamics instead of simply being tacked on externally at a different level of analysis. In other words, the unfolding of the wage labor/capital relation is not carried out on the level of a pure logic of value relations but is itself formed and informed by historical class struggles that constitute the dynamics of development. To be sure, the value categories, here too, unfold the general tendencies of capitalist systems, but they are themselves constructed through a constant reference to class relations. Accordingly, the class concepts and the analysis of class struggles play a *defetishizing* role insofar as they reveal the changing social relations of labor and classes presupposed by the logical value categories, transforming the system into an antisystem, into a critique. Understood in this way, any attempt to systematize the logic of the value categories into an economic theory of the *laws* of capitalist *development* in abstraction from class relations would simply re-reify the analysis and turn Marx into a (rather weak) political economist.

Nevertheless, despite the "dialectical" rather than deterministic interrelation of structure and sociology, the concept of class remains Marx's own last fetish, as the dogmatically presupposed referent of critique and as the necessary form that social struggles transcending capitalist relations must take. Not only does Marx not provide the mediations necessary for the move from class struggles immanent to the reproductive logic of capitalism to those around radical needs pointing beyond this logic; he also does not offer an answer to the question that inevitably arises: Why class? I shall attempt to reconstruct this second model of the relation of structure and sociology in order to show that, despite the separation between historical genesis and system logic, despite the attempt to integrate class relations into the value categories to defetishize them, and despite the effort to ground at least the objective possibility of proletarian class revolution not in philosophy or in a dialectic of history but in the objective development of the labor process (and needs) of capitalism, the relation between the concepts of "class" and system is dominated by the latter and that the class analysis therefore tends to be a key to what will be characterized as the collapse of system logic and future history.

Marx's devastating critique of economic fetishes notwithstanding, the one economic concept never questioned is class itself. For although it is not a value category, the concept of class is socioeconomic, referring to the formation of social groups according to labor, interests, and needs, constituted according to the rationale of a system of production relations, independently of normative, political, or symbolic mediations. Consequently, it remains caught between two antinomic functions: On the one hand, as the constitutive moment of capitalist production relations, "class" serves to illustrate the fetishistic logic of a system that tendentially reduces individuals to their productive functions and interaction to interest conflicts. One could interpret Marx's famous concept of character mask in this light. Insofar as individuals and social classes are presented as "personifications of economic categories," the logic imposed on their interaction (conflicting class interests) is criticized as a fetishistic reduction of individuality to the status of bearers or agents of functions outlined by economic categories. On the other hand, classes and class struggles are to be the source of a radical alternative to this logic, the locus of a new form of individuality, needs, and interaction free from economic fetishes. But if class relations and the value categories are integrated through the concept of character mask, if classes are treated as personifications of social relations of production, a fundamental tension inheres in the very concept of class. Economic determination of forms of individuality and sociality; persons and classes as character masks of economic categories; a reduction of juridical, political, symbolic relations to the logic of economic forms —does Marx's faithful unfolding of this logic imply his belief in the successful reification of modern society, or is it meant as an ironic re-presentation of a rationality he seeks to undermine? One thing is sure, the concept of character mask collapses the *rationality of the system* with the *rationality of social action*, deriving the latter from the former. The integration of class relations into production dynamics has the unfortunate result of implying that only those motives of social action and class formation that correspond to "objective" contradictions of capitalist production relations are *rational*—only action according to interests (imputed from the systemic logic of contradiction even if this logic is constituted by class relations) is *rational* action. Accordingly, the very power of "class" to act as a critical concept vis-à-vis the logic of capitalist production relations is lost. We shall address Marx's attempt to mediate this antinomy in the course of this discussion.

The logic of capitalist production

Marx's interrogation of the structure of labor internal to the capitalist production process begins with the articulation of value forms imposed on the labor process, or its structuration into a valorization process (*Verwertungsprozess*). According to many interpreters, Marx's goal was to render the labor theory of value internally consistent in order to develop an adequate economic analysis of the capitalist mode of production.[5] It is assumed that Marx understood value as "socially necessary labor time" congealed in the commodity. As such, value is seen as the form of appearance of the essence, socially necessary, of abstract labor. And, indeed, one can find innumerable passages in the volumes of *Capital* to validate this essentialistic and economistic interpretation. Marx repeats over and over again that what determines the magnitude of value of a commodity is the labor time socially necessary for its production. Commodities, he insists, must *embody* equal amounts of labor in order to be exchanged. Although human labor itself is not value and has no value, its *congealed* state in the commodity is the essence of value.[6] Accordingly, it is argued that Marx' *Capital* provides a reconstruction of the logic of capitalist economics, growth, and crisis mechanisms. *Capital* offers a critique only in the sense that it points to the systematic exploitation of labor by capitalists. The most serious criticisms of Marx's theory of value by non-Marxists and Marxists alike presuppose this interpretation of the value theory and claim that, as such, value is a metaphysical and tautological concept.[7]

But the substantialist concept of labor value offers only one of several equally justifiable interpretations of the value theory. Indeed, there is a fatal oscillation in Marx's thought regarding the historical referent of the value categories.[8] Marx, in short, wavers between three possible definitions, which could be posed as follows: (1) Value is indicative of a *transhistorical substance* (labor) that is always the source of equality, identity, commensurability, of men and their exchange, that until now has been hidden by political, ideological, or religious significations. According to this position, capitalism at last renders economic relations pure and dominant, allowing for the substance of value, labor, to appear. (2) Value is a *historically specific substance* unique to a capitalist economy that effectively transforms, for the first time, heterogeneous men and their labor into a homogeneous and measurable entity—simple abstract labor, with no other determinant but time. (The value categories here are seen as real fetishistic abstractions.) (3) Value and the homogeneity of labor it presupposes are a representation of a *heterogeneous reality*, a fetish of the capitalist mode of production rooted in the logic of capitalist production and circulation that posits labor power as a commodity, a thing that can be sold on the market for a just price, a wage.[9] For our purposes the third alternative is the most interesting interpretation.[10] Instead of presenting Marx at his worst, as a metaphysician, or as a naive realist confusing tendencies of a system logic (homogenization) for accomplished fact, one might reconstruct Marx at his best. That is, one might consider Marx as a theorist who provides a defetishizing critique of the logic and presuppositions of a historically specific socioeconomic system without recourse to metaphysical or realistic (or naturalistic) assumptions.[11] On the basis of this reconstruction, one could then unfold the limits and difficulties inherent in any attempt to immanently address simultaneously the dynamics of both system rationality and social action, without the obvious drawbacks of the first two positions.

The appearance of products of labor and labor power as commodities and the universalization of the commodity form signal, as Marx ceaselessly repeats, the arrival of a historically new mode of production.[12] For Marx, exchange value and the market are necessary moments of the logic of value relations.[13] To be sure, Marx distinguishes between exchange value and value. But this distinction need not imply an essence/appearance dialectic. Nor does the discussion of forms of value refer to a substance that appears through these forms. Instead, the relation between forms of exchange and production categories comprises a dynamic moving from abstract to concrete determinations of a system logic that forms a totality of significations requiring no external substance as referent.

The analysis in *Capital* unfolds the labor process in its capitalist-determined aspects, as a valorization process (*Verwertungsprozess*) based on the penetration of value relations (the wage labor/capital relation) into the core of production itself. The transition from the process of circulation of commodities to the process of the production of values is a move from a one-sided to a many-leveled determination of the forms of appearance *not of labor but of capital*. The analysis of the valorization process of capital leads not to labor-in-general as the essence of value but to the social relations that allow for the universalization of the appearance of value forms.

Thus the exchange of commodities, without which there is no value form and hence no value, becomes comprehensible through an examination of the production relations on which they rest: the wage labor/capital relation and the calculation and remuneration of labor according to time. Labor time is not the transhistorical essence of value; rather, *value is the supreme fetish* of a society that presumes to relate individual to social labor through the mediation of market relations and seeks to impose a value form on laboring activity (wage form) by reducing all *considerations* regarding labor to the single variable of labor time. Accordingly, Marx's use of the labor theory of value is ironic. His intent is to turn political economy against itself by unfolding the logic of the value theory as fetishistic and by revealing the capitalist social relations—namely, its class relations—that generate such a logic. Marx himself implies that the value theory is absurd:

When I state that coats or boots stand in a relation to linen because it is the universal incarnation of abstract human labour, the absurdity of the statement is self-evident. Nevertheless, when the producers of coats and boots compare those articles with linen, or, what is the same thing, with gold or silver, as the universal equivalent, they express the relation between their own private labour and the collective labour of society in the same absurd form.[14]

This statement provides the clue to his *critique* of value as the historically specific fetishistic form imposed on production by capital. *In effect, value forms represent for Marx the reified logic imposed on social relations of production and exchange by capital.*

We are now at the heart of the concept of fetishism, a concept that applies not only to commodities but to the entire logical set of categories of *Capital.* One must understand the *tendential abstraction of labor* and the *Wertbestimmung* of the product of labor as two moments of a contradictory structure of production in which the relation of individual to total social labor must be mediated by a third, the commodity, which appears independent.[15] If one turns to the concept of abstract (rather than simple or socially necessary) labor and understands it in terms of a societal logic rather than in physiological terms, one can see in the concept of value the hieroglyph of a complex process of *socialization* (*Vergesellschaftung*) that is the real object of Marx's critique—a process that in the first instance takes the absurd form of value relations between commodities. The term *abstract labor* refers to a unique societal logic wherein the particular forms of concrete labor, be they skilled or not, become of secondary importance to labor in the abstract, or the *consideration* of labor in terms of a time ratio without concern for the particular mode of activity, the quality of the product, or its usefulness.

Insofar as abstract labor is a concept with a correlate in the "real," it refers to the fortuitous relation of the individual worker to his work as a result of the process of socialization inherent in the universalization of exchange relations. In the first instance, then, abstract labor is the conceptual correlate of a process of socialization and representation occurring solely through *exchange.* The commodity fetish rests on this *formal* socialization insofar as the relation between individual and social labor appears only through the value relation between commodities. Consequently, the social character of labor (posited, as we shall see, in capitalist production) appears in the absurd form of an objective characteristic of the product of labor.[16] The labor of the individual is not related to the total labor of society or to social needs through direct communicative interaction but is related only through the act of exchange—through value relations between commodities.

For Marx, however, the socialization process inherent in capitalist commodity relations is also the basis of a process of individuation constituting individual actors in exchange as private proprietors, as buyers and sellers of commodities. The analysis of primitive accumulation and precapitalist economic forms revealed the juridical person, the free laborer, the private proprietor, to be the *preconditions* for the universality of capitalist relations of production. They were seen as products of a double process of dissolution and (political) creation of modern legal, contractual relations. Now, however, they appear as the *systematically reproduced* reified product of capitalist circulation relations. Once capitalist relations are established, then, Marx insists that the self-reproductive *economic* and fetishistic logic creates the very agents of its transactions. Accordingly, in the preface to his first volume of *Capital*, he states, "But here individuals are dealt with only insofar as they are the *personifications* of economic categories, embodiments of particular class interests and class relations." [17] We shall confront the equation of class relations and economic categories further on. Let us first consider the significance of this concept of "character mask," according to which economic categories assign the function and place (socialize) to their individual carriers (*Träger*) and determine the juridical, political relations that secure them.

Following the logic of commodity exchange, Marx maintains that the owner-representatives must act according to a socially constructed logic of private interest, mutually recognizing the rights of private proprietors and exchanging for the purpose of interest maximization. Exchange thus constitutes or socializes individuals as free and equal persons interacting according to the interests of buyers and sellers of commodities. "This juridical relation, which thus expresses itself in a contract . . . is but the reflex of the real economic relation between the two. . . . The characters who appear on the economic stage are but the personifications of the economic relation that exist between them." [18]

Because the capitalist and the worker confront each other only as buyers and sellers of commodities, as free and independent persons, the class relation is concealed by the value forms of exchange and can be demystified only through an analysis of production.[19] But if we follow Marx's move from the sphere of circulation, with its individual persona, to the sphere of production via the analysis of the commodity, labor power,

we can perceive a change in the physiognomy of our dramatis personae. He, who before was the money owner, now strides in front as capitalist, the possessor of labor power follows as his laborer. The one with an air of importance, smirking, intent on business, the other, timid, and holding back, like one who is bringing his own hide to market and has nothing to expect but—a hiding.[20]

In effect, the two personae who confront each other in the sphere of circulation turn out to be not just buyers and sellers but capitalist and worker, whose former character masks presuppose the latter—each being so many forms of personification of capital itself.[21]

The interrogation of the capitalist labor process provides the basis for the further determination of the character masks and of the abstraction of labor as the correlate of a second process of socialization. This process is based on the changing division of labor *in* the factory, which directly socializes labor via the internal organization, coordination, and rule over the various moments of the labor process by capital. The first moment in this socialization and abstraction of labor is the constitution of the labor process as the self-valorization process of capital.[22] As is well known, Marx discusses the labor process first in its transhistorical moment as a process of purposeful activity aimed at production of use values.[23]

For our present purposes, what concerns us is the discussion of the capitalist form of the labor process as a *valorization* process—as a historically new and unique formation of production relations.[24] Predicated upon the fact that the worker works under the control of the capitalist and that the product of labor belongs to the latter, the labor process appears, from the standpoint of capital, as a process between things he has purchased, between factors of production. Moreover, in the valorization process, labor is once more abstracted—considered only from the quantitative aspect and important merely in terms of time occupied in work. The systematically reproduced result and condition of the capitalist labor process are as follows: The objective conditions of labor (instruments, means of production, raw materials, etc.) appear as capital, whereas the subjective conditions of labor, labor itself, appear as the worker. *Capital and wage labor are thus the value categories constituted in the production process*, which, like those of circulation, impose a logic (valorization, accumulation) onto the agents who personify them:

The *functions* fulfilled by the capitalist are no more than the functions of capital—viz. the valorization of value by absorbing living labor—executed *consciously* and *willingly*. The capitalist functions only as *personified* capital, capital as a person, just as the worker is no more than *labour* personified.[25]

The individual who performs the functions of capital and the individual who acts as a worker thus appear with the *character masks* of capitalist and wage laborer, as representatives of economic categories and agents of the interests logically deduced from these categories.

It is clear that Marx considers this logic of personification to be the inverted fetishistic logic of capitalist value relations to which both the laborer and the capitalist are subjected.[26] The character masks of the sphere of circulation appear to be straightforward insofar as they refer to individuals viewed from the standpoint of their functioning within the exchange process. But the personification of the categories of capital and wage labor immediately encounters difficulties. On the one hand, given the presupposition of competition, capital must appear as represented by capitalists guided by the particular interest of value expansion and profit maximization. This point is stressed by Marx in his arguments with both political economists and socialists who regard capital merely as a thing, as a static economic category. "But capital in its being for itself is the *capitalist*. Of course, socialists sometimes say we need capital, but not the capitalist. Then capital appears as a pure thing, not as a relation of production which, reflected in itself, is precisely the capitalist." [27] Correspondingly, the category of wage labor must appear as a person, as the worker who is free to sell his labor power but who functions in the process of production as a means of production under the control of the capitalist.

On the other hand, however, Marx insists that capital is separable from the individual capitalist—it can be lost in such a manner that the individual who was is no longer a capitalist. Unlike the exchange of commodities, therefore, wherein each alienates his property *but remains a property owner*, the separability of capital from the capitalist and likewise the possibility for the worker to become a capitalist and lose the status of wage labor imply a *distinction between the agents and their character masks*. Accordingly, capital and wage labor remain curiously independent of whichever individual personifies them!

I may well separate capital from a given individual capitalist, and it can be transferred to another. But in losing capital, he loses the quality of capitalist. Thus capital is indeed separable from an individual capitalist, but not from *the* capitalist, who, as such, confronts *the* worker. Thus also the individual worker can cease to be the being-for-itself of labour, he may inherit or steal money, etc. But then he ceases to be a *worker*.[28]

But what sociological entity is the representative of *capital-as-such* and the *worker-as-such?* The answer is obvious—the class of capitalists and the class of proletarians, both of which *remain*, as do capital and wage labor (and their respective interests), despite the mobility of particular individuals in and out of the respective classes.

It is here that the problem of the relation of structure to sociology, logic to history, system analysis to action theory, and theory to reality makes itself felt. For the logic of interest-oriented action imputed from the value categories to their individual carriers (buyers and sellers, wage laborers and capitalists) becomes even more questionable when transposed to the level of class relations. If, as Marx insists, individual capitalists and workers function in a framework of competition, do the categories of wage labor and capital allow for the imputation of particular, individual, or general class interests to their bearers? Insofar as wage labor and capital are represented by individuals, the logic imposed on their interaction (conflicting private interests) is criticized as a fetishistic reduction of individuality to the status of bearers of economic categories. But since the concept of "class" and the process of class constitution are seen as challenging and ultimately overthrowing this logic, the integration of class relations and value categories and the imputation of class interests from these categories reveal a fundamental contradiction in Marx's thought. For, if classes and class struggles are constituted by the reproductive logic of capital, if the proletariat is fused, homogenized, posited by capital itself as a moment of its own valorization process, if this logic together with the market imposes an interest structure onto the needs of individuals who participate as agents of production, on what basis can one argue that the self-constitution of these agents of production into a class opposed to capital can be anything more than the subjective affirmation of the logic of capital itself? Even if limited to the critical analysis of capitalism alone, with no future-oriented claims, the idea of personification of economic categories by social classes is unacceptable, for it implies that the critical theoretical reconstruction of a system logic is able to get at both the objective, "real" dynamics of that system and the motives, interests, or needs guiding social action in the same operation.

Let us draw out the implications of this position for the class theory. It is clear from the above that the production process rests on a series of inversions: Instead of consuming the means of production, the laborer is consumed by them; instead of appearing as the subject of the labor process, it appears as its object while its product, capital, acts as subject.[29] Thus the inclusion of labor—first in the form of labor power, then as variable capital—in capital's valorization process establishes a fetish different in form but equally mystifying as the commodity fetish, that is, the capital fetish.[30] The capital fetish signals the integration of the working class into the logic of civil bourgeois society, into the valorization of capital, while simultaneously turning the worker into the mere use value of capital, the central instrument of its own reproduction. The worker becomes the personification of wage labor, but of wage labor as a form of capital, reduced to a factor of production and reproduction of value. Marx's analysis of the changing structure of labor accordingly seeks to *defetishize* the capital fetish by pointing to relations of class struggles at the heart of the value categories. Both the reconstruction of the transition from manufacture to machine production, from absolute to relative surplus value as a dynamic of class struggle, and the analysis of capitalist machine production illustrate this process of defetishization.

Marx accounts for the historical transition from capitalist manufacture to machine production by analyzing class struggles over the length of the working day, wages, and working conditions in terms of their effects on and alteration of the logic of the accumulation of surplus value. When demystifying the economistic and technocratic representations of the "industrial revolution" either as a haphazard series of chance inventions or as an objective logic of technical development, he is at his very best. By pointing to the dynamic role of class struggle in this transition, through an interrelation of sociohistorical analysis and the logically deduced economic necessities of capitalist reproduction, he simultaneously defetishizes political economic categories and unfolds what he sees as the system logic of capitalism: a dialectical interrelation of class struggle and value relations. In effect, it is the very success of class struggles in limiting the length of the working day that provides the key to the transition to machine production and the motor to the move from absolute to relative surplus value.[31] To be sure, in competing with each other individual capitalists tend to introduce machinery to cheapen the costs of production, lower prices, and corner the market. At the same time, however, machinery in the form of labor-saving technology is introduced to lower wages and suppress the workers by making them redundant or dependent on a capital-controlled machine process. "It would be possible to write quite a history of the inventions made since 1830, for the sole purpose of supplying capital with weapons against the revolts of the working class." [32] In order to lower costs and to break the resistance of skilled labor, capital introduces machinery, which replaces the subjective principle of the labor process (*manu*facture) with an objective principle, allowing for the employment of more unskilled workers at lower cost. In the transition of manufacture to machinery, it is precisely the stratum of skilled laborers that is crushed, their skills replaced by science and the machine. [33] In short, machinery is, as Marx maintains, "the most powerful weapon for repressing strikes, those periodical revolts of the working class against the autocracy of capital." [34] The transition from manufacture to machine production is thus accomplished according to the double dynamics of competition and class struggle.

But this double dynamic is also internal to capitalist machine production itself. In its initial periods, the high cost of machine technology, together with the new flexibility it lends to the labor process, spurs capital to introduce new sections of the population into the working class (women, children), lowering wages and increasing hours to prevent depreciation and avoid idleness of the machine. Once the working day is limited and laws are imposed regarding child labor, women, and working conditions, the tendency to replace labor by machines is again strengthened. Successful struggles of the working class to attain decent working conditions exert a constant pressure to increase technological development. In this context, class struggle, integrated into the logic of capitalist production relations, becomes the central dynamic force of the development of capitalist machine production. Accordingly, through the critique of this developmental process, Marx is able to get at *two* integral modes of class struggle: the first being the struggle of workers against machines themselves, [35] the second, the struggle over wages, hours, and conditions that spurs the logic of relative surplus value and the increased development of the forces of production.

Despite its acknowledged radicality, however, Marx insists, as he did earlier in the *Manifesto*, that the struggle against the machine is an essentially immature and antiprogressive but happily transcended stage of working-class struggle:

It took both time and experience before the working people learnt to distinguish between machinery and its employment by capital, and to direct their attacks, not against the material instruments of production, but against the mode in which they are used. [36]

What these new radical struggles against the capitalist *mode* of use of machinery are or were, Marx never reveals. But the fact that he refers to the former mode of struggle as immature and even perhaps reactionary reveals a bias inherited from the theory of historical materialism and now systematically rooted in the class theory itself. For once class and production categories are intimately interrelated so that the former supplies the dynamic of the latter, *only those class struggles that further the development of productive forces can be perceived and theorized as historically progressive.* Consequently, as we shall see, the only class struggles that *Capital* can theorize—that is, integrate and deduce from an immanent critique of economic categories—are those that further rather than contest the developmental logic of capitalist production. For the historical materialist, this is not a problem, since the future communist society can emerge only on the basis of fully developed productive forces (and their contradiction of course with productive relations) of capital. For a nonevolutionist critical theory, however, the bias of the analysis presents serious difficulties. For, as Marx maintains in *Capital*, the introduction of machinery produces such a change in the character of social labor that capital is able to break all resistance to itself.[37] And, indeed, the result of this process is the transformation of the structure of the working class along with the changed structure of labor so that the powerful resistance of skilled labor is broken, the reserve army created and re-created, the relative proportion of unskilled to skilled labor vastly increased, and the division between mental and manual labor intensified. Apparently the very success of the working-class struggle leads to its more effective domination by capital. As will become clear, the only possibilities for "radical" class struggles that Marx can locate on this basis derive from the new mode of socialization of labor introduced by capitalist use of machinery. Whether this socialization can accomplish what Marx hopes, or whether it focuses his attention irrevocably on interest struggles on the one hand and only abstract possibilities on the other, systematically precluding the investigation of struggles that challenge the logic of capitalist production, remains to be seen.

The radical transformation of the labor process that accompanies its industrialization by capital involves a new process of socialization of labor and a new form of the capital fetish that can be distinguished from capitalist manufacture. With the "real subsumption of labor under capital," the social forces of labor are developed through the direct application of science and technology, which materially transform the labor process into a mechanized system with *social* dimensions and simultaneously strip from capital (as well as from labor) its individual character.[38] "Production for the sake of production" and the integration of the worker into an objectively organized and materially socialized labor process are the key features of this new form of capitalist production. With the appropriation of knowledge, judgment, and skill involved in directing the labor process by capital, the socialization of labor confronts the individual worker as an independent power of capital:

The social productive forces of labour, or the productive forces of direct social, *socialized* (i.e. collective) labour come into being through co-operation, division of labour within the workshop, the use of *machinery*, and in general the transformation of production by the conscious *use* of the sciences, of mechanics, chemistry, etc. . . . . This entire development of the productive forces of *socialized labour* . . ., and together with it the *use of science* (the *general* product of social development), in the *immediate process of production*, takes the form of the *productive power of capital*. . . . *The mystification implicit in the relations of capital as a whole is greatly intensified here*, far beyond the point it had reached or could have reached in the merely formal subsumption of labor under capital.[39]

The capital fetish attains its full power on the basis of capitalist industry, to the extent that the material process of labor itself, now an automatic machine process, takes on a social character, which appears as the productive force not of labor but of capital! For Marx, "real" as opposed to "formal" subsumption of labor under capital because, at the level of material production, "the life process in the realm of the social," capitalist machinery steps forth as the social subject of the process, the laborer merely its appendage.[40] The inversion between subject and object typical of all capitalist production, according to which it is not the worker who employs the conditions of his work but the reverse, is completed. Since the labor process is turned materially into a valorization process, it acquires the ultimate fetishistic form of value valorizing itself, of the rule of dead over living labor, and of the transformation of the worker's labor itself into a form of existence of capital.

With machine production, then, the relation between capital and wage labor penetrates into the very core of the productive process.[41] The capital fetish signals the socialization of the agents of the productive process, wage laborers and capitalists, into mere embodiments, personifications of capital and wage labor.[42] Thus, according to Marx, the social classes presupposed by the capital relation but originally in-dependent of it (primitive accumulation) now appear *fully integrated into capitalist production relations*—indeed, are *identified with the value categories of wage labor and capital*, or with the *productive functions they perform*. The commodity fetish, or the transformation of social relations into relations between things in an impersonal ex-change process, is complemented by the capital fetish, the expression of an equally impersonal objectified process of production (machinery), which confronts the masses of producers with a regulatory authority and a social mechanism personified by capital.[43] Moreover, the two fetishes interact insofar as individual capitalists confront each other as com-modity owners, thus allowing for an anarchic situation in which the social interrelations of production assert themselves as an overwhelm-ing natural law in relation to individual free will.[44]

Finally, the distribution relations of social wealth in the form of capital (interest, profit, rent, and wages), analyzed by Marx in detail in volume 3 of *Capital*, complete the phantasmagoria of the capital fetishes. Capital, land, and labor as well as interest, rent, and wages appear as pure things, independent of social relations of society, as the sources of value. With these forms of the existence of capital—and Marx insists on the connection between distribution and production forms—the triumph of the dead over the living, of things over indi-viduals, of economic fetishes over social relations, attains its peak. But here Marx should speak for himself:

In capital–profit, or still better capital–interest, land–rent, labour–wages, in this economic trinity represented as the connection between the component parts of value and wealth in general and its sources, we have the complete mystification of the capitalist mode of production. The conversion of social relations into things, the direct coalescence of the material production re-lations with their historical and social determination. It is an enchanted, perverted, topsy-turvy world, in which Monsieur le Capital and Madame la Terre do their ghost-walking as social characters and at the same time di-rectly as mere things.[45]

Like the commodity and capital fetish, the fetishes of distribution con-vert production relations into entities independent of the agents of production and distribution. Presented by political economists as both ahistorical and objective, automatic mechanisms, exchange, production, and distribution forms conceal and fetishize the social relations of domination and interaction between persons that form their basis.

However, we must pose the question of the *status* of these fetishes in Marx's work. For while the thrust of his analysis is clearly to defetishize and demystify the capital relation through a critique of the reconstructed system logic of capitalist reproduction, nevertheless Marx presents the socialization of individuals through production (and the only sphere of the "social" he analyzes is the economic) as an accomplished reification, himself treating individuals as personifications of functions of production, classes as personifications of value categories, and domination relations as purely economic.[46] The domination of the capitalist class over the proletariat is understood as a pure relation of production. In short, the rule of capital over labor is equated with the domination of the capitalist class over the working class, accomplished through the independent reproductive logic of the system of production. According to Marx, therefore, relations of domination in capitalism are no longer accomplished through political or religious forms but appear as relations of production personified by classes. Correspondingly, politics are simply class relations expressed in the sphere of the state. In effect, the technique of demystifying the thinglike appearances of the value categories through representing the unrepresented—the social relations of production and classes—leads to a fetishization of the process of socialization itself into a constituent of the process of production that allocates the position, interests, needs, and objective class status of individuals. We move from one objectivistic framework (economic value categories of political economy) to another (social relations of production, class relations) without leaving or questioning the autonomy or objective character of the sphere in which they are grounded—the economy. For once this "sphere" is treated as self-reproducing, once politics and ideology are seen as the forms of representation of this sphere, then the defetishizing critique of economic categories is doomed to the reproduction of these fetishes, for Marx, as "social relations" between classes. As we shall demonstrate, the implications of this restriction are grave for the model of the future society, if only in the first instance because it implies that social relations finally freed from economic fetishes and class domination would appear in their full transparency. But we shall return to this problem further on.

First, let us turn to the analysis of the new forms of individuation and socialization imposed by capitalist machine production, as well as the objective possibilities this process creates for class constitution and struggles pointing to the future. For it is here that the ultimate capitulation of Marx, through his own class theory, to the fetishes of the system logic he himself constructs becomes most evident. The composition and future potentialities of the working class under "real" capitalist production are presented through an analysis of the contradictions inherent in the division of labor imposed in the factory. On the one hand, as Marx maintains, large-scale industry sweeps away the technical foundation of the division of labor in manufacture, according to which an individual was bound for life to a single operation. Now the tool and the skill of the individual pass over to the machine, freeing the labor process from the restraints of handicraft. The technical reason for socializing the individual laborer into a detail worker disappears. Nevertheless, the capitalist use of machinery reproduces this same division of labor in a more monstrous form by converting the worker into an appendage of the machine—into a detail machine.[47] Here the crucial distinction between the technically necessary and sociohierarchical division of labor imposed by capital for the purposes of its valorization is at work. Marx implies that, for the purposes of domination and exploitation, capitalist relations impose an anachronistic division of labor on the production process, which is neither technically necessary nor inherent in machine production itself.[48] Accordingly, an artificial division of labor is developed with an internal hierarchical structure based on the imperatives of capital's domination rather than on the technical requirements of machinery. The collective worker of manufacture and its cooperative basis is replaced by a working class whose socialization in the new division of labor fragments it into a series of isolated competitive laborers arranged in a hierarchy of super- and subordination, while the social cooperative moment appears as a characteristic of capital. The division of labor into detail tasks, new levels of skills, different pay scales, and varied levels of management fragments the workers, the automation of processes of production turning into a nightmare of insecurity for the individual constantly threatened by replacement with a machine and redundancy of his skills.[49]

This reproduction of a technically unnecessary division of labor constitutes a fundamental contradiction for capitalist production by limiting the very variability of labor it requires for its constantly transformed labor processes. For us, however, it is significant because it leads to contradictions in the assessment of the socialization of the working class that personifies the functions of production. As to the negative effect on labor of the capital-imposed division of labor, Marx is quite explicit:

We have seen how this absolute contradiction between the technical necessities of Modern Industry, and the social character inherent in its capitalistic form, dispels all fixity and security in the situation of the labourer; ... We have seen, too, how this antagonism vents its rage in the creation of that monstrosity, an industrial reserve army, kept in misery in order to be always at the disposal of capital; in the incessant human sacrifices from among the working class, in the most reckless squandering of labor power, and in the devastation caused by a social anarchy which turns every economic progress into a social calamity. This is the negative side.[50]

Certainly, from this standpoint there is little reason to posit the fragmented, alienated, stupefied, dominated wage laborer as the potential revolutionary subject capable of founding a new social order based on a rich and many-sided individuality. There is, however, a positive side to this process. By constantly changing the industrialized processes of production, their technical bases, as well as the functions of the worker and the social combination of the labor process, capitalist machine production repeatedly revolutionizes the division of labor within society, throwing large masses of workers and capital from one branch of production to another: "Modern Industry, by its very nature, therefore necessitates variation of labour, fluency of function, universal mobility of the labourer." [51] Accordingly, a tendency counter to the divisive hierarchical qualification of the labor force appears—that is, a tendency to equalize and reduce to an identical level the work of those laboring on machines.[52] Along with the objective socialization of the labor of the individual, a new technical division of labor becomes "objectively possible"—one that tends to emerge even within capitalist relations but that could only come to fruition with their abolition.

Marx goes into some detail expounding upon this "positive" side of the process of socialization (*Vergesellschaftung*) of labor, explicitly presenting it as the basis for the future-directed organization, power, and structure of labor, which the proletariat, self-constituted as a revolutionary class, will institute in the coming communist society. The new "technical" structure of labor objectively possible in industrial production freed from the forms imposed by capital would consist, according to the model outline in *Capital*, of three sorts of laborers.[53] The vast majority would be machine operatives, employed directly on machines. The tasks of the attendants of machines could be mostly automated, leaving a numerically insignificant class of engineers, mechanics, and scientists who constitute a superior, highly educated stratum standing outside the realm of factory workers but applying their skill and knowledge to the total process. This potential technical division of labor would perpetuate a polarization of mental and manual labor, the operatives' skills appearing as insignificant next to the knowledge of scientific labor and the gigantic productive forces it sets in motion.[54] For the vast majority of workers, machines would replace skilled with unskilled labor.

This ambiguous picture, however, is positively evaluated by Marx, due to its corollary of the variability of labor and the abolition of a system that ties the worker to one task for life. Variable labor—that is, a working population able to shift easily from one occupation to another, from one industry to another, without the disadvantages of insecurity or unemployment that inhere only in capitalist social relations—is the great hope of Marx of *Capital*:

Modern industry, on the other hand, through its catastrophes, imposes the necessity of recognizing as a fundamental law of Production, variation of work, consequently fitness of the labourer for varied work, consequently the greatest possible of his varied aptitudes. It becomes a question of life and death for society to adapt the mode of production to the normal functioning of this law. Modern industry, indeed, compels society under penalty of death to replace the detail-worker of today, crippled by life-long repetition of one and the same trivial operation, and thus reduced to a mere fragment of a man, by the fully developed individual, fit for a variety of labours, ready to face any change of production and to whom the different social functions he performs are but so many modes of giving free scope to his own natural and acquired powers.[55]

In addition to the "liberating" flexibility and variability of labor, Marx points to the establishment of technical schools combined with elementary education as the first step within capitalism to the creation of the possibility to realize the above ideal.[56] Finally, there is the tendency of capitalism to develop the productive forces, allowing for the expansion of needs and the level of consumption for all. Repeatedly Marx insists that the civilizing aspect of capitalist production lies in its development of the productive forces, new needs, and social relations that provide the elements for a new social order.[57] The development of industry, the rationalization of agriculture, the reduction of socially necessary labor time, and the increase in overall social wealth constitute the positive side, of course embedded in a framework that has thus far posited development at the cost of the individual.

Far from attempting to reconcile the two opposing tendencies of socialization of the working class, or the differences between the "objective possibilities" and the capitalist forms of machinery, Marx maintains that they constitute the internal contradiction and dynamic of capitalist relations of production. More important, *the objective contradictions between the two constitute for Marx the logic of the abolition of capitalist production relations, implying a class struggle whose teleology is the realization of the objective possibilities of machine production and division of labor outlined above.* The fundamental contradiction of capitalist production, deduced from the logic of the value categories, is the contradiction between the "socialized forces of production" and the limits imposed on their development and use by their "private appropriation by capital." The following aspects of this contradiction emerge: (1) Capital, for purposes of domination, imposes an anachronistic division of labor on the working class, throwing up barriers to the smooth expansion of its own productive process. (2) Capital shortens the hours of necessary social labor only to lengthen them for the purposes of valorization. (3) It accomplishes the triumph of man over nature only to turn the laborer into the slave of the productive forces. (4) Capitalist machine production increases social wealth and knowledge while impoverishing the worker mentally and materially. (5) Capitalist reproduction leads to the progressive expropriation of capitalists, revealing the social character of the labor process and the arbitrary nature of private appropriation. (6) Capital destroys small-scale domestic industries, the last resorts of the redundant population, removing its own safety valve. And finally, (7) capital appears as the greatest barrier to its own developmental tendencies by forcing the exigencies of its self-valorization onto its development of technology.[58] The latter refers to the famous tendency of the profit rate to fall, an argument based on complicated computations of the value theory that do not concern us here.[59] It is worth noting in passing, however, that for Marx this tendency never constituted a breakdown theory but implied the likelihood of crises that could appear as periodic forcible solutions to the existing contradictions that restore detroyed equilibrium.[60]

Put in a more general way, the contradiction of capital with itself lies in the tendency toward the absolute development of the productive forces over and against the aim of preserving the value of the existing capital and expanding it. Stoppages, crises, depreciations of capital, decrease of variable in relation to constant capital, the necessity to accumulate value in the form of use values—these immanent barriers to capitalist production are constantly reproduced. Hence, the *real barrier* to capitalist production is *capital* itself.[61] Its contradictions, unfolded in *Capital* through an analysis that interweaves class and value categories, provide allegedly the basis both for the abolition of capitalism through a working-class revolution and for the creation of a socialist society in which production and individual development are unlimited.

These contradictions, however, are not presented as mere features of or as immanent to capitalism but contain, as previously indicated, a future-directed teleology inherent not in the crisis theory but in the class analysis. For the third and only "revolutionary" basis of working-class constitution and class struggle theorized by Marx in *Capital* is the unification of the proletariat on the basis of the socialization and homogenization of labor immanent in the mechanized process of production. As representatives of the socialized productive forces, as personifications of social labor, the proletariat's "objective" interest must be to abolish the limits imposed by capital to the further development of the productive forces and their conscious organization according to a central plan. Since the actual division of labor imposed by capital on the proletariat, according to Marx's own analysis, results in its division, stratification, and hierarchization, Marx is unable to point to actual struggles or needs that either unify the class or involve a revolutionary project. Instead, he deduces a logic of class struggle from the logic of contradiction of the developmental value categories, imputing class interests from the productive forces the class allegedly represents. The ultimate implications of the integration of the concept of social class into the dynamic of production, of the transformation of classes into personifications of production relations, in short, of the logic of *capital* as a logic of class struggle, become clear as soon as this logic of internal development and contradiction dictates the dynamic of class constitution and historical transformation. The old formulations of historical materialism, specifically the contradiction between forces and relations of production, return as the historicized immanent dialectic of class confrontation within capitalism, teleologically predetermining the "revolutionary subject," form of organization, and mode of transition to the future. A critically reconstructed system logic is collapsed with present and future history; a critical sociology of class is turned into the panlogistic science of the future.

Designated as the revolutionary subject in advance, the working class, despite the de facto hierarchical divisions and internal stratification imposed by capitalist domination relations, is to follow the logic of the productive forces it abstractly represents and constitute itself as a class on the basis of the tendencies toward homogenization and socialization of labor inherent in machine production, representing also the ripened material conditions and social organization of labor to be reproduced without capitalist forms in the future. Not only does the socialization of the labor process render the individual capitalist, according to Marx, superfluous, not only does the development of the credit system along with joint stock companies reveal the social character of production, not only does the external process of expropriation of capital by capital appear as the step just prior to the expropriation of capital by socialized labor, but the development of cooperative factories within capitalist production reveals how the *new form springs from the womb of the old.*[62] In effect, the critique of political economy historicizes the dialectic, separating genesis from system logic, only to reunite them for the future, insisting on the immanence of the future in the system logic of the present: "But the historical development of the antagonisms, immanent in a given form of production, is the only way in which that form of production can be dissolved and a new form established." [63] The class of proletarians, as representatives of social production, will, once socialized and homogenized in the labor process, carry out their obvious historical task: "there can be no doubt that when the working class comes into power, as inevitably it must, technical instruction, both theoretical and practical, will take its proper place in the working-class schools." [64] The anarchy of the division of labor in society (the market) will be replaced by the conscious decisions of these socialized products of the division of labor in the factory, the newly associated producers.[65]

To be sure, the associated producers in question—that is, the working class as it emerges out of capitalist industry—hardly appear able to carry out their assigned task. For the objective possibilities outlined in *Capital* for the modern factory operative, despite the goals of technical education to render his labor variable, do not overcome the fact that he remains, after all, an unskilled laborer, able to move to different branches of production because of the overall simplification and similarity of the tasks of attending machines and not because of his knowledge and development. The gulf between the machine operative and the scientific worker at the other end remains immense. In this context, the glorification of the socialization process of labor, which lays the groundwork for the "social individual," implies that the social individual is merely an empty abstraction or representative of the productive forces. That alienation, division of mental and manual work, in short, most of the drawbacks of labor in capitalist industrial production, remain in the model of communism flowing from this analysis and explicitly unfolded in *Capital* is obvious from Marx's famous distinction between the "realm of necessity" and the "realm of freedom" in the future, a distinction that marks labor with unfreedom and assigns "the development of human energy" as "an end in itself" to a realm beyond labor.[66] According to this model of communism, then, we have a situation in which direct labor remains as a form of activity, in the realm of necessity, subject to an alienating division of labor. Of the "realm of freedom," all we are told is that it is not a realm of production; otherwise it is left completely undetermined. And not accidentally—for the very logic of the critique of political economy, which restricts itself to the immanent unfolding of the categories of production to the point of development where the contradiction between social labor and capitalist appropriation can be theorized and the class struggle between its representatives asserted, precludes reflection on political, juridical, symbolic, or cultural forms insofar as they transcend the object of analysis itself, the critique of the categories of political economy.

Both the model of communism and the class that will realize it reveal the problems inherent in such a critique. On the one hand, the actual organization of the working class by capital involves a variety of skills, pay rates, privileges, and statuses, as well as the triumph of the capital fetish. To argue, on the other hand, that these divisions are artificial, attributable to the imperatives of capitalist domination rather than to technical necessity, is not to overcome them. And Marx can point to no process of defetishization in the activity and demands of the empirically existing working class that parallels his theoretical critique. Certainly the technical and scientific skilled workers have needs and particular interests that are different from those of the unskilled laborer. Marx avoids the difficulties these divisions pose for the very concept of the proletariat only through a category error— through the collapse of the structural tendency toward homogenization of labor with the sociological level of class stratification. In effect, in Marx's own time, as well as in our own, the discrepancy between structure and sociology means that the wage labor/capital relation becomes concretized in a complexity of different status and interest groups rather than in two clear-cut opposing classes! But surely the way for the so-called proletariat to recognize its "common class interests" over and against its particular interests and divisions could not be through the reading of *Capital*! Once again, it seems as if the logic of interest conflicts derived from the economic categories and the representative concept of class lead to the disastrous conclusion: the necessity (never asserted but obvious logically) of a party to represent universal class interests over particular interests of fractions of the class.

The limits of capitalist subsumption: the problem of land

The difficulty in meshing the production (value) categories with social classes becomes demonstrably evident in the third volume of *Capital*, where Marx attempts to write a chapter on class but finally gives it up and leaves it unfinished.[67] The manuscript of volume 3, unpublished in Marx's time, breaks off with only two completed pages of the chapter entitled "Classes." But Marx did not die at his desk in the process of writing this chapter; on the contrary, he lived many years beyond the date of this manuscript and wrote several other texts in the meantime. The question becomes: Why was Marx unable to write the chapter on classes? I shall attempt to demonstrate that the problem was not biographical or "historical" but theoretical—in short, rooted in Marx's concept of class itself and not simply in its application to a heterogeneous empirical reality.

Throughout the first volume of *Capital*, the concept of class, as already indicated, appears repeatedly as the personification of capitalist production relations, interrelated and often identified with the forms of the wage labor/capital relation. The theoretical difficulties with such a concept of class, however, do not make themselves felt until the third volume, when, having devoted himself to an analysis of forms of distribution of surplus value, Marx presents a concept of class that appears now as the personification not of production but of distribution relations! Instead of the two-class model corresponding to the wage labor/capital relation, Marx, throughout volume 3 of *Capital*, speaks of the three major classes of modern society: landlords, industrial capitalists, and wage laborers.[68] It would be plausible, to be sure, to maintain that, in speaking of the personifiers of money capital, interest capital, merchant capital, and industrial capital as various social classes, Marx really meant only the various stratifications of the capitalist class. The same, however, cannot be said for the landlord class, the direct "personification" of one of the most essential conditions of production—land in the form of private property.[69] For Marx maintains that, although the exploitation of agricultural wage labor on the basis of the rationalization of agriculture is the ultimate source of the *revenue* of the landed proprietor (be he directly a capitalist farmer or merely the entitled owner of land rented and exploited by a capitalist intermediary), although rent is merely a portion of the overall *surplus value* of society like interest and profit, nevertheless, in this case proprietorship of land, in distinction from any productive function, is the basis of this class and does not of itself constitute capital! Mere ownership allows this class to pocket a product of social development.

Indeed, this class, with its form of property (land) and its form of appropriation (ground rent), constitutes an obstacle to the further rationalization and capitalization of agriculture and becomes a source of constant interest conflicts with capital, despite the fact that its form of property constituted the starting point for capitalist accumulation.[70] As the direct personification of private property denuded of any productive function, the class of landlords represents the internal contradiction between production on a social scale initiated by capital and private property acting, like capital itself, as a barrier to the further development of production.[71] But the crucial distinction between the class of landlords and the fractions of the capitalist class is the following: It is as the owner of a natural force in the form of a monopoly, and not as the embodiment of one of the social factors of production, that the landed proprietor constitutes a special class and claims a share of the social product. Marx goes so far as to maintain that, even if the capitalist himself should be the owner of the natural force in question (land), he would pocket an extra portion of the social surplus in his capacity as an owner of a natural force, not as a capitalist![72]

But what can this mean? Marx implies here that even if a separate social class of landed proprietors did not exist, even if capitalist farmers owned the land they invest in, nevertheless, a percentage of the social product would accrue to them as personifiers of the natural force they own, as implicitly a class of landlords. This is the clue to the impossibility of regarding landlords either as a fraction of capital or merely as a historical anachronism, as an empirically existing but transcendable social stratum (transcendable in capitalism, that is). It must not be overlooked that for Marx the concept of class is never "innocent," it is never interchangeable with that of a "social stratum" or an empirically existing group that forms fleetingly with no specific relation to the key functions or logic of the system. Landlords, like the other classes described in volume 3, represent the crucial moments of a social process of distribution, which is theorized as a moment of the historically specific capitalist process of accumulation and realization. But, and here is the problem, the landlord class is more than that, for as a class the landlords represent the second greatest transhistorical source of social wealth next to labor—nature.[73] As such, it is an alien force within the womb of the historically specific socialized forms of capitalist production, which cannot be overcome (i.e., socialized) until the existence of capital itself, or of private property, is abolished.

In other words, landed property and its class representatives appear as the internal limit to the central logic and, for Marx, progressive moment of capitalism—its logic of socialization (*Vergesellschaftung*) of production and of production relations. The ceaselessly repeated insistence that capital is not a thing but a social relation of production cannot be said of landed property, for land, according to Marx, is nature, the nonsocially created source of wealth. Property in land is a distribution form, not a form of production. To be sure, the historically modern form of landed property is "adequate" to the capitalist mode of production, having in common with capital its purely "economic form," appearing as monopolized property freed from all traditional and political associations, accessories, etcetera.[74] But, in the former case, private property appears as the appropriation of nature by the few and the personification of nature by this class; in the latter case, it is the private appropriation of the socialized productive forces that is personified. Marx's concern in the last part of volume 3 of *Capital* is to demystify the fetishes deriving from the tripartite distribution process, according to which land, labor, and capital appear as the independent sources of rent, wages, and profit. Through a critique of political economic theories of distribution, he seeks to demonstrate that distribution is determined by specific social forms of production and production relations and, as such, is always a distribution of the total social product in the form of surplus value. In short, he uses the value theory critically against its original proponents to defetishize their reification of social relations and to demonstrate the sociohistorical character of distribution determined and conditioned by capitalist class relations, insisting that the wage labor/capital relation determines the

entire character of the mode of production. But, once again, the immanent logic of the defetishizing critique rests on the problematic concept
of class as the personification, this time, of the distribution relations
in question—problematic in the first instance because the three-class
model conflicts with the two-class model of personification of the wage
labor/capital relation, leading to an insoluble (for Marx) contradiction
in the very determination of what is a class. Thus, in the fragment on
classes, Marx begins with the results of the third volume, namely,
three great classes whose respective sources of income are wages, profit,
and ground rent—proletarians, capitalists, and landlords—and proceeds to attempt to justify this conception of class in the face of the
multilevel stratification of England, the historical referent of his critique. He states:

The first question to be answered is this: What constitutes a class?—and
the reply to this follows naturally from the reply to another question,
namely: What makes wage-labourers, capitalists, and landlords constitute
the three great social classes? [75]

But immediately he shows that distribution forms as the criteria would
be inadequate, for on that basis physicians, officials, and the like would
be classes, as would the infinite fragments of interest groups and ranks
in the overall social division of labor.[76] And here the manuscript breaks
off.

Clearly, what perturbs Marx with such a stratification model is its
conflict with the concept of class as the dynamic correlate of production relations. But what is most disturbing is neither the obvious sub-
divisions and fragmentations of social strata present in any given historical situation nor the conflict between the concept of class as the
personification of production as opposed to distribution relations. The
latter two concepts could be reconciled, if it were not for the second
function of representation of the landlord class as personifying, in addition to a capitalist distribution relation, a noncapitalist, nonsocialized
force—nature. For here, the limit not just to the capitalist form of
rationalization but to the totalization of the capitalist dynamic of socialization makes itself felt, a limit that runs counter to the dynamic
of Marx's work as well. For if private property in land, whether in the
form of small-scale peasant property or large-scale landlordism, is the
presupposition of capitalism, then the presence of classes (the peasantry and the landlords) that cannot be integrated into capitalist production relations—that is, cannot be seen as personifications of value

categories since they are not socialized according to the internal dynamic of capitalist reproduction but represent its limit—has to be admitted. But, as previously argued, landed property is also a byproduct of capitalist reproduction, and hence its class representatives are not really anachronistic. If, as classes, they personify neither dead nor living labor, then the concept of class with which Marx has been operating breaks down.

Indeed, if we ask why Marx insists so strongly on the limits that the class of landed proprietors pose to the capitalist mode of production and expansion and consider his answer—that insofar as this class represents a thing, nature, it limits the socialization and rationalization process—then it becomes obvious that Marx again falls prey to the fetishism he seeks to overcome. For land is no more a pure thing than, let us say, raw materials, yet the owner of raw materials (e.g., a mine) is considered to be simply a capitalist if he employs labor to exploit the mine, whereas the owner of a large estate who also employs labor to farm it is given a double determination—capitalist receiving profit, landlord receiving rent. Obviously, on the logical level, Marx could have included landed property under the same category as ownership of raw materials. He did not do so, not because land is objectively more of a pure natural thing than a mine but because of historical reasons—such as a never-overcome traditional attitude toward landed property and the resistance of owners of landed property to their reduction, leveling, and integration by the capitalist fetishistic forms. Or perhaps Marx was forced to consider property in land as a special case because of an implicit perception of the resistance presented by landed proprietorship to the rationalization of the possession relation of the individual to nature, that is, against its reduction to the level of pure economic quantitative relations with no symbolic meaning other than economic interest. Of course, landed proprietorship in the form of small-scale peasant property has historically provided the most striking example of such resistance against capitalist forms of production, rationalization, and proprietorship. Since the large-scale landlord certainly rationalized agricultural production, employed wage labor, and produced for a market, it seems arbitrary that the mere fact of land ownership is enough to distinguish the landlord from the capitalist. But peasant property and Marx's relation to the peasant class reveal his astonishing attitude toward land to be an implicit form of an awareness of historical resistance to capitalization, represented for Marx by land ownership *tout court*.

In the third volume of *Capital*, landed property appears simply as either large- or small-scale, both forms representing an obstacle to the free unfolding of capitalist social relations, rationalization, and socialization of production. Since, for Marx, these latter processes are the necessary precursors to a higher form of society, those classes representing obstacles to it become the "reactionary" objects of his scorn. The landlord class escapes with the accusation of being simply parasitic (having no productive function), but the peasantry is treated with unabashed ridicule: "small landed property creates a class of barbarians standing halfway outside of society, a class combining all the crudeness of primitive forms of society with the anguish and misery of civilised countries." [77] Its basic sin is its lack of the means and knowledge to apply social labor productively.[78] Thus it is not because land is an independent source of wealth next to labor that landlords and peasants constitute classes opposed to capital but because these groups have historically resisted capitalist forms of production, continually reviving precapitalist traditions and modes of relating to land; they are therefore conceived of by Marx as an alien force. Since landed property could not be fully rationalized in the usual capitalist manner, since it could not fit neatly into the categorical framework of *Capital*, which presents all economic forms of possession and distribution via the value categories as fetishistic expressions of social relations, it represented to Marx an unmastered—that is, a not purely economic—residue of precapitalist forms.

Ironically, Marx thought he could dispense with the peasantry by calling it anachronistic and by pointing to a logic of its dissolution—the proletarianization of labor and concentration and centralization of land ownership—though he was unable to write off the class of landlords through this logic. This is ironic, for history reveals the opposite to be the case: Large-scale landed property (in the West) has been effectively capitalized, the distinction between the aristocratic landlord and the capitalist farmer having vanished, whereas the peasantry has remained as a constant source of resistance to "capitalization" in all European countries.[79] As we shall see, a fundamental source of Marx's difficulty here lies in the identification of the capitalist process of socialization and rationalization of production as the formal precursor of the full socialization of society to take place in communism with the abolition of private property altogether. For only on the basis of the assumption that the capitalist socialization process is the internal contradiction to capital as private property, and the projection of this logic of socialization into the future, could Marx develop such scorn of landowning classes, especially small-scale landed proprietors, which prevent and resist the universalization of this socialization process. In short, the positive evaluation of the socialization of labor accomplished by capital, together with the total integration of the concept of class and the value categories through the concept of personification, prevented Marx from theorizing the historical resistance to this logic by peasant and some landlord strata as a valuable social protest. Having chosen the side of "universality" of the logic of capitalist rationalization against particularity (private property), the struggle of a class in defense of its particularity, of a class which could never, qua class, represent universality, could have no meaning for Marx's class theory. Instead, he fetishized the concept of land as nature, as a thing whose possession as private property is represented by classes that are "objectively" anachronistic but are constantly reproduced in the present. The logic of representation, be it of production relations, of distribution relations, or of nature, consequently leads to an antinomic concept of class that could not be used to theorize the struggles of the very groups composing the classes in question!

Communism and the opening to authoritarian politics

Even if we restrict ourselves to the concept of class (two-class model) flowing out of volume 1 of *Capital*, the tension between the logical categories and their sociological correlates remains. The dynamic of the socialization of labor does not find adequate expression in an empirically homogenized working class even in Marx's own argumentation. Were the proletariat indeed homogenized and unified through the immanent development of the labor process, this would still be a unification, a constitution, of the class by, within, and according to the imperatives of capital. Socialized through a logic of production, the imputable interest of this class would perhaps be to overthrow capitalist property and market relations, but only in order to further the productivist project imposed on it by capital in the first place. For the representatives of socialized labor, of the productive forces, no other "class interest" can be imputed. In effect, the careful logical distinction between the production process and its capitalist form, between the technically necessary and social/hierarchical division of labor, leads to the unfortunate implication that the productive forces (machine industry and socialized labor) developed in the womb of capitalism will be taken over as the model of association and production by the "associated producers" in communism once private property and value forms are abolished. Indeed, the very notion of "associated producers" (including its possible implication of workers' control) reveals the ultimate bias of the logic of the text, if not of Marx personally. For, once more, the individual (here the "social individual") is understood as, or reduced to, the status of a producer, collectively planning and organizing the socialized productive forces according to an immanent goal of production and expansion of production inherited from capitalism, for no other norms, values, or goals appear to guide the activity of the producers qua producers. That Marx of *Capital* always refers to the individuals of the future as "associated producers"—that is, under the sign of production—signals the inability of his analysis to transcend the categories and attributes of the object of its critique. (Both the "democratic centralism" of Leninist parties and the antiparty council-communist model suffer from this universalization of the socialization of labor and the worker into the sole mode of association for the future.) The idea of a class making a revolution in the general interest of the class, against interest and class relations as such, is only the expression of this problematic.

The model of communism flowing from the three volumes of *Capital* suffers from the antinomies internal to the class theory and the critique of political economy. The image of a collectively planned, fully socialized society, instituted by the class representatives of the socialized productive forces, freed from the tyranny of private property, liberated from the fetishes of commodity and capital, in which the rationality of production no longer confronts the irrational barriers of capitalist valorization and in which the fully transparent organization[80] of social and material life processes replaces their mystification, is simply a rationalistic myth combined with a technocratic utopia. The famous "social individual," the immanent product of the socialization process, turns out to be the leveled, averaged individual sans class, that is, divested even of this last moment of particularity, determined by the structure of labor, with the sole attribute of being a producer, subject to the tyranny of social relations now not only in the sphere of production but also in what used to be the unregulated sphere of exchange, the market. Since Marx never discussed the "private" or the "particular" except as that which has to be abolished with the abolition of capitalism, one can only presume that in the fully transparent socialized communist society envisioned in *Capital* it would no longer exist.

But, one must ask, through what mode of organization, through what mechanism, do the associated producers accomplish the suppression of exchange, of the private realm, and how are they to collectively plan production and distribution? The answer, which Marx does not give in *Capital* but has given elsewhere and which now flows from the very logic of socialization and representation (i.e., from the class theory), is, of course, some form of the state. The explicit statism of historical materialism is here replaced by an implicit statist logic. For, clearly, the only organ capable of planning and representing the fully socialized productive forces and their distribution in the place of both capital and the proletariat is the state itself, the old state or a new one understood as an organ of planning at the very least. And since the administration of things is always administration of men, this state would retain its hierarchic character. The logic that integrates social class into production relations, turning classes into representatives of productive forces, collapsing present and future history in the teleology of interest conflicts derived from these production relations, and identifying politics with class relations of domination, culminates (at least logically) in a statist principle and technocratic ideology wherein the state represents the interests of the proletariat in its planning function, parading as the simple administrator of socioeconomic affairs. The industrial mode of production and its socialized labor process would have to be preserved by the central planning agency, which substitutes its own "rational redistribution" for the capitalist property, market, and distribution relations.[81]

The pretensions of a critical science to be able to reconstruct not only the system logic of capitalism as a fetishistic mode of domination but also the logic of its overthrow, rooted in the material preparations and mode of socialization within capitalism, culminate in an image of the future in which sociality is automatic, immediate, and universal. The dialectization of the concept of class, or the integration of classes into the logic of production relations and their socialization under the law of value, institutes a productivist vocation in the working class that in no way breaks the fetishistic logic of political economy but raises it to the conscious goal of the future.[82] The very concept of class, flowing out of *Capital*, linking the form-giving value categories of production with sociological counterparts and imputing interests and goals from the contradictory logic of the former to the latter, reproduces rather than challenges the productivist and economic reductionist logic of capitalist representations as the determinant of the future. The historicization of the dialectic in *Capital*, a positive achievement insofar as the system categories of capitalist production are distinguished from precapitalist forms, cannot come to fruition. For the dialectization of the concept of class has the result of recollapsing logic and history, in terms of the present and the future. Inevitably the antinomies among science, philosophy, and critique in Marx's oeuvre as a whole reappear in the concept of class and the class theory, turning a critical concept into the dogmatic ground of both relations of domination and revolutionary transformation.

Marx succeeded in making class struggle the immanent dynamic of capitalist development, but only insofar as it represents interest struggles derivable from the relations of production themselves. But the very *immanence* of this class concept renders it incapable of getting at radical contestations pointing beyond capitalism, other than those that seek to continue its productivist logic without the barriers presented by capital.

The surrender of the neo-Hegelian dogma of the proletariat as class subject is in itself hardly the way out of the difficulty, if one retains the logic upon which this dogma is grounded—that is, the effort to immanently ground the preconditions and objective possibilities and forms of the future society through a dialectical critique of the system logic of capitalism in general or through a critique of the ideology of political economy in particular. For what could emerge from such a critique could never be anything more than a socioeconomic or technocratic utopia, including the already mentioned utopia of the *Grundrisse*. For even here the only organizing principles for the new society appear to be those of (1) the unfolding and satisfaction of needs, (2) disposable time, and (3) production for use rather than for its own sake. In the *Grundrisse* model necessary labor time will be measured by the needs of the social individual, while the power of social production will be so great that, in addition to satisfying the needs of all, disposable time would increase for everyone. Still, economy of time along with planned distribution of labor would remain the first economic law for the future society. Although this would differ from value calculations of direct labor time in capitalism, nevertheless, social organization of labor must be planned and time economized, this time by the "general intellect." The limits of the defetishizing critique become immediately apparent, for the terms applied to the communist future as well as the socialization basis of the individual derived from the critique—needs, time, and production for use—*remain socioeconomic*. Twist and turn as we may, the class theory as a theory of revolution is unavoidable in this framework,[83] for the Marxian concept of class is the logical correlate of depoliticized, socioeconomic categories of the spheres of production and exchange, whose dynamic is presented as the dynamic of society as a whole and whose logic is seen as the logic of the total social system. The entire logic of defetishization of the value forms thus culminates necessarily in a fetishistic class theory and in an economistic vision of the future in which needs, time, and production for use appear as self-regulating principles, as the automatic outcome of a process of dissolution of the present, requiring no further reflection on the goals, norms, principles of justice, or modes of political interaction in the future. The logical culmination of the critique of political economy, whether in the *Grundrisse* or in *Capital*, is not a political utopia but a socioeconomic one based on the socialization of society unhindered by private property or classes, and the emergence of the social individual whose immediate, direct, and transparent sociality does away with the necessity of political mediations.

One could, of course, argue that Marx does reflect on politics for the future and tries to provide at least an alternative principle of justice to that of capitalism insofar as he replaces the principle of "to each according to his work" and equivalence exchange with "to each according to his needs." This principle, presented in the *Critique of the Gotha Program* as the guiding principle of the accomplished stage of communism freed from the forms of the transition period where the other principle still operates, corresponds quite well with the *Grundrisse* model of communism and the praxis philosophical moments of Marx's theory. But this alternative is quixotic. For the image of a future society oriented to universalized need satisfaction and production-for-use presents no real alternative to capitalist logic; it only unfolds the underside of that logic, of the value forms, abstracting them into a fetishized alternative to exchange relations. "Use value," "needs," "production for use" are just as much capitalist significations as "value," "profit," "production for its own sake." [84] Ironically, it is precisely because Marx did not set out in *Capital* and the *Grundrisse* to develop an alternative system of norms to the principle of equivalence exchange implicit in political economy that he is led to immanently deduce an alternative principle of distribution (to exchange) from the internal categories of capitalism itself. Accordingly, he makes the double error of assuming that needs and use value exist as pure economic entities and that they may be calculated in a society that has overcome the capitalist deviation of production for surplus value. In short, he forgets that use value is also capitalist-determined and that needs are always constituted in an interpretive symbolic framework and are never simply objective, economic, and calculable. Just as the image of precapitalist societies oriented to production-for-use but based on a limited structure of needs and mystifying forms of political and religious domination is a projection backward of political economic significations, so too the vision of a future society oriented to the satisfaction of infinitely expanding needs, based on the great productivity of the forces of production and the abolition of classes, is a projection of capitalist significations onto the future. To project these significations into the future is to impute the capitalist-determined mode of individuality to the "social individual"—that is, self-creation and self-objectification through labor and needs at last oriented to useful ends.

Indeed, via the class theory, Marx succumbs to the very core of fetishistic logic—economic reductionism and desymbolization of sociopolitical cultural life. For he assumes in the first place that objectifications along the dynamic of labor alone found the world as objective and man as historical, relegating all of nonlabor to a representative, superstructural level of activity or thought. And, in the second place, he assumes that this "objective reality" created through the dialectic of labor contains its own criteria of wealth and emancipation: disposable time and need satisfaction. In short, instrumental rationality becomes posited as the true rationality adequate to human potential in a society at last oriented to production for use. In this sense Marx was not able to transcend the fetishistic logic of capitalism, its productivism, its rationality. For the vision of a future whose sole explicit principle of justice is "to each according to his needs" is based on the image of a society that can dispense with the trappings of law, a society that is the overcoming (*Aufhebung*) of civil society with its bourgeois institutions, a society in which the unity of public and private and the transparency of social relations allow one to dispense with the burden of politics altogether. The principle of "each according to his needs" is an answer only to the question of distributive justice,[85] and a bad one at that. For the theory of needs that posits individual need as the criterion of justice according to which each is the best judge of his own needs presupposes either that individual needs are mutually compatible and good or that they too require an external criterion for the evaluation and hierarchization of needs. If such a principle restores integrity to the individual (in the former case) and precludes the logic of substitution of the particular needs of the individual by the interests of the class, it does so at the price of creating a mythology of abundance in an Eden of harmony. In the latter case, the necessity of an external principle for the hierarchization of needs deprives the concept of need of its advantage over the concept of interest, for once again another agency will legislate the true, just, or good needs for individuals themselves. Unfortunately, the absurdity of the first interpretation easily leads to the authoritarian alternative of the second.

In short, Marx's effort to think a utopia where questions of political interaction, norms, and values resolve into those of distributive justice, itself reduced to the automatic fetishistic principle of needs, suppresses the normative moment of needs and the political question of which needs, which capacities, which qualities, which attributes should be fostered. It suppresses the deeply political question of what is a good society. This problem has been recognized by thinkers as diverse as Castoriadis and Habermas.[86] For Castoriadis, the essentialistic value theory that posits abstract labor as the universal transhistorical essence of man and the theory of historical materialism—that is, a dogmatic philosophy of history unable to thematize the difference between the social and the natural and therefore positing natural laws of history— are the two assumptions that lead Marx to suppress the political in his consideration of the two steps of the communist future.[87] But I would argue that it is not necessary to reconstruct such an obviously problematic version of Marx, nor is it advisable. For it opens the way for Marxists to "save" Marx by reconstructing the praxis philosophical or critical elements of his thought without historical materialism. Although my conclusions concerning the utopia of needs are similar to those of Castoriadis—namely, that Marx's theory founders on its own fetishistic attempt to suppress political questions—I interpret the causes somewhat differently. They are rooted not in an essentialist metaphysics or a rationalistic philosophy of history (rather, both could be abandoned without resolving the problem) but in the nature of the critique and in the class analysis of modern society. For, as I have tried to show, even without the theory of historical materialism, even without an essentialistic value theory, the reconstruction of Marx at his best cannot avoid the difficulties mentioned. Internal to the critique of political economy itself is a never-resolved antinomy: that between the recognition that needs, individuals, institutions, representations, societal logics and so on are historically specific to particular social formations and the attempt to ground the future immanently in the "objective possibilities," immanent contradictions, and internal dynamics of the present. Though it is not objectionable for a social theory to attempt to locate objective possibilities for the transformation of the structure of labor in possibilities of automation, for example, it *is* problematic to seek to ground radical needs and revolutionary subjectivity in the same systemic analysis. Such a grounding invariably reduces the creative, historical, political dimension to the logic of the systemic categories.

It should be obvious, though, that the class theory is deeply implicated in this problematic. Insofar as the concept of the proletariat is concerned, the mythical character of its role as the universal class is evident. It is not just the proletarian myth that is at issue here, however, but the claims of any Marxian-type class theory. For the class theory is what leads Marx to assume that relations of domination are simply class relations, that politics are always politics of class domination (i.e., the representation of interests generated elsewhere than in the political realm), that social interaction and social movements can be explained in terms of production relations, that the abolition of classes means the end of domination. Even if this is not accomplished by a class subject, it is the basis upon which the need for politics itself can appear unnecessary once classes are abolished. The problem lies not simply in Marx's various models of communism but in the very heart of the class analysis of capitalism and in the mode of theorizing to be found there. For the projection of a technocratic utopia onto the future, in which the administration of things replaces politics (the administration of men), derives from the systematic exclusion of "the political" in Marx's analysis of the present. In short, it derives from the one-dimensional concept of political power as the power of particular groups (classes) in the guise of universality. The technocratic utopia of a society organized along the automatic principle of need satisfaction and rational distribution of labor suppresses the political decisions and normative dimensions of needs and interaction in a manner similar to Marx's reduction of civil to bourgeois society, of politics and ideology to the expression or reflection of economic relations, and in the location of the dynamic of this society in the class relations of its mode of production.

The contradictions flowing from the attempt to integrate social classes into production categories, as their personifications, are clear: From the immanent dialectic of class confrontation only interest conflicts can be derived, not radical needs. Moreover, the attempt to ground radical needs in the structure of labor neither avoids the fundamental difficulties of the imputation of motives of social action from the system logic of a mode of production nor escapes the fetishistic reduction of motives to socioeconomic imperatives. For the *Grundrisse* and *Capital* are in accord in taking the systematic tendencies of reification as accomplished fact insofar as social action is concerned. The never-abandoned idea that capitalist rationalization actually eliminates the magical, religious, juridicial, normative, political "mystifications" guiding social action and integrating individuals into society reveals the basic weakness of the class theory. Based on the one-sided image of a capitalist economy reproducing itself out of itself, the concept of class presupposes that rational interests or needs (in this case they are interchangeable) prevail over normative, cultural, social, symbolic, political elements in the determination of social action. But such a bias is unavoidable as soon as one has reduced cultural, political, and "ideal" aspects of society to the ideological epiphenomena of production relations. Herein lies the real productivism of Marx, and the reason why the critical sociology of class turns into a fetishism of class relations. For once the determinants of social classes are posited as production relations, the defetishization of economic categories through the concept of class can yield only reified economic needs or interests that do not point beyond the logic that is being challenged.

The tensions and antinomies in Marx's work can be systematically related to the exaggerated claims of a defetishizing critique and an overburdened, "dialectical" class theory. The hidden assumption that allowed Marx to think he had at last united philosophy, science, and critique is of course the idea that theoretical abstractions are "real abstractions," that the leveling economic representative logic of political economy actually rationalizes, homogenizes, and demystifies heterogeneous reality, calling for a critique that defetishizes the final source of mystification, the economy. Given the presumed reality of this system logic or the logic of a system of representations, asserted to be ideological but with real counterparts, Marx could think that in the concept of class as the personification of real economic categories he had discovered the sober truth of bourgeois society and the dynamic of its abolition. He could presume to have united in a single grand effort a systemic theory of capitalist reproduction, a defetishizing critique of political economic categories (an antisystem), and a theory of revolution, all of which come together around the concept of class and the project of a defetishizing critique of the ideology representing society's real abstractions—political economy. He could, in short, presume to ground a radically different future in the logic of the present, mistaken as the movement of reality rather than the logic of a system of representations. Hence the tension between the political project of the creation, through revolutionary praxis, of a new emancipated society and the scientific project of grounding this possibility not in philosophy or in the evolutionary laws of history but in the objective developmental tendencies of the socioeconomic reality of capitalism.

This leaves us facing the most serious problem of Marx's work—that of the very project of the critique of political economy. It should be clear by now that political economy appeared to Marx as the ideology par excellence to be criticized with respect to modern society because he assumed modern *society* to be capitalist, in the sense of being fully determined by the capitalist *mode of production,* and because he assumed that the categories of political economy were real abstractions whose critique could yield or represent the hidden class relations of domination and revolt underlying the system. But when critique postulates the logic of its object, as an allegedly reified system of representations, as real, and then universalizes this logic into that of society as a whole, the project of defetishization must fail. For the risk of any such critique oriented toward reproducing and defetishizing a systemic logic, but on its own grounds, is that of perfecting rather than transcending the logic it seeks to immanently unfold. In accepting the political economic postulate of a self-regulating, self-reproducing economy rather than challenging this assumption as a myth,[88] Marx simply reproduced the political economic reduction of political, cultural, normative, religious determinations as irrelevant or determined by the economy. The revelation of the internal contradictions and even class relations on this basis could not defetishize the economic categories because the myth of a self-reproducing economic system was not only challenged but extended, beyond the claims of political economy, to the ultimate determinant of political relations themselves. Through the class theory of domination, Marx totalized all of society from the standpoint of one sphere, the economy or the mode of production. He assumed that the capitalist mode of production reproduces itself, its social actors, and their necessary motivations out of its own economic logic. Accordingly, he could have only an instrumental concept of politics as a tool of class domination, just as the only forms of socialization of the class individuals he was concerned with were those of the market and production relations. The critique of political economy could only uncover the tensions of the sphere to which political economy addressed itself—it could point to economic crisis tendencies, class relations of domination and contestation, but no more. But the desire to immanently ground in a system logic revolutionary potentials of social action without interrogating the normative, political, and cultural modes of integration of individuals into their society, in addition to the logic of the economy, necessarily culminated in a fetishistic class theory and a technocratic utopia for the future. In short, to consider classes as personifications of production relations meant the reduction of the individual to economic determinations, and the panlogistic collapse of social interaction (between classes) to the logic of contradiction of economic categories.

Marx's early attempt to distinguish between modern and premodern forms of stratification through the differentiation between religiously and politically constituted orders and socioeconomic classes lacking direct legal representation remains invaluable. So too does the attempt to unfold and criticize the logic of the economic ideology of his time, political economy, through the analysis of the fundamental capitalist production relation—the wage labor/capital relationship. And finally, the attempt to demonstrate the nonaccidental character of the emergence of social classes and structures of domination in formally democratic societies is of the greatest importance. The problem lay in the integration of these three attempts, together with a theory of development and revolutionary transformation, in one single totalizing logic, the logic of a "mode of production." For such a totalistic theory dangerously excludes the possibility (which we of the twentieth century ought to know well) that there might be other modes of domination than socioeconomic class relations, other principles of stratification in addition to class (nationality, race, status, sex, etc.), other modes of historical creation and interaction than labor and revolutionary praxis, other sources for the motivations guiding social action, other forms of political interaction (participation) than hierarchical power relations, and other modes of contesting capitalist society than class struggles around radical needs emerging in the dialectic of labor.

Conclusion: Toward a Critical Stratification Theory

This study concludes by calling for a new beginning, for the development of a critical stratification theory freed from the dogmatic assumptions shackling Marxian class theory. It is not, however, an argument for dismissing Marxism. The underlying assumption of my work is that a new critical sociology of stratification can proceed fruitfully only if it is informed by the Marxian project, its insights, and its limits. Precisely because the Marxian class theory was so ambitious—too ambitious—a thoroughgoing analysis of it provides important clues as to what must be avoided and what must be confronted by new attempts at class analysis.

Marx's insights into the forms of power, dynamics, and social struggles of modern society hinged upon assumptions regarding the relation between stratum and structure, social contestation and social change, system contradictions and social action. Yet the Marxian method of relating these elements has proven inadequate. I have argued that attempts to construct a global class theory of contemporary capitalism along the lines of the Marxian model must fail. The Marxian synthesis of systemic crisis theory with a theory of social action (class struggle) in the framework of one critique took for granted the existence of a single, underlying total system—the capitalist mode of production—whose logic penetrated and structured all spheres of life. Correspondingly, all elements of civil society and the state could be understood as bourgeois institutions subordinated to the logic of the capitalist organizational principle. This view led Marx to privilege political economy as the object of critique and to identify socioeconomic class relations as the key to the structure of domination and forms of resistance in modern society. Marx assumed that the analysis of the steering mechanism and stratification principle of modern society reveals the basis for the construction of social identity of collective actors involved in radical social movements. He implied that an alternative to this thoroughly capitalist system must entail a complete break with "bourgeois" culture and institutions. The normative contents of social life that Marx wanted to defend, but which his theory could no longer locate immanently in civil society, were thus carried by a metasocial, teleological philosophy of history.

It would be extremely irresponsible today to perpetuate this image of modern society and its alternative. Neither the structure of the social system nor the social movements in Western capitalist societies conform to this overly simplified model. Moreover, all metasocial guarantees of norms and values have lost their cogency. The work of systems theorists has shown that the modern social system is differentiated into a set of subsystems of which the economy is only one, not necessarily determinant, element,[1] whereas theorists of collective behavior have stressed the complexity of motives, interpretations of need, norms and world views that inform social action.[2] To be sure, none of these analyses comprises a critical theory of society, but anyone interested in such a theory would have to take the fruits of contemporary social science at least as seriously as did Marx in his own time (political economy). A "post-Marxist" approach to stratification should be able to *identify* the structural contradictions, crisis tendencies, and mechanisms of stratification within contemporary social systems; to *assess* the potentials for and of social movements without presupposing the primacy of either the economy or socioeconomic class struggles. It must also be able to *justify* the principles guiding the partisanship for a given social and political project against others.

There have been genuine advances in this direction. Claus Offe, Jürgen Habermas, and Alain Touraine have attempted to provide the elements of a critical theory adequate to contemporary society by appropriating the advances made in social analysis while avoiding fatalism, dogmatism, or apology.[3] What is most striking about all of these theorists is that they have recognized the difficulties inherent in attempts to bind together the standpoints of system and action within a unified theoretical framework. Instead, a kind of tacit division of labor seems to have taken shape among (1) efforts to develop a noneconomistic crisis theory able to articulate the logic of the complex interrelation of the subsystems and mechanisms of stratification in advanced capitalism; (2) efforts to provide an adequate substitute for metasocial guarantees of standards; and (3) a theory of social movements that transcends the limits of socioeconomic class analysis. The first approach thematizes the logic and limits of reform strategies in the framework of a political crisis theory and, in its Habermasian version, articulates the procedural rules (communicative ethic) for the justification of validity claims of norms. But these approaches are unable to translate their results into terms that could address social contestation. The third approach excels in identifying the cultural stakes and creative role of social movements in identity construction and reinterpretation of social norms but cannot connect these movements to the map of stratification or to the specific institutional constraints of the social system in which they occur. What remains unclear, then, is how these approaches might inform one another. I would like to discuss the strengths and limits of these theoretical strategies in order to point to the tasks ahead for critical stratification theory.

Attempts to develop a new political crisis theory are based on the realization that the Marxian theory is unable to yield an adequate account of the structures of power or the mechanisms of stratification in late capitalist societies. The key change that prevents the identification of forms of stratification by simply looking at production units and market situations is the new relation between state and society in contemporary capitalism. The increasing autonomy of the administrative subsystem (the state) engaging in pervasive regulation of social and economic processes implies that an analysis that focuses on empirical power relations between societal interest groups (classes) as a prepolitical phenomenon constituting the material base of the political "superstructure" will be unsatisfactory.[4] What is now required is an approach that analyzes the politically mediated nature of society and the implications of the new relation between economic and administrative/political subsystems for social stratification.

Claus Offe's critical appropriation of systems theory is, I believe, the best example of such an approach. His work is geared toward identifying the structural dimensions of stratification and power distribution and the systemic contradictions and crisis potentials of late capitalism. The obvious parallel between Offe's critique of systems theory and Marx's critique of political economy (which could perhaps be seen as the systems theory of the nineteenth century) should not, however, be overdrawn. Whereas Marx focused primarily on the crisis tendencies in the economic system, treating everything else as its environment, his defetishizing critique of political economy purported to identify the action potential of social classes. Offe's critique of systems theory is both more complex and less ambitious. His model of the social system includes not one but three elements: the economic, the political/administrative, and the normative/legitimating subsystems.[5] His analysis of the *crisis potentials* inherent in the interrelation among these subsystems refrains, however, from deducing the *conflict potential* or social identities of social actors. The reasons for this modesty are compelling. Under the conditions of late capitalism, the growth of the administrative/political subsystem and its penetration of the economy implies the noncorrespondence of the contradiction between wage labor and capital and the constitution of social classes. In short, one cannot deduce all of the social strata or the conflict potential of groups from the contradiction within the capitalist economy, because this subsystem is no longer isolated from political/administrative mediation.[6] The penetration of the economic subsystem by the state complicates the lines of inequality by making them multidimensional. Accordingly, it is necessary to identify the *political mechanisms* of stratification to grasp the new structural dimensions of the distribution of power and privilege. The specific logic of the "political selectivity" of interests by the state becomes the focus of analysis.[7]

The crucial step beyond orthodox Marxism is the thematization of the political/administrative system as a *source* of stratification and power rather than as a mere reflection of socioeconomic inequalities. In other words, the specific organizational structures and institutional articulation of the state involve a systematic logic that selects, creates, and rewards certain kinds of interests and excludes others.[8] The state is viewed as a network of steering mechanisms whose role in securing the continuance of the organizational principle of the capitalist economy,[9] by compensating for the dysfunctional by-products of capitalist reproduction, has vastly increased. But, precisely for that reason, it cannot be analyzed through the categories of the critique of political economy. Instead, the political/administrative institutions that prevent the universal participation in consensus formation and prestructure the opportunities for specific strata to utilize the state's services or benefit from its regulatory acts need to be analyzed directly. This in part accounts for the compatibility of formal democracy and capitalism, since the nineteenth century.

Accordingly, Offe provides a convincing structural analysis of the way in which the institutions of the political system (parliaments, parties, unions involved in collective bargaining) act as "filter systems" that select or bar certain types of interests, needs, or motives from political articulation. Excluded from articulation are those needs or interests that are not fully organizable, demands that are general in nature, demands lacking functional significance for the economic or political system, and claims that are not associated with a particular status group or are made by groups that are not capable of conflict.[10] In addition, the administrative system of the interventionist state is analyzed in terms of "positive" contributions to the structuration of interests.[11] Through its role in politically distributing income for key groups of workers (state participation in collective bargaining) and in granting subsidies to business, through general political regulation of the level of disposable individual income, and through the expansion of political factors (at the expense of the market) in providing for the availability of key facilities for the satisfaction of vital needs (education, housing, health, transport), the interventionist state sets up a new logic of social inequality.[12] Offe argues, in short, that the "vertical" system of class inequality (capitalist class relations) has been overlain and complicated with a "horizontal" political system of stratification that creates disparities between "vital areas." Along this axis, social inequality and stratification of interest groups relate directly to the varying share of political demands filtered down from institutional sectors to any given functional group—the greater share directed to those groups that are functionally indispensable and/or capable of constituting a "risk" to the continuance of the system.[13] Structural curbs are placed on vital areas, social groups, and categories of needs deemed incapable of generating dangers to the system as a whole. The latter are not articulated within the political system and are denied access to its services.

To be sure, vertical inequality remains, reinforced by preferential selection and satisfaction of interests compatible with the capitalist organizational principle. Class differences along the horizontal axis continue to dictate the differential life chances of individuals to compensate for inadequate levels of state services and responsiveness. But politically determined disparity between sectors, functions, and interests granted state attention and the "modern pauperism" of depressed areas follows a different logic. The lines of interest organization and potential conflict emerge on the terrain of the state itself.[14] This means that the proliferation of interest groups no longer directly follows the path articulated by the old class criteria (relation to the means of production). The analysis of political selectivity reveals mechanisms of stratification that underly the constitution of relevant interests within the "political marketplace." The important point is that these interests do not simply "enter" the political system from elsewhere (the economy) but are in part constituted by that system itself.[15] This implies a three-tiered stratification system: (1) classes or interests developed along the horizontal axis through market/production relations; (2) proliferation of interest groups across class lines generated in part by the administrative system; and (3) marginal areas, social groups, and needs constituted as such by the selective processes of state intervention but without the possibility of being articulated vis-à-vis the political/administrative system.

The reconstruction of a crisis theory in the form of a critique (determination of the limits) of the regulatory capacities and "reform" strategies of the interventionist state serves two related purposes. First, it allows one to articulate the *logic* of contradiction underlying the seemingly haphazard proliferation of conflicting interest groups. Second, it thematizes the constraints upon state strategies of "crisis management" deriving from the imperative of absorbing and neutralizing the dysfunctional effects of capitalist reproduction. Systemic crisis theory, however, must renounce any claim to assess the chances or goals of social contestation that does not take place within the overall framework of interest articulation and political reform. Such an approach can articulate the logic of interest conflicts that occur on the terrain of contradictory system imperatives. But this is a far cry from the pretensions of a Marxian-type class theory. The critique of crisis management strategies can certainly indicate the structural inequalities that are created by the shifting but systematic marginalization of specific areas, groups, or types of demands. Nevertheless, it cannot thematize the conflict potential of self-constituted groups that emerge, as it were, outside the interstices of the system. The critical systems theorist is limited by his object domain to identifying the trajectory only of those "events" (interest conflicts) that the logic of crisis management (reform) itself occasions or articulates.[16]

Accordingly the analysis of the "permanent crisis of crisis management" does not involve either a breakdown theory or a theory of revolution. It is, instead, a theory of the limits of structural reform. The basic assumptions are the following: Crises are developmental tendencies that threaten the identity of the subsystem that provides the organizing principle of the society as a whole by increasing the importance of subsystems that generate events occurring outside its framework. Structural contradictions are located between rather than solely within subsystems. It is Offe's thesis that the regulatory problems resulting from the inadequacy of exchange mechanisms (capitalist organizational principle) in securing system integration in advanced capitalism require increasing autonomy of the administrative and normative subsystems to compensate for dysfunctional effects of capitalist socialization processes.[17] Late capitalism is characterized by the move from "positive" to "negative" subordination of flanking noncapitalist subsystems.[18] This means that structural elements are produced in response to inadequacies within the dominant economic subsystem, which can be irrelevant, antithetical, or even dysfunctional to the maintenance of capitalist relations. These system-foreign, external regulatory mechanisms must be kept from becoming fully autonomous. The crisis theory accounts for the limited effectiveness of regulatory strategies by tracing out the contradictory logic imposed on the political/administrative subsystem by the imperative of preserving a capitalist economy. Each subsystem imposes conflicting demands and constraints on the other: The administrative system cannot determine its strategies through technocratic planning because it must yield to private investment decisions; the political system cannot operate through a genuine democratic consensus of the citizenry for it must shield administrative decisions that select particular interests over others from public scrutiny; the economic system must contend with a type of development that behaves defensively toward the use of its own results in the social structure.[19]

Thus the self-obstructing character of state regulation (what I will call "structural reform") geared toward maintaining the capitalist system through "noncapitalist means" provides the basis of a political crisis theory. In short, political crisis refers to the inability of the state to compensate dysfunctional social consequences of private production through fiscal, administrative, or "consensus-generating" resources without (a) infringing on the capital relation or (b) transferring contradictions into the administrative system itself and (c) undermining the legitimation necessary for the functional capacity of the state. Once the state assumes partial responsibility for steering the economy, the unavoidable proliferation of interest groups making demands for preferential treatment strains the economic resources at its disposal (fiscal crisis).[20] The administrative planning of the economy comes up against the barrier of private control of information and investment decisions. The nonidentity of the symbolic and instrumental functions of the state and the growth of both with the increase of administrative tasks carry the danger of a collision course between the necessity of broadening consensus to legitimate visible steering functions that arbitrarily select certain interests over others and of keeping the contours of capitalist production stable. The new forms of state intervention increase the importance of loyalty-binding functions that it itself undermines by increasing the likelihood of a reflection on norms vis-à-vis its preferential strategies (potential legitimation deficit). The fiscal crisis of the state and the decreasing ability of the mass party or trade unions to provide social identities and integrate mass participation are signs of the crisis of crisis management.

The theory of the crisis of crisis management is at its best in articulating the range and limits of potential strategies to resolve these steering problems by the "reform of reform." They include strategies for reprivatization or corporate backlash in economic policy decisions (neoliberalism); attempts to revise the liberal democratic constitutional norms and rules of the political system (institutional redefinition, regression, and reduction of "rights"); strategies of administrative decentralization oriented toward displacing demands on the central state to regional or local government; and neocorporatist strategies to shape and channel the system of interest representation and conflict resolution that bypass parliaments and formal law by politically institutionalizing select interest groups to share responsibility for decisions and failures.[21] It is clear that the constant shifts among these alternatives come up against a common barrier; within the framework of liberal-democratic forms of political organization each strategy carries the risk of exacerbating a legitimation deficit. This could be avoided only by a wholesale abandonment of formal democracy or of the capitalist economy—namely, radical change. But that is precisely what reform strategies were introduced to avoid—hence the constant instability and ineffectiveness of crisis management.

The specific weakness of this approach is the inability to elaborate upon the significance of a legitimation deficit for potential or actual social actors. Little can be said within the framework of a crisis theory that analyzes the political/normative subsystem from a functionalist standpoint regarding the validity of its norms and values or the potential impact on social actors of an obvious violation of universal legitimating principles by political steering mechanisms. Even *critical* system theory screens out consideration of the role of counterfactual validity claims.[22] In this context, a legitimation deficit means only the lack of sufficient mass loyalty for the political/administrative system.

This is a question of *behavior* that is either functional or dysfunctional from the point of view of system maintenance. The assessment of *social action* involving the contestation of institutionalized interpretations of norms and values of a system cannot be made. The relation between the universalistic claims of the political system and the conflicting interpretations of these claims by those "within" and those excluded remains unthematized. The critical systems theorist is limited by his object domain to identifying the trajectory *only* of those events (interest conflicts) that the logic of crisis management or structural reform itself articulates. Struggles over the definition and genesis of social norms are relegated to the status of nonevent. Social movements, as opposed to political contestation, appear necessarily as signs of destruction, deinstitutionalization, and regressive forms of identity construction. They can be presupposed or pointed to as unavoidable occurrences but not directly analyzed from the standpoint of the crisis of crisis management. Thus the critique of the selectivity of political/administrative subsystems fails to provide a means to address new need interpretations, norms, motives, claims, or action excluded from articulation within the state itself. Nor can it distinguish between the logic of reform that serve crisis management functions and *institutional* reforms, above all those initiated from below, that articulate "counterpowers" (André Gorz), democratize and/or delimit steering mechanisms, and alter or even challenge the organizational principle of a society by altering both the nature of the social partners and the definition of the rules of the game (norms) in society, economy, and polity.[23] (Institutional reforms change, in short, the legitimate norms regulating social interaction.) Such a distinction could only be provided from the combined standpoints of action theory and an institutional analysis that investigates the source and genesis of institutional change initiated by social movements. From Offe's standpoint, however, all institutionalized reform is, by definition, "structural reform from above," serving however inadequately, crisis management functions. Thus the critical system-theoretical approach is limited to the following: It can account for the steering problems and dysfunctional effects of crisis management strategies; it can articulate the mechanisms generating conflicting interest groups (stratification); and it can point to the logic of the shifting marginalization of excluded social actors viewed as *victims*.

By limiting itself to the standpoint of system rationality, however, this approach inadvertently reinforces the technocratic illusion it seeks to criticize, namely, the possibility of severing structural innovations geared to crisis management from institutional reform and social movements. All of the strategies of reform of reform mentioned above involve changes in institutional arrangements only to the extent that they are oriented toward freeing steering mechanisms from institutional constraints (further disembedding economy and administration from society) and toward suppressing the thematization of institutional arrangements altogether. The institutional order is, in short, posited as an environment to be controlled. Offe's inadequate distinction between the political and the administrative subsystems (the former embeds the latter in societal norms) accounts, in part, for the screening out of the second type of reform. From this standpoint, "progressive" institutional reform that would further embed steering mechanisms in a normative order (open to reinterpretation and critique) and expand (universalize) and democratize the procedures and actors involved cannot be posed.

The limitations of this approach can be summed up in a few words: methodological unwillingness to take into account the claims of action theory unless the norms motivating action and the collective actors that carry them can be fully integrated into a system-theoretical framework. The alternative theoretical strategies of Habermas and Touraine take up these two dimensions, the normative/consensual and the conflictual aspects of action, separately. But while each of them succeeds in filling some of the gaps left by a critical functionalist model, they do so at the price of new aporias. As a result, each of their solutions can be criticized from the point of view of the other. Let me address each in turn.

Habermas attempts to correct the bias of the systems-theoretical approach by reformulating the concept of crisis to include the relevance of social action and by returning the dimension of a normative concept of rationality to the critique of contemporary society. He argues that one can speak of crisis only when members of a society experience structural alterations (reform) as critical for continued existence and feel their *social identity* threatened. An adequate concept of crisis must thus grasp the connection between "system integration," or the specific steering mechanisms of a society, and "social integration," or the legitimating normative structures and principles in terms of which needs are interpreted and motivations generated within the symbolically structured life world. In other words, the theorist must be able to relate crises in social identity to steering problems in such a way that the distinct logics of social action and system functioning are not blurred. Habermas's critique of functional reason thematizes the independent and, in his view, more comprehensive logic of communicative interaction and moral development—that is, the socialization of individuals through the medium of values and norms in need of justification upon which the functional imperatives of system integration depend.[24] The assumption that norms still direct social action and that the administrative system, despite its efforts to shield itself from democratic claims, still rests on normative structures (provided by the sociocultural system) for social integration is essential to the revised theory of legitimation crisis.[25] Underlying this theory is the presupposition that the administrative generation of meaning is impossible. Thus the increasing penetration of steering mechanisms (administrative and market) into aspects of social life formerly organized through communicative interactive processes and the functionalization of realms of action other than material reproduction processes (culture, reproduction, education) carry the danger of disturbing and drying up the sources of the creation of meaning.[26]

This new crisis concept requires a new definition of the social system, however. Habermas thus revises the concept of "organizational principle" to combine on a more abstract level references to steering mechanisms (functioning) and social identity (action-orienting norms). The organizational principle of a society identifies (a) the institutional boundaries for the possible expansion of steering capacity and (b) the range of variation for the interpretative systems and learning potential involved in moral development that secure social identity.[27] On the basis of this concept, a crisis exists if steering problems involve threats to social integration or the impairment of consensual foundations of normative structures. The "crisis of crisis management," then, is only a necessary and not a sufficient condition for a crisis of the whole system, or even a full-scale crisis of the political subsystem.

Habermas accepts Offe's thesis that a "rationality deficit" of the administrative system lies in its inability to steer between contradictory imperatives (the need to depoliticize its interventionist policies and to avoid critical reflection on the part of society on proposed goals). He also accepts the argument that state intervention renders the original Marxian class theory inappropriate. But the failure of the state to satisfy the interests of competing groups does not of itself result in a challenge to social identity or legitimacy. Nor does it directly trigger confrontation between clearly defined social antagonists. A political crisis theory would have to show that the expansion of administrative steering processes threatens the very processes through which meaning, values, norms and motivations are generated. In short, the mechanisms that generate mass loyalty and establish the requisite structures ensuring social identity and the motivational syndromes required by the state and economy (civil and familial privatism) would have to be disturbed.

Like Offe, Habermas argues that whereas state intervention improves the management of economic crises it increases the likelihood not only of a rationality but also of a legitimation deficit. Assuming responsibility for crisis management renders the state vulnerable to the programmatic demand it has placed on itself. The administrative handling of steering problems formerly left to the market simultaneously suspends the ideological support of equivalence exchange and places in question the structure of the depoliticized public realm. With every penetration by the state into sociocultural life, the administrative system risks thematizing new issues formerly withheld from public reflection—educational curricula, city planning, environmental policy, social services, energy problems, growth *policies*, etcetera. The partial recoupling of the economic system to the political and the penetration by the political system into cultural areas disturb the reservoir of automatically accepted traditions necessary for legitimation. Administrative steering itself, irrespective of its success or failure in satisfying interests and crisis management, produces unsettling effects and could trigger public controversy. But these legitimation deficits would lead to crisis and reactivate the public realm only if accompanied by a motivation deficit—that is, a gap between the motivations required by the state and the economy and those provided by the sociocultural system.

The main proposition regarding the likelihood of a motivation deficit is that "bourgeois" culture was never able to reproduce itself from itself and legitimate capitalist society but, rather, was always dependent on remnants from previous cultural traditions.[28] Accordingly, Habermas tries to show that the key motivational syndromes of "civil and familial privatism" (political abstinence and orientation to career, leisure, consumption) crucial to the legitimation of steering processes in advanced capitalism are breaking down.[29] This is due in part to the erosion of the organic context in which these traditional attitudes were produced and the impossibility of administratively regenerating them, the undermining of cultural traditions and specifically bourgeois ideologies, and the inability of bourgeois culture to rely on its own secular motivations or to provide functional equivalents for spent traditions.[30] State interventionism not only in the economy but in sociocultural life is simultaneously a threat to the separation of administrative decision making from the motives of citizens *and* a contributing factor to the decline of traditions and ideologies essential to the legitimation of administrative choice.

On the other hand, it is presupposed that the level of moral development involved in bourgeois culture continues to be relevant and could be undone only through a violent process of enforced regression.[31] Although market ideology and formal democracy no longer serve as a firm foundation for legitimacy in late capitalism, the memory of collectively attained universalistic value systems (implying the common communicative substratum of postauratic art, scientism, and postconventional morality) cannot be simply erased.[32] The legitimation of authority entails practical truth claims regarding the correctness of the norms and values in whose name it is exercised. In formally democratic states, there is an underlying presupposition that the polity is the bearer of public morality and may institutionalize only generalized interests. Once the level of justification or the kind of reason accepted as the basis of legitimacy has become the criterion of generalizability (universality) of interests, then truth claims no longer rest on the specific content of norms but rest on the process of adjudication. The natural or self-evident character of what is a general interest has been destroyed. But the penetration of steering mechanisms into more and more aspects of social life triggers controversy over the very processes of ascertaining the generalizability of norms, interests, and goals[33]— hence the conflict between the normative structures and universal principles inherent in *modern social identity* and the *political-economic system* of late capitalism that privileges and selects some interests over others.

The resultant crisis of motivation could be resolved only by uncoupling the socialization process from the cultural system, or by moving from bourgeois formal law to the institutionalization of procedures adequate to the principles of a universalistic political morality.[34] The former possibility would mean the end of individuality as we know it, for normative structures would no longer be internalized by individuals through their socialization; rather, identity-constituting socialization would be severed from norms and truth claims altogether. Habermas argues that such a possibility cannot be discounted at this point. In order to provide another alternative, however, he tries to reconstruct the evolutionary logic of moral development implicit in the trajectory of alterations within cultural systems. The theory of evolution and the concept of a communicative ethic (discursive redemption of validity claims regarding social norms and need interpretations as a counterfactual principle of universalization) [35] are elaborated to indicate the direction that an emancipatory outcome of a motivation/legitimation crisis must take. But Habermas can argue for a positive outcome to the pending motivation/legitimation crisis only in the most abstract sense—that is, he can show that the developmental logic of world views does not in principle exclude the continuation of a mode of socialization related to norms or the transition to a new stage of (postconventional) politically relevant, moral development.[36] Habermas cannot appeal to the presence of specific norms or values within the contemporary institutional framework of advanced capitalist society that might ground the likelihood of a progressive rather than an authoritarian resolution to the crisis. This is because he has rejected the tactic of immanent critique on the basis of the thesis that both the content and the form of traditional legitimations—prebourgeois and bourgeois—are now in crisis. The self-evidence of universalistic values can no longer be assumed because the extrasocial guarantees in which they had been grounded (natural law, the concept of man or of the subject, the philosophy of history) have broken down.

As Habermas has demonstrated in his earlier work on the public sphere,[37] the principles of individual autonomy, personhood, democracy, freedom, enlightened and critical public opinion, were rooted in social institutions that gave these norms a certain *veritas in re*. The structures of the intimate sphere, civil society, the public realm, the state, and their interrelation were the original loci for the fundamental rights embedded in formally democratic constitutions, as well as the source of legitimacy underlying the state. Habermas has more recently come to believe, however, that these institutions have been so transformed through state intervention and rationalization as to render the previously mentioned norms increasingly abstract and remote. Like Offe, Habermas assumes that the public realm and political as well as legal ideologies have been functionalized and that truth claims have been replaced by cynicism in social science and in ideologies. Bourgeois values have "gone into retirement"—there are no norms or values to which an immanent critique might appeal with the expectation of agreement. The political system too suffers from a radicalized war of gods. This leaves Habermas with the paradoxical conclusion that the level of moral development that he works out has, today, tendentially, no institutional embodiments on the macrosocial level.

Unlike Offe, however, Haberman is unwilling to screen out the practical dimension of social theory or action. In order to assert the possibility of a progressive outcome to crisis tendencies in late capitalism, the only alternative that Habermas seems to have left is to turn to the microsocial or social psychological level. In other words, he seeks to demonstrate the presence of the fundamental convictions of communicative ethics within typical socialization processes. The tactic of reconstructing the evolutionary logic or rationalization of communicative interaction in terms of the discursive rationality entailed in the form of argumentation procedures adjudicating validity claims (of truth, rightness, justice) presupposes that the ideal of a new stage of postconventional individual and collective identity not only *should* but, to a certain extent, *already has* emerged.[38] If this could be demonstrated, then the "communicative ethic" would not be just another "extrasocial" guarantee playing the same role as the philosophy of history in previous Marxian critical theory. To the extent that this principle *informs* social action, it could serve as a counterfactual standard for the critique of institutions inhibiting democratic participation in will formation and for the process of adjudicating new need interpretations and constructions of social identity articulated by social movements.

Habermas believes that one can find evidence of the motive-forming power of communicative ethics in certain sections of the student, youth, feminist, and countercultural movements of the last twenty years.[39] He points to changes in the socialization processes in the educational system and the family and to the complexity of the role system in advanced capitalism as factors that increase the likelihood of a postconventional outcome to adolescent development. To the extent to which the movements based on this new paradigm of socialization acknowledge the universalist foundations of morality and legality and seek to generate democratic participatory procedures for the articulation and generalization of interests and norms, they are viewed as "offensive" and progressive rather than merely reactive.[40] Clearly, what is of interest to Habermas is the logic of justification of the interpretation of values and norms within these movements and not their substantive content or source. Not the motivations but the logic of motives is addressed by this theory. In short, the relevant progressive social movements are significant as *carriers* of (universalistic) cultural potentials and moral evolution that are developed on the more abstract level of cultural rationalization. Habermas is not interested in the specific institutional innovations of social movements, be they new forms of democratic association, or new forms of social interaction and the like. Indeed, it is precisely this *creative* dimension of social movements that is ignored by his theory. Thus, all that could be argued from the standpoint of the social identity of some social actors, is that the authoritarian and particularistic features of political/economic/cultural systems of advanced capitalism have permanently lost their legitimacy, increasing the likelihood of protest and/or withdrawal vis-à-vis these institutions.

Of course, Habermas's point is that the counterfactual structures of discursive rationality represent an evolutionary potential of the species in general. They thereby provide a criterion for assessing the legitimacy of institutions and the claims of social movements that develop in response to crises. I would argue that this is no small gain. It is not the task of this type of theory (or any other) to decide in what precise forms postconventional procedural norms and values should be institutionalized or to provide a model for the most appropriate institutional articulation of an emancipated society. Nor is it true that this version of a crisis theory blocks in advance all possible relationship to its addressees.[41] It is in itself an important step, furthermore, that the incorporation of the standpoint of social action into an overall critical systems-theoretical approach is able to demonstrate the possibility of a progressive—that is, not antimodern—resolution to crises in social identity triggered by the destructive penetration of the life world by overly complex steering mechanisms. And the importance of articulating universalistic criteria for the procedures of resolving conflicts and adjudicating norms cannot be overestimated. *No critical stratification theory can do without such criteria with which to defend partisanship for given social movements (or class struggles) and goals against others.* Moreover, Habermas's theoretical path provides the only alternative to the dangerous myth of a future conflict-free homogeneous society, insofar as it articulates principles regarding procedures of compromise between the interest conflicts bound to emerge in any complex society.

Nevertheless, the limits of this theoretical strategy are clear. Despite the reformulation of the concept of crisis, the analysis of legitimation problems does not address the processes through which given institutionalized norm interpretations are challenged and new interpretations articulated. It can only point to structural changes that disempower old norms and forms of legitimation. Unconcerned with the content of norms, the reconstruction of the logic of moral/cultural development cannot enter into or explain the *dynamics* of social movements in and through which the battles over interpretations of old norms and the creation of new norms and cultural models are fought out. Nor can the crisis theory clarify the relation between structures of domination or stratification and emergent social movements raising concrete issues, involving particular groups, and contesting specific institutional structures of heteronomy. Habermas's theoretical strategy can explain the likelihood of crises in social identity and assess the abstract cultural possibilities available for alternative identity constitution. But despite the attempt to introduce an action framework into crisis theory; despite the importance of providing a standard with which to assess the *character* of social movements, Habermas's framework does not include a place for social movements—they play no constitutive role regarding legitimation, the functioning of the public sphere, or the creation of norms. Moreover, it predisposes him to assess nonpolitical movements that are not clearly carriers of cultural/moral evolution (those that do not address the state, do not take shape as political parties or claim civil rights) as at best defensive, at worse regressive reactions to crises. The argument that legitimation deficits would lead to crises if accompanied by motivation deficits implies a standpoint that abstractly opposes social integration (correspondence of norms and motivation) to social disintegration. Given the corollary thesis of disempowered institutionalized norms in late capitalism, social movements are perforce relegated to a residual category of action that is either anomic or merely reactive. In other words, social movements are viewed as crisis phenomena tout court. But only a theory of the creative potential of social movements vis-à-vis the institutionalization of society (new norms) could make sense of the hope that crises (legitimation or other) might reactivate the public realm.

Habermas states that the new social conflicts appear at the "seam between system and life-world." [42] But once modern civil society is analyzed exclusively in terms of steering mechanisms, once the personality system alone is posited as the carrier of universalistic culture, then the macroinstitutional locus of the tension between "norm" and "reality" cannot be thematized.

Both Habermas and Offe have pointed to a potentially very disturbing consequence of crisis management: The displacement of conflicts to the periphery (marginalization) and the possibility that groups in which conflict potentials emerge might not be the bearers of enlightened action. Habermas should indeed criticize contemporary social movements as particularistic and antimodern to the extent that they do not exhibit the elements of postconventional morality and discursive rationality. But he is wrong to therefore dismiss altogether those social movements that incorporate some antimodern characteristics. Historically, such movements have been capable of immense learning experiences, and in any case their normative foundation today is generally based on internal contradictions. Although their specific claims and self-understanding are indeed often antimodern and neoromantic, their forms of organization and their underlying stress on new forms of democratic participation in all policymaking (technological, ecological, military, urban, economic), in fact embody postconventional norms. The movements are therefore capable of becoming the objects of sympathetic immanent critique. Moreover, if universalism is not to remain an empty formula, it must involve solidarity with all particularity, provided that particular groups or movements are willing to tolerate others and are open to dialogue. And, indeed, their existence is a further clue to the continuity of civil society on the level of institutionalized norms that are capable of motivating not just individuals but large groups. By dividing the focus of action theory between the abstract level of cultural development and the microsocial level of individual socialization, Habermas blocks the analysis of those institutions and collective practices that make his norms realizable.

An alternative to this approach is to make collective actors and their forms of struggle the starting point of the analysis of society and to enter thereby directly into interpretation of the nature, projects, and stakes of social movements. By replacing the construct of society as a social system driven by an inner logic with the image of society as a field of social action, Alain Touraine has attempted to analyze the social praxis involved in the *genesis* of norms and the conflicts over their interpretations.[43] Like Offe and Habermas, Touraine is guided by the realization that the relation between *system* and *class* presupposed in Marxism is untenable, but he radicalizes the opposition between the two, arguing that it is impossible to speak at the same time of the contradictions of a system and of *social* action and conflict.[44] Moreover, any attempt to assess the normativity of social action by appealing to a "higher order of facts," be it metaphysics, a philosophy of history, or a theory of evolution, will necessarily lose sight of the social praxis involved in the creation and dynamics of a society. Thus

Touraine chooses a pure action-theoretical approach in order to place social relations and social movements at the center of the analysis of society.

The strengths and weaknesses of this approach are evident in Touraine's reconceptualization of Marxian class theory. The most important service provided by Touraine is the articulation of the distinctiveness of the social dimension of modern civil societies, comprised of and constituted by social struggles vis-à-vis the genesis of action-orienting norms. Two images of society that reify social action in the above sense are thereby rejected: (1) the systemic model of society torn apart by structural contradiction; and (2) the idea that conflicts occur only within cultural values that are directly imposed on the whole of society. By focusing on social movements, Touraine hopes to combat the fatalism of contemporary analyses of society that stress domination, structure, the state, or adaptation. The latter capitulate to the rationality of domination that rejects the very concept of the social creation and independent functioning of society as liberal mythology and replaces the discussion of social interaction with analyses of order and exclusion, power elites and integrated, submissive, or anomic, rebellious but impotent masses. It is precisely the continued importance of the promise of the democratic dream of a self-constituted society that Touraine's theory of social movements hopes to defend. It remains to be seen, however, whether the theoretical strategy he adopts is adequate to this task.

Touraine's avowed purpose is to establish

a Post-Marxist analysis which would finally attribute to class relations and social movements and hence to conflictual action for the social control of a cultural field the central importance that these relations and movements were still unable to attain in Marxist thought and which is denied to them by those who no longer see any other enemy than the state.[45]

Social relations are no longer understood in terms of position in the structure of labor or relation to the means of production.[46] Rather, they are seen as normatively oriented interaction between adversaries within a cultural field open to opposed interpretations. Thus Touraine redefines the concept of class in terms of a general theory of social action,[47] disassociating it from economic mechanisms, structural contradictions, or imputed interests. Indeed, his analysis moves in the opposite direction from those of Offe and Habermas: Far from viewing the expanded role of the state in contemporary society as the sign of the disorganization of socioeconomic classes, he uses the "advantage of hindsight" (the presence of new social movements) to correct the Marxian "error" of defining classes in economic terms in the first place.

Accordingly, classes are defined purely in terms of social action, as the social division and relation between those who identify historicity with their own interests and those who seek to regain control of historicity that has been denied them. Struggles over historicity—the pattern and definition of knowledge, type of investment, and cultural model of a society—constitute the class relations of each system of historical action. "Class struggles" and "social movements" are synonymous expressions for the conscious contestation involved in the "self-production" of society or the work society (sets of social actors) performs on itself by inventing its norms, its institutions, and its practices.[48] The sociology of action situates class struggles at the center of the functioning of society and of the process through which society is *created*.

To be sure, Touraine does not deny the importance of the object domain of critical systems theory—crisis, contradiction, power, reification, and so on. But he wishes to rescue the analysis of the domain of social action from its subordination to historical development by Marxism, to order by functionalism and structuralism, and to power by poststructuralism. To this end, he constructs a strict distinction between the diachronic and synchronic axes of analysis. What Marxian class theory analyzed under the heading of system, contradiction, revolution, development, is now located on the axis of diachrony. For Touraine, the administrative state and political action (structural reform/revolution) related to it are the proper analytical referent of the analysis of order and/or systemic change. In short, the state is presented as the central agent of development from one system of historical action to another *and* as the key institution involved in the maintenance of order.[49] From the standpoint of diachronic analysis, all social categories are situated in relation to the state. It is here that the opposition between ruling elites directing the state and historical change and a dominated "mass" governed by the ruling elite takes shape.[50] Revolutions, as distinct from social movements, address the state and refer to the change from one social system to another.

The functioning of society (self-production of its historicity), the creation and interpretation of action-orienting norms, class relations, and social movements are located on the synchronic axis of analysis. Here the key social antagonism is between a ruling class that identifies itself with historicity and a popular class struggling to institute an opposed interpretation of the cultural model that each side has in common. These struggles do not, however, build up the social system of the *future* as they do in the Marxian model. Rather, they represent alternative ways of interpreting the norms and institutionalizing the cultural model of the *present*. It is important to note that class struggles do not have the state as their direct object. For the state is located on a different axis than the arena of social struggles. The purpose of this distinction is to articulate a mode of social conflict that (a) does not have as its ineluctable goal the seizure of state power, (b) is distinct from strategic or instrumental action,[51] and (c) is not a sign of the malfunctioning of society but rather the expression of its health.

In this respect, Touraine's insight into the difference between *social struggles* and *political action* (triggered by and addressing state policies) is quite helpful. The distinction between the two axes allows him to stress the significance of forms of struggle independent of the crisis management strategies of the political system. Social movements, or class struggles, do not "succeed" (or fail) only to the degree to which they become political movements posing the question of power. As we have seen, from the standpoint of crisis theory, such struggles appear as peripheral to the reproduction of the system. From the standpoint of action theory, they acquire a vastly expanded importance: Social movements are the process through which social groups constitute *themselves* and their social identities and implicitly challenge the hierarchical stratification mechanisms and institutionalized norms of a given social order. Far from being signs of anomie, disintegration, or destructive rebellion or revolution, social movements are seen as the creative source of new norms and new identities. To vindicate this claim, Touraine refuses to focus on the growth of the state and its ability to quash or contain social movements. The proper object of partisan *social* theory is, in his view, to articulate the potential and dynamics of class struggles/social movements that enlarge the autonomous social space of civil society (understood in pure action terms) in which the content of norms and the control over cultural orientations is at issue. Thus, what appears as marginal (or, if threatening to order, cooptable/repressible) from the standpoint of system reproduction moves to the center of the stage for the theorist of social action.

Nevertheless, Touraine concedes a certain two-sidedness to class struggles. "Class relations have both a light and a dark face. The light face reveals the clash between conflicting classes for the control of historicity . . . the dark face is that of the people's defense against the dominant order." [52] But theories that focus on the "negative" struggles of actors vis-à-vis the selectivity and exclusionary mechanisms of a dominant order deemphasize the most important dimension of class struggle: the "positive" affirmation of a project.[53] Although the two analytically distinct axes of diachrony and synchrony tend to converge in what Touraine calls "the double dialectic of social classes," there is never a perfect match between the governing elite and the dominant social class, or between the antiestablishment actions of the masses and popular class struggles. Apparently their interrelation becomes an issue to the sociology of action only in the context of a historical transition between two societal types. One then confronts "historical struggles" in which social movements contesting the control of a new cultural model "mix" with other struggles (revolutions) associated with mechanisms of change, addressing the pattern of development being imposed by the state and a ruling elite.[54] In this case the relation between the state and social classes becomes an issue despite their location on different axes. Nevertheless, for the theorist of social movements, the task in such a context is to distinguish and address the "light face" of positive class struggles that will constitute the key contestations of the new historical society.

There is, of course, another motive underlying the action-theoretical reconceptualization of the concept of class. Touraine wants once and for all to dispense with the class-in-itself/class-for-itself dichotomy that derives from the analysis of objective class interests deduced from structural contradictions. For any such deduction of class interest renders the development of "correct" class consciousness a problem leading to the usual Leninist solution. By placing steering mechanisms and conflicts over patterns of development onto the diachronic axis, Touraine frees class theory from the burden of identifying a revolutionary agent—class struggles/social movements revolve around the functioning, not the abolition, of a society. The gap between imputed and empirical class interests disappears: Any group of actors that contests the historicity of a society engages in class struggles. By making the claims of conflicting social groups the starting point of synchronic analysis, Touraine believes he can avoid the Marxian dilemma altogether.

But the old problem of criteria for identifying the *unity* of *class* struggles underlying the variety of contestations within a society returns. The tension between "system" and "class," order/change and social movements, is not resolved but simply displaced by action theory. It reenters in the very definition of society vis-à-vis a single shared cultural model (why one?) contested by two (why two?) opposing social classes. If one proceeds from the purely immanent analysis of social contestation, as Touraine insists one must, the action theorist is faced with a dilemma. Having screened out any reference to system or structure, practical philosophy or evolution theory, the action theorist is left with no means for identifying the unity of struggles underneath the multiplicity of contestations of a society. Nor does one have any basis for choosing to support one social movement against another. Touraine in particular must offer grounds for the implausible assertion that "the greater the diversity of struggle, the more each society is animated by a single social movement for each social class." [55] He cannot succeed, however, without violating his own methodological postulate of sociological immanence. Corresponding to an analysis that places historicity, institutions, and organizations in a hierarchical order of importance, forms of struggle are classified in terms of the degree to which they approximate contestation over the normativity of a given cultural model, the highest form being a social movement. Yet Touraine's claim that the presence of several social movements would have to imply the co-existence of several societal types within a historical social formation is guilty of the same tautological and dogmatic argumentation that characterizes orthodox versions of the Marxian theory of social formations. [56] Moreover, the two-class model implies a privileged vantage point to the sociologist of action who is somehow able to see the unity of social conflicts that appear quite discrete to the actors themselves. And, indeed, the method of "sociological intervention" advocated by Touraine to "raise" a preselected variety of concrete struggles to the "level" of a social movement and to increase their awareness of the stakes of the struggle is only a barely concealed sociological Leninism. [57] The principle of selection at work here is the researcher's "insight" into the nature of the cultural field shared by the antagonists but obscured by their submersion in their opposing class ideologies. Although the pure sociology of action, unlike systems theory, is capable of accounting for the movement character of social action, it is in fact less able to account for the plurality of social actors than the systems theorist. [58]

Despite the above criticisms, we must not lose sight of the advantages of an action theoretical framework such as Touraine's. What Habermas and Offe analyze under the heading of increased state penetration of civil society, or the colonization of new areas of social life by steering mechanisms, is, to Touraine, only a one-sided interpretation of contemporary society. From his point of view, the proliferation of social contestation over noneconomic and nonpolitical themes such as ecology, housing, health, education, women's roles, and so forth, are signs of an increased reflexivity regarding the social construction of reality and of an expansion of the social space (öffentlichkeit) of disputable norms to include previously reified domains of everyday life. The emphasis on the synchronic dimension of social movements, and on the contestation over normativity, enables the action theorist to grasp the potential importance of new social movements whose social identity is not constructed around steering mechanisms and whose telos is not to take state power or to organize around corporate interests. However, the pure action framework precludes an adequate theoretical articulation of key empirical insights into what is new about the new social movements, namely, the fact that they are not merely crisis behavior, and that they cannot be understood along the lines of the Marxian model of revolution.

This weakness derives in part from the construction of social action from the standpoint of antagonistic social movements with radically opposed institutional models. Excluded is the possibility of consensus and compromise between a plurality of social actors or movements, as well as reflection on the institutional procedural norms and structures crucial for both. But such concerns would take us out of the realm of the movement character of social action to reflection on institutional reform. Although Touraine's political posture, to his credit, calls for both institutional reforms and social movements, his rigid theoretical dichotomy between order and movement, diachrony and synchrony, prevents an adequate analysis of the relation between the two. So, too, does his historical typology.

Touraine's action theory runs into even greater difficulties when it attempts to construct a plausible definition of societal types. Yet it is crucial that a theory that wants to vindicate the primacy of the synchronic analysis of social movements provide criteria for distinguishing between societal types. Indeed, Touraine maintains that a new societal type has emerged, ushering in what he calls "the era of social movements." [59] This claim is backed up by a typology of "modern" societal types—merchant, industrial, postindustrial—that are hierarchically ordered according to the level of reflexivity vis-à-vis historicity exhibited in each. In order to avoid the charge of evolutionism, Touraine insists upon the radical discontinuity between these societies. Yet one look at this typology reveals both an implicit evolutionary bias that is, in his own schema, indefensible and a covert reliance precisely on the results of systems theory for the distinction between societal types.

The explicit criteria employed by Touraine for defining societies are their "cultural model," their type of investment, and the nature of the social movements animating them. Thus "merchant" societies are defined by a cultural orientation of exchange and a mode of investment (supported by the state) that occurs at the level of distribution of both goods and rights.[60] The metasocial guarantees of such societies are political; class struggles involve movements for civil freedom and countermovements for political power and domination. On this basis, Touraine defines struggles for civil liberties and political rights as movements or class struggles only for merchant societies.

Industrial societies represent themselves by the place occupied in an evolution described as progress.[61] Thus the metasocial guarantee of industrial society is the overarching meaning of history viewed not as a product of social relations but as the criterion by which to judge them (specifically vis-à-vis progress in the development of the forces of production). Accordingly, class struggles are situated at the point of material production and revolve around issues of socioeconomic justice. The two contending classes (workers versus boss/organizers) compete for control over the development of the forces of production; both struggle for what they consider to be a just institutionalization of industrial society. In this context, struggles over political and civil rights descend, according to Touraine, to the institutional/organizational level, losing the character of social movements.

A similar demotion of the importance of the workers' movement occurs with the emergence of the third societal type—postindustrial society (or programmed society).[62] Here investment is made at the level of production management rather than work organization, and class domination consists in controlling the management of the production and data-processing apparatus. Thus workers' struggles lose their class character and become either managerial (trade unionist) or political/reformist.[63] What is striking about the cultural model of postindustrial society, is the new representation of society as a system capable of producing and generating its own normative guidelines. This means that there are no longer any metasocial guarantees of social order. Class struggles thus occur over the control of the production of society (historicity) itself. The main struggle in programmed society is between different kinds of apparatuses (technocracy) and users (the public) distributed in all spheres of society. Such struggles are, to Touraine, truly social struggles because they are no longer carried out in the name of political or economic rights and are no longer tied to actors defined by specific attributes.[64] Instead, the main class actors are simply those who control the apparatus and those who resist it in the name of a population's right to choose its own kind of life.

Three objections immediately come to mind regarding this typology. First, as previously stated, despite the rejection of systems analysis and evolution theory, it is obvious that the discussion of cultural models and forms of investment relies on both. For example, the effort to give some content to the concept of "postindustrial society" clearly draws from analyses of new structural elements in the organization of production and in the relation between state and society.[65] But, by relying on system theory covertly, Touraine is forced to do without its major strengths—the analysis of mechanisms of stratification and of constraints upon social action. Similarly, the rejection of both evolution theory and practical philosophy renders the key criterion of his own implicit evolutionism—the (increasing) reflexivity of cultural models and social actors—indefensible. Clearly Touraine employs the concept "postindustrial society", and the technocracy/self-management opposition describing the new social movements, in order to get beyond the obsession with antimodern communal identity of contemporary social actors. But without an adequate standard of universality, he can offer only an illusory transcendence of particularism.

Second, the absence of a serious analysis of the institutional dimension of society entails the loss of precisely those criteria that are crucial for the distinction between social systems. Any possibility of relating the map of social stratification to the social movements of a society are thereby foreclosed. The most glaring example of this deficiency is the argument that each societal type is characterized by a single type of class relations.[66] All industrial societies, according to Touraine, whether the regime is capitalist or socialist, have the same form of class domination and contestation: "From the point of view of class situation, there is no difference between American workers and Soviet workers." [67] Such an assertion is utterly meaningless, however, from the standpoint of the action-theoretical analysis of social class, for the forms of struggle, the definition of actor and adversary, and the normative stakes of contestation are radically different in these two systems.

Third, the breakup of "modernity" into three discontinuous "historical societies" involves an utterly arbitrary and indefensible hierarchization of forms of struggles, types of demands, and concrete social conflicts. It would be easy to show that struggles for political rights, civil rights, and self-management were and are key elements in workers' movements, just as demands for social justice and rights inform many of the new social movements. In short, it would be just as plausible to stress what movements for civil, political, and social rights have in common—namely, the attempt to democratize political, economic, and social life—as to make their differences the sign of unique societal types and to deny the character of social movement to any such struggles. But this would require the resolution of the most striking contradiction pervading Touraine's sociology of action, namely, the insistence on the radical discontinuity of societal types and the (very vague) concept of modernity that seems to apply to all of them.

It should now be clear that action and systems theory suffer from opposite weaknesses. The latter can identify stratification mechanisms and structural crisis tendencies and, in the Habermasian version, provide criteria for distinguishing between emancipatory and regressive alternatives to the present system. The former can thematize the social character of social movements occurring at the heart of society that are, to a certain extent, screened from the latter point of view. The question remains as to whether critical stratification theory must be left with this dichotomy. One obvious alternative is that of synthesis. As Klaus Eder has shown, Touraine's theory of societal types and social movements could easily be reconciled with an evolutionary theory of the Habermasian type without much violence done to either.[68] Touraine himself has made the capacity of human societies to develop (and adapt) through learning processes and to generate their own orientations, normativity, and objectives with increasing reflexivity the "starting point of the sociology of action." [69] On this basis, it is possible to argue that "modernity" is given when cultural orientations have become disputable and to interpret changes in societal types, cultural models, and forms of social contestation as a learning process implying the development of cognitive and moral competences. Accordingly, Eder reinterprets Touraine's societal types as stages in the process of the realization of the constitutive structures and potential of modernity, involving an evolutionary logic of cognitive (increased reflexivity) and moral (increased autonomy) development. Social movements are seen as the central conflicts within a field of possible experiences that institutionalize new cultural and moral competences. They provide the missing active component in the Habermasian theory of evolution—that is, the process through which structures of historical action are changed. On the other hand, the evolution theory resolves the central contradiction of Touraine's approach by supplying the *concept* for the unity of discrete "historical" societies—modernity—as well as the criteria with which to judge whether forms of contestation imply a new, nonregressive social movement.[70]

This synthesis is accomplished at a price, however: Social contestation is granted the status of a social movement only if it moves society to the next evolutionary stage—only if it is a historical movement. The projects and forms of social struggle that do not fit the bill are, ipso facto, devalued as either "not yet" or "distorted forms of" social movements. Thus Eder's analysis loses the synchronic dimension of social movements and, along with it, Touraine's insight into the *creativity* of social movements. Through the imposition of a teleological framework, social movements become once again, the *vehicle* of evolution, that is, what is necessary to move to the next stage of historical development. Moreover, the most objectionable proposition of the Tourainean approach remains unchallenged, namely, the concept of societal type and the claim that each is animated only by one class struggle. Indeed, Habermas's concept of modernity does not seem to mesh too well after all with Touraine's insistence on discontinuity between societal types. From the standpoint of evolution theory this problem is perhaps not very pressing, for what is of interest is only the historical movement that accounts for the leap from one stage to the next. But, for a critical theory of *society* concerned with the synchronic dimension of stratification and struggle, the drawbacks of such a proposition are immense. For Eder's synthesis of Touraine and Habermas builds on a side of each that, for different reasons, diminishes the importance of the *plurality* of forms of contestation from below that aim at the reconstitution of social life and creation of new forms of interaction *within* contemporary society. At the same time the dimension of system logic/reproduction is lost. The multiplicity of existing social movements is devalued to the extent that they do not undertake the task of unification or totalization (Touraine), or fail to represent purely universal claims (Habermas). But the truly universal dimension of these movements, which is to be found on the level of their continuity with the democratic movements running through the fabric of modernity, is itself lost by a stage model that stresses fundamental discontinuity between the epochs of modernity. So too is the *institutional* locus of the *continuity* of modernity, namely, the normative dimension of society in light of which social movements take shape, constitute, and reinterpret the norms structuring social life.

It is indeed striking that all of these theorists place the concept of *civil society* at the center of their analyses of modernity. Yet they all refrain from analyzing the institutionalization of civil society, which constitutes the normative continuity of modernity and is the terrain of social struggles. There are substantive and methodological reasons for the omission of this domain of analysis in each case. For Habermas and Offe, the thesis of the repoliticization of society and economy points to the degeneration of the institutions and symbolic structures of civil society: the bourgeois public realm has been structurally transformed; bourgeois world views have gone cynical. In other words, Habermas argues that institutionalized norms are now without obligatory power due to the overextension of purposive-rational subsystems and the penetration of steering mechanisms into the life world.[71] The institutional order is relevant to his theory only to the extent that it is disempowered. For Touraine, civil society is simply identified as the space or locus of action for social movements; his focus is on the process of contestation over opposed reinterpretations of norms and new institutionalizations, but not on what has been institutionalized. The institutional continuity of modernity has been screened out by his theory of radically discontinuous societal types. Let us not forget, moreover, that Touraine rejects the sociological tradition of institutional analysis leading from Durkheim to Parsons, as comprising a sociology of order that perceives social movements only under the guise of deviance or anomie. Touraine consequently is steered away from the analysis of the specific concrete institutional dimension of modern civil society which he nevertheless presupposes. To be sure, the above-mentioned tradition has emphasized the rule-governed, controlled, prescriptive, consensual basis of institutionalized social action. From this standpoint society would be inconceivable without the institutionalization of norms (and their internalization) that secure everyday life insofar as they provide a necessary minimum of routinization and orientation.[72] Touraine rightly rejects the *corresponding* opposition between the given (albeit conventional) rule-governed order vs deviation/chaos, that flows from this tradition. For this opposition implies the irrationality of social movements as well as a unitary rationality within a given form of society expressed in its institutional order. But the analysis of institutionalization does not perforce imply this opposition. Yet both systems theory (Offe) and action theory (Touraine) or even their tenuous combination (Habermas and Eder) tend to screen out the institutional level of analysis insofar as the emphasis is placed on either steering mechanisms and the abstract requirements for social integration, or on social contestation and evolutionary mechanisms.

Indeed, system and action theory must remain antinomic if the institutional dimension, or, rather, what Castoriadis refers to as institutionalization, is not included as an analytic component of social theory.[73] Every society, according to Castoriadis, institutionalizes a symbolic socially sanctioned "order," which combines functional, rational components with an imaginary (*imaginaire*) component. The "social imaginary" or the instituted symbolic order of a society (or of any permanent association) exceeds the content of given symbols and cannot be identified with any given set of functions. It is a historical creation that constitutes the conventional social system of meanings, norms, and determines, in the sense of giving significance to, the various aspects of social activity, including purposive-rational, and strategic action. Far from comprising an ideological superstructure superimposed on a "real" substructure, the instituted social imaginary provides the ordering principle of both "real" and symbolic dimensions of social life.

Thus far we have not gotten beyond the sociology of institutions. However, Castoriadis's emphasis is different from that tradition, and it is this difference that makes a difference. In short, he stresses the social historical *creation* of institutions by social actors rather than the necessity of institutions to social order. Thus the institutionalization of a society presupposes the imaginary capacity crucial to the creativity of sociohistorical actors.[74] The fact that society is institutionalized can be made conscious, reflexivity vis-à-vis the social imaginary is possible but, contrary to the rationalist's dream, it cannot become fully transparent. The world is neither pure chaos nor completely meaningful—creative social action requires not fatalism, but hope. The "imaginary institution of society" refers, then, simultaneously to the creativity of human praxis and to the specific historical and action-orienting self-representations and norms of a given society.

Institutional analysis in this sense can be seen as a third analytic level, equally indispensable for critical theory as are systems or action theory. The logic of institutional continuity and discontinuity of modernity is not reducible to either the variation of functions, abstract capacities, or conflictual social action. A society is not only integrated and contested, it is also institutionalized. This means that the social imaginary of a society is carried by concrete empirical institutions (such as law, customs) yet is not reducible to any given set of empirical legal or organizational forms. It also means that the bare opposition between the two sociologies of social action: consensus theories of order vs theories of social movements (irreconcilable antagonism between alternative consensuses)[75] can be avoided by a third possible formulation of the relation between social actors and societal institutions: autonomy and reflexivity. From the standpoint of the creative institutionalization of society, autonomy does not mean simply the self-positing of the law by the individual nor the voluntary embrace of laws through recognition of their necessity. Rather it implies a specific relation to institutionalized norms by the members of a society, entailing reflexivity and the possibility of changing one's criteria within the horizon of possibility of given institutionalizations. If we accept the definition of modernity provided by Habermas and Eder—as the institutionalization of reflexivity regarding institutions—then the democratic potential of modern civil society lies precisely in the possibility of social actors to alter their own institutionalizations (criteria as well as forms).[76] Accordingly, it is in principle always possible to subject *social* institutions of modern civil society to immanent critique, with the proviso that the action-orienting norms and cultural values at issue be open to discursive redemption. Indeed, I would argue that, precisely because he has provided a theory of communication that articulates procedures (albeit modeled on the philosopher's own form of discourse) to secure the universality of universalistic validity claims, Habermas has made immanent critique possible once more! Immanent critique can no longer stand on its own—it requires support from practical philosophy as well as critical systems theory and the analysis of the movement and creative character of social action. But the war of gods and the absence of metasocial guarantees do not have to be taken to mean a permanent disenchantment (and cynicism) or reification of *social* life. Let us not forget that rationalization for Max Weber not only entailed the loss of a unified meaningful world that could expect automatic agreement, it also implied that man must now *create* the meaning of his world—reflexively. And certainly "modernity" implies precisely this reflexive creation and institutionalization of society and meaning.

It is of course not possible to provide a theory of civil society in the space of this conclusion. But I would argue that such a theory is indispensable to a critical stratification theory. For modern Western society is distinctive precisely because it has been *institutionalized* through democratic revolutions and ongoing social movements as *civil society*, differentiated from yet in relation to the modern state. The crucial elements of the social imaginary of modern civil society have been the articulation of plurality in the context of unity and universality, individual and social autonomy, status equality and reflexivity vis-à-vis norms and institutions.[77] The social imaginary of modern civil society is thus more than the sum of the three cultural models described by Touraine and exceeds the "rationality" of the capitalist mode of production emphasized by Marxism.[78] From this standpoint, the institutionalization of civil society provides the underlying unity for the epochs of modernity as well as the normative promise that allows one to say that such-and-such an institution or social movement is not yet modern (Habermas, Eder).

To be sure, the institutionalization of the key features of civil society —*legality* (private law; civil, political, social equality and rights), *plurality* (autonomous, self-constituted voluntary associations), and *publicity* (spaces of communication, public participation in the genesis, conflict, reflection on and articulation of political will and social norms)—has been contradictory to the extent that the institutions of a new, differentiated capitalist economy and, in some countries, the institutions of the absolute state infringed upon societal independence and sought to functionalize it. Yet the parameters of social action described above have not been fully suppressed except in authoritarian statist systems of the twentieth century. On the contrary, a countermovement to the functionalization of society has been with us from the start. As Polanyi was the first to show, the attempts to extend the principles of civil society to steering mechanisms by social movements have been unending and not unsuccessful.[79] The concrete institutions and movements carrying civil society have, to be sure, varied greatly. Nevertheless, the institutions of civil society in the West structure to varying degrees nearly every organization and inform every progressive social movement. On the one hand, they have served to embed the differentiated state structure in a framework of norms that compel it to operate in a legally defined space, sharing power with nonstate elements and controlled by publicity, private and public law, and political freedoms. On the other hand, they have carried the normative potentials (open to continuous reinterpretation and social contestation) without which both the evolution of socialization patterns and the learning processes of social movements of the Western type would be unthinkable.

Moreover, the tension and link between forms of stratification and self-constituted groups challenging the legitimacy of structural inequality and authoritarian hierarchy can be accounted for by these institutions of civil society. The continual redefinition of the equality of "rights," social justice, participation in decision making, all of which challenge the inherited stratification system of a society, and the countermoves by the forces of order have as their referent the institutions and principles that have not stopped being elaborated and fought over since the beginning of modernity. Surely the *continued* importance of the workers' movement must be understood as an attempt to introduce the elements of civil society into the last untouched bastion of ascribed privilege and power—the economy.

I have argued throughout this study that Marx's reduction of civil society to capitalism distorted his insight into the specifically modern form of class relations, and into the difference between economic and social relations. This led to the development of an overburdened and dogmatic class theory. Marx collapsed two quite distinct dynamics of modernity—capitalist rationalization and the countervailing process of democratization initiated through social movements. The birth of civil society was understood by Marx to entail the depoliticization of society and the monopoly of political life by the state. But the birth of society also entailed the emergence of new forms of association and of public life (bourgeois öffentlichkeit) that were institutionalized in democratic constitutions as sets of rights, parliaments, due process, and publicity. The formally democratic state is thus more than the sum of sovereignty, repression, plus steering mechanisms. The theory of social movements accounts for the ongoing creativity of social actors in developing a plurality of new forms of democracy such as councils, local assemblies, democratic associations, and so forth. To be sure, the capacity of the steering mechanisms to denude democratic institutions and social movements of their legitimate normative content and independence has been demonstrated often enough. But it is insufficient and dangerous to attempt to restore the autonomy of civil society by advocating a rigid concrete separation between a pure social space of autonomous self-constituted groups and the steering mechanisms of economy and state.[80] The tendency of social movements proliferating in Western society today is to renounce the institutional dimension of society altogether as fully coopted by mechanisms of domination that cannot be reformed and hence must be bypassed. Attempts to reconstitute the social space without reference to the further institutionalization of civil society would indeed be regressive. Thus the theorist must resist the temptation to follow this path by rigidly separating the realm of freedom from the realm of necessity,[81] action and life world from system and steering, and handing the latter over to the powers that be. The idea that the realm of necessity can only be restricted but not restructured, that alongside it new collectivities can develop democratic forms of life freed from organizational and institutional imperatives, is misguided. For unless they dirty their hands and raise the dual question of structural and institutional reform, social movements and their critical theorists will be relegated, in the long run, to the very marginality against which they rebel. The sovereign power of the state and the coercive power of the capitalist economy they hope to bypass have the nasty habit of returning to frustrate their projects.

Both Touraine and Habermas are aware of this problem. Indeed, both have rejected the antimodern cast of communitarian, social movements mired in specificity, particularistic identity, and "difference," denouncing power but refusing to enter into the fray by addressing the organizational, institutional structures of society and state. Such movements have contributed little to strategies of reform from below that go beyond the institution of counterpowers and seek to restructure and further develop the elements of civil society in economy and polity. Social movements are not political movements, but without reform of political/economic steering mechanisms the very social space in which they operate and which they seek to expand is endangered. Yet one cannot simply call for the "great alliance" among party, union, and movement, between reformist struggles against authoritarian tendencies in the state or economy and social movements for self-determination, without articulating the institutional domain (and alternatives) in which these forces might meet while retaining their difference. The history of social movements as well as of direct democracy (whether of the polis or council type) has shown that any single form of democracy or movement has its exclusionary mechanisms—direct democracy excludes the inactive; workers' councils exclude the nonworker. The analytic dimension of institutionalization allows for the theorization of a plurality of democratic forms which, if partially institutionalized in every domain of social and political life, could serve as countervailing powers vis-à-vis one another. In this sense, the analysis of institutions and their immanent critique is an indispensable component to the theory of social action in general, and of association or society in particular.

It has been the thesis of this conclusion that neither the system category nor the class concept accounts for the multiplicity of institutions, structure of stratification, or forms of social contestation around which the society is both reproduced and challenged. The Marxian critique of an antagonistic social system that generates illegitimate inequalities through its exclusionary mechanisms remains an invaluable step for any attempt to theorize the crisis tendencies of societies that have institutionalized the principles of modernity in a contradictory manner. Today this critique must be transcended by a theory that explores the institutional domain that Marxism confused with the capitalist economy and identified as bourgeois/capitalist society. For the possibility of a modern but postcapitalist democratic society can be made plausible only if, beyond the analysis of systematic dysfunctioning and of the new normative potentials of social movements, we are able to show that the implicit dynamism of the institutions of civil society, of democratic political cultures do not exclude the possibility of a socialist and pluralist civil society.

Notes

Introduction

1. The works of the Frankfurt School theorists, including Franz Neumann, Friedrich Pollock, Herbert Marcuse, Max Horkheimer, and Theodor Adorno in the 1930s and 40s, reflect this sentiment. For a concise account of the historical challenge to the orthodox Marxian class theory, see Jürgen Habermas, "Zwischen Philosophie und Wissenschaft: Marxismus als Kritik," *Theorie und Praxis* (Berlin: Luchterhand, Verlag, 1969), pp. 162–215.
2. Marxists have been remarkably unable to assess the New Left in terms other than traditional class categories. For two excellent post-Marxist accounts, see Alain Touraine, *Lutte étudiante* (Paris: Editions du Seuil, 1978, and Claude Lefort et al., *May 1968: la Brèche* (Paris: Fayard, 1968).
3. I am thinking of the neoconservative broadside and the movement of the "moral majority." The best summary of the former remains that of Peter Steinfels, *The Neo-Conservatives* (New York: Simon and Schuster, 1979).
4. The ecology movement, the disarmament movement, and the women's movement are three contemporary examples of social struggles that cannot be grasped through the class theory.
5. I use the term *neo-Marxism* to distinguish attempts by Marxists to revise or reconstruct the original theory in light of historical development from the official orthodoxy of Soviet communism. Neo-Marxists seek to contribute to a renaissance of Marxian theory in order to rescue the original project from its degeneration into the official ideology of authoritarian communist regimes. In short, neo-Marxists try to restore the link between the critique of capitalism and emancipation to Marxism by revitalizing and, at times, adding to the Marxian categories.
6. See chap. 1, herein.
7. Herbert Marcuse, *One-Dimensional Man* (Boston: Beacon Press, 1964).
8. Jean Cohen, "The Legacy of Herbert Marcuse," *Dissent*, Winter 1981, pp. 90–93.
9. The mutual attraction in the 1960s between politically active radicals searching for the means to comprehend their society and Marcuse's analysis of the structure, ideology, and dangers of late capitalism created a powerful synthesis that gave sections of the New Left many of its distinguishing characteristics.
10. Marcuse seemed to concur with Weber's cynical assessment of representative

democracy and interpreted his concept of legitimation along the lines of the historical materialist conception of ideology. This overinterpretation of Weber's "iron cage" tended to underestimate and even conceal the structural and historical differences between the United States and the Soviet Union. Although intended as a critical analysis, Marcuse's *Soviet Marxism* (New York: Random House, 1971) has, consequently, a decidedly Trotskyist thrust and an implicit convergence theory.

11. Serge Mallet attended lectures by Marcuse given at the Ecole des Hautes Etudes in Paris in 1963. He published a reply in 1965 in *Praxis*, nos. 2–3, reprinted as "Socialism and the New Working Class," in *Essays on the New Working Class*, ed. D. Howard and D. Savage (Saint Louis: Telos Press, 1975). Gorz, too, considered that his work was both influenced by and in response to that of Marcuse; see André Gorz, *Strategy for Labor* (Boston: Beacon Press, 1967), pp. 3–35.

12. Gorz, *Strategy for Labor*; Serge Mallet, *La nouvelle classe ouvrière* (Paris: Editions du Seuil, 1969) and Stanley Aronowitz, *False Promises* (New York: McGraw-Hill, 1973).

13. In his most recent book, *Adieu au proletariat* (Paris: Editions Galilée, 1980), Gorz embraces the position that the realm of necessary labor is by definition the realm of alienation and cannot be altered but may only be reduced.

14. For a critique of this strategy, cf. Jean Cohen, "Agnes Heller's *The Theory of Need in Marx*, *Telos* 33 (Fall 1977): 170–84.

15. Gorz's about-face in *Adieu au proletariat* is ironic in this regard. He seems to have abandoned all strategy for workers' control at the point of production as impossible because labor is necessarily alienated.

16. I consider the main weakness of council communism to be the attempt to generalize forms of organization (workers' councils) perhaps adequate to the corporation into a model of organization for society and the state. Local and regional councils might indeed be a sign of the democratization of political and social life, but they cannot, in my view, dispense with structures of formal law and representative institutions in other organizations that are necessary to protect the rights of the individual against the group and to provide for the articulation of universal norms and general interests.

17. Gorz, *Adieu au proletariat*.

18. Eric Olin Wright, *Class, Crisis, and the State* (London: Verso, 1979) and "Intellectuals and the Class Structure," in Pat Walker, ed., *Between Labor and Capital* (Boston: South End Press, 1979), pp. 191–212; Nicos Poulantzas, *Political Power and Social Classes* (London: New Left Books, 1973), *Classes in Contemporary Capitalism* (London: NLB, 1975), and *State, Power, Socialism* (London: NLB, 1978).

19. For the source of this idea, see Louis Althusser, *For Marx* (New York: Random House, 1969).

20. Wright, *Class, Crisis, and State*, pp. 1–29.

21. Poulantzas, *Political Power*, pp. 67–68. See also Nicos Poulantzas "The Capitalist State: A Reply to Miliband," *New Left Review* 95 (1976): and Nicos Poulantzas "The New Petty Bourgeoisie," in A. Hunt, ed., *Class and Class Structure* (London: Lawrence and Wishart, 1977).

22. Poulantzas, *Classes in Contemporary Capitalism*, pp. 14–17.

23. For an amusing critique of this position, see Frank Parkin, *Marxism and Class Theory* (New York: Columbia University Press, 1979). While Parkin's criticisms of structuralist class theory are to the point, his book employs anti-Marxist rhetoric that deals with superficial issues and is unable to address the theoretical problems underlying them. Supposedly a "Weberian" class theory, Parkin's book turns Marxism into a set of dogmas to be rejected, on the one hand, and ends up affirming some of the worst Marxist assumptions, on the other. Parkin wonders, for example, why there has been so much fuss about the state on the part of neo-Marxists, assuring us that one can analyze it in class terms after all. Like those he attacks, Parkin never thought to reconstruct the theory he abandons, thus reproducing some of its worst dogmas in his own work.

24. Wright, *Class, Crisis, and State.*

25. Ibid., pp. 53–54.

26. Ibid., pp. 15–29.

27. Ibid., pp. 43–44, n.33

28. Ibid., pp. 88–91.

29. Alvin Gouldner, *The Future of Intellectuals and the Rise of the New Class* (New York: Seabury, 1979). Ivan Szelényi and Georg Konrád, *The Intellectuals on the Road to Class Power* (New York: Harcourt, Brace, Jovanovich, 1979). Barbara and John Ehrenreich, "The Professional-Managerial Class," in *Between Labor and Capital*. For a collection of essays by S. M. Lipsett, Aron Wildavsky, Jeanne Kirkpatrick, B. Bruce-Briggs, Daniel Bell, among others, on the theme of the new intellectual class, see *Society* 16, no. 2 (Jan.–Feb. 1979): 14–15. See also *The New Class?* ed. B. Bruce-Briggs (New Brunswick, N.J.: Transaction Press, 1979).

30. The idea that intellectuals compose a stratum between capital and labor is not new. Nor is the argument that they have succeeded in constituting their particular form of knowledge (theoretical, transcontextual) as a source of privilege or prestige. A sociological analysis of the occupational standing, educational advantages, cultural patterns, strategies of exclusion and closure, and structural position of intellectual strata would be worthwhile. This is quite different, however, from a class analysis of the sort being discussed here.

31. As Ivan Szelényi remarked in an unpublished manuscript on Gouldner's *Future of Intellectuals*.

32. Antonio Gramsci, *Prison Notebooks* (New York: International Publishers, 1971); K. Mannheim, *Ideology and Utopia* (New York: Harcourt, Brace, 1936).

33. Szelényi and Konrád, *Intellectuals on the Road to Class Power.*

34. Arguing that the status, authority, and power of intellectuals vary historically with the social formation in which they are situated, Szelényi and Konrád offer a typology of the various stratification mechanisms that constitute intellectuals into an order, stratum, or class (ibid.). The development of market economies in the West occasioned, according to these authors, the transformation of intellectuals from an order (in traditional society) into a semiautonomous stratum of free professionals. In this context, the market is seen as the key stratification mechanism relevant to intellectuals. With the development

of "state monopoly capitalism," a number of redistributive mechanisms are introduced that further stratify intellectuals. Only in the East, however, where such mechanisms are unified and exclusive, do intellectuals constitute a class.

35. Statements to the effect that the *economic* conditions for the formation of intellectuals into a class are absent in the West because the redistributive mechanisms of state monopoly capitalism have not brought with them a class position for a teleological redistributor reveal the economistic and structuralist Marxist bias of the analysis. Ibid. p. 76. The category of "rational redistribution" does not, of course, come from Marxism. It derives from a Weber/Polanyi synthesis. Cf. ibid., introduction.

36. This analysis rejoins Gouldner's in the attribution to Marxism of the anticipation and even the creation of this central structure of domination. The claims of scientific socialism, the demand of sacrifice of particular to general interests, the goal of centralized planning and nationalization, and the advocacy of the abolition of the state/civil society duality are cited as proof of this assertion. Despite the instance that the class position of intellectuals requires the *presence* of the unifying structure, genesis and structure are collapsed through the imputation of just such an interest to all Marxism.

37. The implication seems to be that the party would wither to an ideological, symbolic entity and become a mere administration. Apparently, the absolute rule of the party elite has already given way to a compromise with technocracy wherein the former exercise only a hegemonic authority. All that technocrats need do to break the hegemony of the party elite and replace it with the class rule of intellectuals is to develop an alliance with ideological and dissident intellectuals. But, when disputing the class status of intellectuals in the West, our authors claimed that scientific planners in the East, unlike Western managers, are not required to get a maximum return on each dollar and that the planner decides on the criteria for investment. With the transition to intellectual class rule, however, efficiency would assert itself. However, since the goal-setting function of the planner/redistributor would remain, it would seem likely that the technocrats, once in power, would acquire additional goal-positing tasks formerly carried out by the party. They would thus serve double duty—as experts and as teleological monopolizers of the power to articulate norms. A pure technocracy would thus be theoretically and practically impossible. For a discussion of the general weaknesses of this approach to the analysis of state socialist systems, cf. Andrew Arato, "Critica immanenta e socialismo autoritaria," *Problemi del Socialismo* 22, no. 4 (1981): 85–108.

38. Although it violates their intentions, the use of the concept of class to designate the interest groups proliferating in state socialist "modes of production" brings back the old theme of determination by the economy in the last instance. The concept of class, then, returns the economistic bias to the analysis and obscures the new stratification mechanisms at work in systems lacking civil society.

39. See Bruce-Briggs, *The New Class?*

40. The list is extremely long, extending from Edmund Burke, *Reflections on the Revolution in France* (New York: Bobbs-Merrill, 1955), to Raymond Aron, *The Opium of the Intellectuals* (London: Secker and Warburg, 1957). Most

of the neoconservatives use Tocqueville as their main referent. This is a misuse of a major thinker for political conclusions contrary to his line of thought, for it was Tocqueville's thesis that intellectuals in France prior to the French Revolution engaged in abstract political reflection that was both dangerous and destructive because they were *denied* access to meaningful participation in public life—because they did not have political experience. Thus the myth making of intellectuals regarding politics derived not from their excess power but from their exclusion from the public realm. The receptivity to their ideas among the populace derived from the same deficiency—the absence of democratic public spaces for participation and for the genesis of public virtue. This is hardly the Burkean problematic.

41. The theorist who first formulated this theme was Talcott Parsons. Cf. his *Evolution of Societies* (Englewood Cliffs, N.J.: Prentice-Hall, 1977).

42. Ehrenreich and Ehrenreich, "Professional-Managerial Class," pp. 5–48. See also Jean Cohen and Dick Howard, "Why Class?" in *Between Labor and Capital*, pp. 67–96.

Chapter 1   Civil Society and Its Discontents

1. The term *bürgerliche Gesellschaft* can be translated as bourgeois, or civil, society. Following Hegel, Marx means by this term the emergence of a modern economy and society. For a history of this concept, cf. Manfred Riedel, "Bürger, Staatsbürgern, Bürgertum" and "Gesellschaft, bürgerliche," in *Geschichtliche Grundbegriffe* (Stuttgart, 1972, 1975), vols. 1, 2. I reject the structuralist position that Marx's late works have broken with Hegel by dropping the concepts of civil society, alienation, and concern wth the Hegelian dialectic. For this position, see Althusser, *For Marx* and *Reading Capital* (New York: Random House, 1970), passim.

2. G. W. F. Hegel, *The Philosophy of Right*, trans. and ed. T. N. Knox (New York: Oxford University Press, 1967).

3. The pendulum has shifted back and forth between arguments for the discontinuity of Marxism (Diamat and, more recently, Althusserian structuralist versions of Marxism as science) and for the underlying continuity of the Marxian project (Marxism-as-philosophy and/or Marxism-as-critique, typical of socialist humanist interpretations and the approach of critical theorists of the Frankfurt School). Whether they stress continuity or rupture, all of these approaches entail "symptomatic" readings of the texts, geared toward "saving" Marxian theory.

4. Hegel, *Philosophy of Right*, pp. 122–55.

5. Hegel, *Philosophy of Right*, p. 189, par. 289.

6. Ibid., p. 122, par. 181; p. 124, par. 187; pp. 125–27, pars. 190–93. For an excellent discussion of this problem, cf. Manfred Riedel, *Bürgerliche Gesellschaft und Staat bei Hegel* (Berlin: Luchterhand Verlag, 1970), passim.

7. Hegel, *Philosophy of Right*, pp. 122–55.

8. Shlomo Avineri, *Hegel's Theory of the Modern State* (Cambridge: Cambridge University Press, 1972), p. 135.

9. Joachim Ritter, *Hegel und die französische Revolution* (Frankfurt: Suhrkamp Verlag, 1972).

10. It is crucial here to remember Hegel's distinction between *morality* and *ethics* —the former refers to private values guiding individual action, the latter to public norms. Hegel's point against political liberalism and political economists is that the market cannot integrate social life on its own.

11. For an outstanding critique of Hegel along these lines, see Jürgen Habermas, *Strukturwandel der Öffentlichkeit* (Berlin: Luchterhand Verlag, 1962), pp. 144–58.

12. Ibid.

13. For the opposite approach, see Hannah Arendt, *The Human Condition* (Chicago: University of Chicago Press, 1958).

14. They could, to be sure, be interpreted as the basis for modern corporatism. Avineri, *Hegel's Theory*, attempts such an interpretation, but does not come to grips with the main problem discussed here.

15. Marx argues that the fallacy of mediation is that it does not resolve contradictions but displaces them to other levels, pretending to overcome contradictions while in fact preserving them. Marx, *Contribution to the Critique of Hegel's Philosophy of Law*, in Karl Marx and Friedrich Engels, *Collected Works* (New York: International Publishers, 1975), 3:88.

16. See also L. Kolakowski, "Marxist Roots of Stalinism," in *Stalinism*, ed. R. C. Tucker (New York: W. W. Norton, 1977), pp. 283–98. Unlike Kolakowski, I do *not* believe that any attempt to implement the basic values of Marxism would generate a political system much like Stalinism. But he is right in arguing that authoritarianism inheres in any attempt to totally suppress an autonomous civil society, whether by absorbing civil society into the state or the state into civil society.

17. Marx, "On the Jewish Question," in Karl Marx and Friedrich Engels, *Collected Works*, 3:146–75.

18. Althusser, *For Marx*, pp. 41–87.

19. Marx, *Contribution to the Critique of Hegel's Philosophy*, p. 18.

20. Althusser, *For Marx*.

21. Helmut Reichelt, *Zur logischen Struktur des Kapitalbegriffs* (Frankfurt: Europäische Verlagsanstalt, 1973), pp. 19–73.

22. This principle derives from the natural law tradition, which both Hegel and Marx appropriate despite their criticisms.

23. The former insofar as the alienability of labor and property and the satisfaction of need, guaranteed by private law, are left to the decisions of formally free and equal individuals; the latter insofar as self-determination achieves the political form of sovereignty of the people, to which legitimate authority must constantly appeal as its basis.

24. Habermas, *Theorie und Praxis*, pp. 283–306, and Albrecht Wellmer, *Critical Theory of Society* (New York: Herder and Herder, 1971), develop this concept of ideology critique to characterize Marx's approach. They do not, however, take cognizance of the changes in the concept and object of critique as Marx's work develops.

25. It is Marcuse's position that philosophy is transcended in Marx's works be-

cause it is embodied in socioeconomic categories. Herbert Marcuse, *Reason and Revolution* (Boston: Beacon Press, 1969).

26. They are not, in other words, the sign of a fixed concept of human nature or an empiricistic problematic, both of which posit the presence of man as the unchanging subject of history.

27. See chapters 2 and 3, herein.

28. Marx, *Contribution to the Critique of Hegel's Philosophy*, pp. 81, 117. Labor, in this early text, is excluded from the definition of the specifically human. Only with the 1844 *Manuscripts* does labor enter into the concept of self-objectifying praxis through the theory of objectification.

29. Hegel, *Grundlinien der Philosophie des Rechts* (Frankfurt: Suhrkamp Verlag, 1970), pars. 205, 303, 291, 296, 297.

30. See chap. 4, herein.

31. Marx, *Contribution to the Critique of Hegel's Philosophy*, pp. 50–51.

32. Ibid.

33. Marx, "Jewish Question," p. 166.

34. Ibid., p. 168.

35. Ibid., p. 156.

36. Marx argues that, through the universalization of the franchise and the creation of an enlightened public through a free press, individuals could attain direct participation in public affairs and thus repoliticize their life in civil society. This model would add spaces for direct participation to the structure of formal democracy and involve only the abolition of the bureaucracy that appropriates political life through its administrative monopoly on decision making. Marx, *Contribution to the Critique of Hegel's Philosophy*, pp. 30, 61–63, 121. But Marx quickly abandoned this approach and never returned to reflect on the importance of public spaces within civil society to check state power. Unlike Alexis de Tocqueville (*Democracy in America* [New York: Doubleday, 1966]), he never perceived the problem of the tyranny of the majority and thus sought no limits to its power, if it happened to be the proletariat.

37. See chap. 6, herein.

38. The debate regarding the nature and significance of the 1844 *Manuscripts* revolves around the issue of whether the critique of political economy derives from an investigation of the historically specific features of the capitalist system or whether it rests on an eschatological and teleological philosophy of history. The recent proponents of the former position are Reichelt, *Zur logischen Struktur*, and Ernst Mandel, *The Formation of the Economic Thought of Karl Marx* (New York: Monthly Review Press, 1971). The second approach is represented by Althusser, *For Marx* and *Reading Capital*, and Jindrigh Zeleny, *Die Wissenschafts Logik und "Das Kapital"* (Frankfurt: Europäische Verlagsanstalt, 1973).

39. K. Kosik, in *Die Dialektik des Konkreten* (Frankfurt: Suhrkamp Verlag, 1967), provides a brilliant analysis of the philosophy of praxis in Marx. Kosik, however, developed an ontology of labor as praxis that unified Marx's work as a whole. He does not address the antinomies in Marx's methodologies as a consequence of this view.

40. Marx, *Economic and Philosophic Manuscripts of 1844*, in Marx and Engels, *Collected Works*, 3:231–32.
41. Ibid., p. 270.
42. Marx, "Jewish Question," p. 199. See also *Contribution to a Critique of Hegel's Philosophy*, p. 183.
43. See Gyorgy Markus, "Der Begriff des 'Menschlichen Wesens' in der Philosophie des jungen Marx" (Berlin: Internationale Marxistische Diskussion 53, Merve Verlag, 1976), pp. 41–90, and "Human Essence and History," *International Journal of Sociology* 4, no. 1 (Spring 1974): 89.
44. Marx, *Manuscripts of 1844*, pp. 241–42, 256.
45. Althusser, *For Marx*, passim.
46. The model of communism in the *Manuscripts* as the overcoming of alienation, the realization of species life, and the abolition of the wage labor/capital duality is normative but abstract vis-à-vis the analysis of civil society in the same texts. Marx, *Manuscripts of 1844*, pp. 231, 306.
47. Markus, "Human Essence," passim.
48. See Agnes Heller, *Toward a Marxist Theory of Value*, in *Kinesis: Graduate Journal in Philosophy* (Southern Illinois University, 1972), pp. 8–76.
49. Because primitive societies do not display these features, they appear to the Marxist as unhistorical. The interrelation of ritual and myth, the reproduction and development of symbolic meaning, in short, the cultural history of primitive society, is thus closed to the theory of objectification in this form.
50. The theory that species development is carried on the level of society has been challenged by those who argue that it is the very extension of the productive forces within the framework of alienation that militates against progress on the level of society, especially with the transition from liberal to late capitalism. Adorno, Horkheimer, Benjamin, and Marcuse point to the irretrievable losses accompanying the "civilizing process." For Adorno especially, there has been such a manifold destruction of cultural values that the "whole has become the false." Theodor Adorno, *Minima Moralia* (London: New Left Review Editions, 1974), p. 50.
51. See chap. 3, herein.
52. Ibid.
53. "From this moment onwards, consciousness *can* really flatter itself that it is something other than consciousness of existing practice.... from now on consciousness is in a position to emancipate itself from the world to proceed to the formation of 'pure' theory, theology, philosophy, morality, etc." This is the case as soon as intellectual mental labor and material labor devolve on different persons, according to Marx. Marx, *The German Ideology*, in Marx and Engels, *Collected Works*, 5:45.
54. Ibid., p. 92.
55. Ibid., p. 36.
56. Jürgen Habermas, *Knowledge and Human Interests* (Boston: Beacon Press, 1971), pp. 25–42; and Wellmer, *Critical Theory*, pp. 67–121. Their criticism refers to the self-understanding of Marx, who viewed his own theory along the lines of a positivistically understood model of natural science and thereby blurred the distinction between natural and social science, as well as that be-

tween science and critique. There is a great deal of debate over the issue of whether Marx advocated a new science, the unity of science, and/or the preservation or transformation of technology. For a view opposite to that of Habermas and Wellmer, cf. John O'Neil, *Sociology as a Skin Trade* (New York: Harper and Row, 1972).

57. Science, according to Althusser, is that mode of pure theorizing that dispenses with the concept of or reference to a subject, abandons the "empiricist" assumption that knowledge is a real part of the real object, and is detached from social conditions. It is ironic that precisely those characteristics that Marx of *The German Ideology* attributes to ideology Althusser attributes to science, and in reference to the same texts! Althusser, *Reading Capital*, p. 38.

58. Kosik, *Die Dialektik des Konkreten*, p. 57.

59. This is the position, above all, of Reichelt, *Zur logischen Struktur*, passim. The structuralists, to be sure, distinguish between *genesis* and *structure*, but in comprehending the structure as a mode of production whose categories can be used to analyze past history the fruit of the distinction is lost.

60. Marx, *Capital* (New York: International Publishers, 1967), 1:8–9.

61. Marx, *Grundrisse: Foundations of the Critique of Political Economy*, trans. Martin Nicolaus (London: Penguin Books, 1973), pp. 81–115.

62. Ibid., pp. 107–8. The reference here is to the dialectic of abstract and concrete—thought does not, of course, follow the process by which the concrete comes into being but presupposes the presence of the system as a totality in order to produce a systemic theoretical product. Whereas the structuralist takes this to imply a total separation between pure theory and "reality," between the object of knowledge and the real object, between theoretical and "real" abstractions, a more adequate interpretation is that of J. F. Lyotard, who claims in an unpublished manuscript that the categories of the system presuppose a historical present and are oriented toward informing praxis but do not attempt to express historicity directly. Lyotard, "The Place of Alienation in the Marxist Overthrow."

63. Marx, *Grundrisse*, pp. 85–86.

64. Georg Lukacs, *History and Class Consciousness* (London: Merlin Press, 1968), pp. 83–110.

65. Marx, *Theories of Surplus Value* (Moscow: Progress Publishers, 1968), pp. 117–18.

66. Althusser, *Reading Capital*, passim.

67. See chap. 6, herein.

68. Reichelt, *Zur logischen Struktur*, p. 14.

69. Whether this means that the critique of political economy has solely a negative thrust or seeks also to unfold a positive theory of development is an open question. Lukacs, *History and Class Consciousness*, upholds the latter view; Lyotard, "Place of Alienation," the former.

 "Madame la Terre" and "Monsieur le Capital" are terms used by Marx in the third volume of *Capital* to refer to the fetishization of rent and profit within political economy. Marx, *Capital*, 3:829–30.

70. Reichelt, *Zur logischen Struktur*, p. 85.

71. Lyotard, "Place of Alienation," p. 4.

72. Ibid., p. 37.
73. Marx, *Grundrisse*, p. 409.
74. Ibid., p. 245.
75. Marx, *Capital*, 1:78–79.
76. Jürgen Habermas, *Legitimation Crisis* (Boston: Beacon Press, 1975).
77. For an excellent discussion of this problem in relation to natural law theory and Hegel, see Albrecht Wellmer's manuscript, "Ethik und kritische Theorie."

Chapter 2   The Philosophical Presuppositions of the Class Theory

1. See Marx to Joseph Weydemeyer, March 5, 1852, in Karl Marx and Friedrich Engels, *Selected Correspondence* (Moscow: Progress Publishers, 1955), p. 64.
2. C. B. MacPherson, *The Political Theory of Possessive Individualism: Hobbes to Locke* (New York: Oxford University Press, 1962), p. 229. MacPherson shows the interconnections among the theory of property right, individualistic anthropological presuppositions, and the acknowledged exclusion of the working classes from full membership in the state, given their lack of property and, hence, independence. I do not, however, take MacPherson as *the* authority on Locke. Neither Locke nor the Scottish moralists (Smith) were mere apologists for capitalism or property.
3. Lorenz von Stein, *The History of the Social Movement in France: 1789–1850* (Totowa, New Jersey: Bedminster Press, 1964).
4. Henri de Saint-Simon, *Social Organization and the Science of Man*, ed. F. Markham (New York: Harper and Row, 1964).
5. Marx, *Contribution to the Critique of Hegel's Philosophy*, pp. 45, 50.
6. Avineri, *Hegel's Theory*, pp. 155–56; Hegel, *Philosophy of Right*, pp. 132–33, pars. 206–7, and additions. Nevertheless, Avineri persists in referring to the estates described by Hegel as classes, even going so far as to repeat the error of the original English translator of Hegel's text, T. Knox, who translates the word *Stand* as "class" when it appears under the heading of the state. Avineri does so simply because Hegel sees estate membership as based on talent rather than heredity, as was the case with feudal estates. This prevents Avineri from perceiving the contradictory character of Hegel's concept of *Stand*, however.
7. Hegel, *Philosophy of Right*, pp. 131–32, pars. 202–6. See also Riedel, *Burgerliche Gesellschaft*.
8. Hegel, *Philosophy of Right*, pp. 197–98, par. 303. Throughout this discussion, Hegel uses the word *Stand*; the word "class" (*Klasse*) does not appear.
9. Ibid., p. 150, pars. 243–45. Here the term in German is *Klasse* and not *Stand*. Only in reference to the poor, who do not belong to an estate, does Hegel use the term *Klasse*. Compare with the German edition: Hegel, *Grundlinien der Philosophie des Rechts*, pp. 389–90, pars. 243–45. Hegel uses the term *Klasse* in one additional context to refer to the "business classes" (together with whom the creation of a *Pöbel* interrelates) only when he is considering them in absence of corporate membership. Here, in par. 253 (p. 395, German ed.), Hegel argues that only if the business strata do not belong to corporations can they be seen as a mere class, a conglomeration of particular interests swayed and motivated by greed and success measured in wealth alone. The point he is

making is that membership in a corporation and in an estate returns ethical consciousness to otherwise privatized individuals.

10. Hegel, *Philosophy of Right*, pp. 149–50, par. 243, my emphasis.

11. Ibid., pp. 148–50, pars. 241, 244.

12. Ibid., p. 277, par. 244, addition.

13. Ibid., p. 150, par. 245.

14. Ibid., p. 277, par. 244, addition.

15. Ibid., p. 150, par. 245.

16. Marx, *Contribution to the Critique of Hegel's Philosophy*, p. 80.

17. This limited use of the concept of class to refer to stratification in *capitalist* society characterizes not only the works prior to the theory of historical materialism but also the "mature" writings: *Grundrisse, Capital,* and *Theories of Surplus Value.*

18. Marx, *Contribution to the Critique of Hegel's Philosophy*, p. 70. "It is an historical advance which has transformed the *political* estates into *social* estates, so that, just as the Christians are equal in heaven, but unequal on earth, so the individual members of that nation are *equal* in the heaven of their political world, but unequal in the earthly existence of *society.* The real transformation of the *political estates* into *civil* estates took place in the *absolute monarchy.*"

19. Fascism presents the clearest example of this step backward from universalistic morality through the attempt to reintroduce corporate structures into civil and political life.

20. Marx, *Contribution to the Critique of Hegel's Philosophy*, Introduction, p. 184. It is of course questionable whether the French Revolution can be considered a revolution of a class, specifically the bourgeoisie, or not. Certainly many social strata were involved in the revolt, from the *sans-culottes* to radical lawyers, all of whom do not constitute a single class. But insofar as capitalist social relations became prevalent as an outcome of the revolution and, above all, estates were abolished, one can consider it to be "bourgeois" in outcome if not in terms of agency. It should be clear, however, that Marx rejects the Jacobin solution to the incompleteness of a formally democratic political revolution from above carried out by the state. In an insightful critique of Jacobinism, Marx states that once the dust clears, the successes of such a revolution will prove to be illusory and civil society will reassert itself. Would that such were indeed the case for the second permanent revolution in history, the Russian. Marx, "Jewish Question," pp. 155–56.

21. Ibid., p. 186.

22. For an excellent analysis of Soviet society as a new form of domination, see Claude Lefort, *Éléments d'une critique de la bureaucratie* (Geneva: Librairie Droz, 1971), pp. 130–91, 287–316. See also Cornelius Castoriadis, *La société bureaucratique* (Paris: Éditions 10/18, 1973–76), vols. 1–4.

23. Marx, *Contribution to the Critique of Hegel's Philosophy*, Introduction, p. 183.

24. Ibid.

25. Hegel, *Philosophy of Right*, pp. 127–28, pars. 192–96.

26. Ibid.; and Jean Jacques Rousseau, *Du contrat social*, ed. R. Grinsley (Oxford: Oxford University Press, 1972).

27. Agnes Heller, *The Theory of Need in Marx* (London: Allison and Busby, 1976), passim.

28. For an excellent analysis of the concept of interest in natural law theory, cf. Helmut Neuendorff, *Der Begriff des Interesses* (Frankfurt: Suhrkamp Verlag, 1973), passim.

29. Cf. the introduction by Helmut Reichelt, ed., to Hegel, *Grundlinien der Philosophie des Rechts* (Frankfurt: Ullstein Buch, 1972), pp. v–lxxiv.

30. Heller, *Theory of Need*, p. 59.

31. Marx, *Grundrisse*, p. 244.

32. Marx, *The Holy Family*, in Marx and Engels, *Collected Works*, 4:267.

33. André Gorz and Herbert Marcuse have both taken up the concept of need unfolded by Marx and integrated it into their analyses of modern capitalism. (cf. Introduction, herein). Against Gorz and Marcuse, Heller argues that one cannot designate groups of needs as radical from the standpoint of capitalism but only from the standpoint of the value concept of need. That is, needs are radical not solely because capitalism cannot satisfy them but because they point beyond the capitalist structure of need and interest relations. Cf. Cohen, "Heller's *Theory of Need*."

34. Heller, *Theory of Need*, p. 60. For a further analysis of the use of the concept of interest in Marx, see Cohen, "Heller's *Theory of Need*."

35. Marx, *Theses on Feuerbach*, no. 3, in Marx and Engels, *Collected Works*, 5:4.

36. Heller, *Theory of Need*, p. 38.

37. Marx, *Manuscripts of 1844*, p. 295.

38. Ibid., p. 304. See also Marx, *Grundrisse*, p. 109.

39. Marx, *German Ideology*, pp. 42–43.

40. Heller, *Theory of Need*, p. 28. See also Markus, "Human Essence."

41. Marx, *Manuscripts of 1844*, p. 277. Standards of beauty and form enter even into the production of objects destined to satisfy physical needs.

42. Ibid., pp. 273–79.

43. Ibid., p. 273.

44. Ibid., p. 240. Marx also states: "An enforced *increase of wages* . . . would therefore be nothing but better *payment for the slave*, and would not win either for the worker or for labour their human status and dignity." Ibid., p. 280.

45. Ibid., p. 238. The antimodern element in Marxism is clearest here, in the rejection of differentiation via the division of labor.

46. Marx, *German Ideology*, p. 80, my emphasis.

47. Marx, *Manuscripts of 1844*, p. 280.

48. Ibid., p. 308. Hence, the very presence and concept of so-called survival needs indicate a reduction of individuals to the status of animality.

49. Ibid., p. 306.

50. Heller, *Toward a Marxist Theory of Value*, p. 18.

51. Ibid.

52. Marx, *Manuscripts of 1844*, p. 316.

53. Ibid., p. 313.

54. Marx, *The Poverty of Philosophy*, in Marx and Engels, *Collected Works*, 6:211.

55. Marx, *Holy Family*, p. 37.

56. Marx, *Contribution to the Critique of Hegel's Philosophy*, Introduction, pp. 184–85.
57. Ibid., p. 184.
58. Claude Lefort, *La politique et la pensée de la politique*, Extrait des lettres nouvelles, II année, nouvelle serie 32, p. 26.
59. Ibid., pp. 35–36.
60. Habermas, *Knowledge and Human Interests*, pp. 25–65.
61. Ibid., p. 47.
62. Ibid., p. 42.
63. It was, above all, Marcuse who popularized the master/slave dialectic in this form as an interpretation of the radical potential inherent in laboring activity through a Marx/Hegel synthesis. Cf. Marcuse, *Reason and Revolution*, pp. 258–312.
64. Habermas, *Knowledge and Human Interests*, pp. 53–54. This position can be attributed only to the early Habermas. With the text, *Legitimation Crisis*, Habermas's position on the class theory changes. Cf. Conclusion, herein.
65. Habermas, *Knowledge and Human Interests*, p. 97.

Chapter 3   Class and History

1. Marx to Weydemeyer, March 5, 1852, in Marx and Engels, *Selected Correspondence*, p. 64.
2. This is the central thesis of Althusser, *For Marx* and *Reading Capital*.
3. Although the theory of historical materialism dominates the various texts of the period between 1845 and 1857, I focus on *The German Ideology, Theses on Feuerbach*, and the *Communist Manifesto*. The main interpreters of Marxism as science are Althusser and the French structuralist Marxists, including Nicos Poulantzas, Maurice Godelier; Helmut Reichelt and Jindrigh Zeleny (*Die Wissenschafts Logik*).
4. Marx, *Theses on Feuerbach*, pp. 3–5.
5. The best discussion of this antinomy is Wellmer, *Critical Theory*, pp. 67–121.
6. Ironically, or perhaps understandably, this embrace of political economy's orientation occurs in texts that no longer have political economy as the direct object of critical analysis. This is especially true of *The German Ideology*.
7. Althusser and Markus develop two opposing interpretations of the shift heralded by the *Theses on Feuerbach* and *The German Ideology*. The famous sixth thesis, which argues that the "essence of man" is not an abstraction inhering in each individual but in reality is the ensemble of social relations, leaves the activity constituting social relations unspecified. Thus Althusser insists that this thesis implies a shift from anthropology to the scientific study of society, whereas Markus maintains that it replaces Feuerbach's essentialism with a new philosophical anthropology. Cf. Althusser, *For Marx*, passim, and Markus, "Der Begriff des 'Menschlichen Wesens.' "
8. "The whole internal structure of a nation depends on the stage of development reached by its production. . . . How far the productive forces of a nation are developed is shown manifestly by the degree of division of labor." Marx, *German Ideology*, p. 32.

9. Ibid., p. 43.
10. Ibid., pp. 39–40.
11. Ibid., p. 39.
12. Ibid., pp. 74, 81. For a critique of this approach, see Wellmer, *Critical Theory*, passim.
13. Marx, *German Ideology*, pp. 53, 89.
14. "The term civil society emerged in the 18th century, when property relations had already extricated themselves from the ancient and medieval community. *Civil Society as such only develops with the bourgeoisie; the social organization evolving directly out of production* and intercourse, which in all ages forms the basis of the state and the rest of the idealistic superstructure, has, however, always been designated by the same name." Ibid., p. 89; my emphasis.
15. Ibid., p. 53.
16. Cf. Wellmer, *Critical Theory*.
17. Ibid.; Habermas, *Knowledge and Human Interests*.
18. The debate between the structuralists (Althusser, Perry Anderson) and the "culturalists" (E. P. Thompson) regarding the theory of class and class struggle exemplifies this antinomy without resolving it. Neither side, moreover, questions the concept of class or sees any links between this concept and the difficulties that each side faces regarding historical analysis. For a discussion of this debate in its most recent form, see my "Thompson, *The Poverty of Theory*," *Telos* 49 (Fall 1981): 189–96.
19. Marx, *German Ideology*, p. 54.
20. Marx, *Manifesto of the Communist Party*, in Marx and Engels, *Collected Works*, 6:482.
21. But it is also meaningless to deduce from this fact that intellectuals are a class. This is the analysis of Gouldner, *Future of Intellectuals*.
22. The most explicitly technologically determinist version of the forces/relations model can be found in Marx, *Poverty of Philosophy*, 6:166.
23. Georg Lukacs, *History and Class Consciousness* (London: Merlin Press, 1968), p. 238.
24. Karl Polanyi, *The Great Transformation* (Boston: Beacon Press, 1944), passim.
25. Lukacs, *History and Class Consciousness*, p. 249.
26. Cornelius Castoriadis, "On the History of the Workers' Movement," *Telos* 20 (Winter 1976–77): 20.
27. Ibid., pp. 14–16.
28. Marx, *German Ideology*, pp. 65–66, 76.
29. Castoriadis, "History of the Workers' Movement," p. 16.
30. Marx, *German Ideology*, p. 76.
31. Ibid., p. 77.
32. Marx, *Manifesto*, pp. 485–87; also Castoriadis, "History of the Workers' Movement," p. 23.
33. The fruitful tension between need and interest is also dissolved.
34. Marx, *Manifesto*, p. 48.
35. See chap. 6, herein, for a discussion of this problem as it relates to the systemic analysis of capitalist production relations.
36. Marx, *Manifesto*, p. 503.

37. Ibid., p. 490.

38. See chap. 6, herein.

39. Marx, *Manifesto*, p. 496.

40. Ibid., p. 498.

41. Ibid., p. 499.

42. Marx, *German Ideology*, p. 49.

43. Building on the insights of Castoriadis and Jean Baudrillard, Alain Touraine in *The Voice and the Eye* (New York: Cambridge University Press, 1981) has presented the most interesting attempt to develop a theory of social movements that is based on the distinction between change and development. (Cf. Conclusion, herein.)

44. The rather unfruitful debate over reform vs. revolution that penetrates the history of Marxism has its roots here. The pre-Bolshevik debate among Lenin, Luxemburg, Bernstein, and Kautsky, as well as the post-Bolshevik disagreements exemplified by the splits in the Marxist parties (Bolsheviks vs. Social Democrats) and, finally, the furor raised by the idea of Eurocommunism all have in common the Jacobin model of revolution (shared, of course, by the Bolsheviks) oriented toward state takeover, over and against which the idea of "reformism" receives its content. It is impossible to summarize this literature. André Gorz (*Strategy for Labor*) and Alain Touraine (*The Voice and the Eye*) both take significant steps beyond this sterile opposition by attempting to redefine reform (Gorz) and revolution (Touraine).

45. The best recent discussion of the analytic approaches to the French Revolution and of its symbolic meaning is François Furet, *Pensée la Revolution française* (Paris: Gallimard, 1978).

46. Marx, *Manifesto*, p. 489.

47. The problem of defining absolutism as a mode of production has haunted even the best of avowedly Marxist theorists. Cf. Perry Anderson, *Lineages of the Absolutist State* (London: New Left Review Editions, 1974), pp. 15–60. Anderson challenges the classic Engelsian dictum pronouncing absolutism to be a class equilibrium between bourgeois and feudal domination, arguing that it is the perfected form of feudal domination. Insisting on the category of "mode of production" and, correspondingly, of class rule, he forces his otherwise rich analysis into the sterile form of class categories, obviously doing an injustice to the political moment of absolutist rule that escapes socioeconomic determination and forms of domination.

48. Jean Baudrillard, *The Mirror of Production* (Saint Louis: Telos Press, 1975), pp. 153–54.

49. Marx, *Manifesto*, p. 489.

50. Ibid., p. 493.

51. Marx, *German Ideology*, p. 61.

52. Ibid., p. 52.

53. Ibid., pp. 47–48.

54. Ibid., p. 87; my emphasis.

55. Baudrillard, *Mirror of Production*, p. 144. Cf. also Marx, *Poverty of Philosophy*, pp. 211–12.

56. Baudrillard, *Mirror of Production*, pp. 155–56.

57. Ibid., pp. 158–59. See also Castoriadis, "History of the Workers' Movement," pp. 23–27.

58. Of course, E. P. Thompson's *Making of the English Working Class* (New York: Vintage, 1963) is the shining example of a Marxist historical text that takes these features into account.

59. Castoriadis, "History of the Workers' Movement," pp. 23–27.

60. For the best analysis of this problem and a summary of the literature, see Mihaly Vajda, "The State and Socialism," *Social Research* 45, no. 4 (Winter 1978): 844–65. For a structuralist and quasistructuralist approach to the state, cf. Nicos Poulantzas, *Fascism and Dictatorship* (London: New Left Books, 1974), and Wright, *Class, Crisis, and State*. Of course, non-Marxists pointed out long ago the deficiencies of Marxism vis-à-vis the analysis of the state. Cf. Sheldon Wolin, *Politics and Vision* (Boston: Little, Brown, 1960), passim. The best Marxist approach, one that avoids the issues of class and state and focuses on the structural relation between the state and the capitalist system, is that of Claus Offe, *Strukturprobleme des kapitalistischen Staates* (Frankfurt: Suhrkamp Verlag, 1973), passim. For Ralph Miliband's response to Poulantzas's structuralist approach, see Miliband, "The Capitalist State: Reply to Nicos Poulantzas," *New Left Review* 59 (Jan.–Feb. 1970): and "Poulantzas and the Capitalist State," ibid., 82 (Nov.–Dec. 1973).

61. Marx, *German Ideology*, p. 90.

62. Marx, *Manifesto*, p. 59.

63. This image does not apply to nineteenth-century capitalism, where throughout Europe and England nonbourgeois strata retained the reins of political power, exercising it in such a way that they could hardly be seen as mere agents of capital. Nor does it apply to late capitalism, where the emergence of new social strata and the changed relation of state and society immeasurably complicate the analysis of political power.

64. In a number of places Poulantzas has attempted to argue that Bonapartism is the norm rather than the exception to bourgeois domination. Be that as it may, this is perhaps a structuralist Marxist position, but it certainly was not Marx's belief. Poulantzas, *Political Power*, pp. 79–81, 107–8, 279–86.

65. C. Wright Mills, *The Power Elite* (New York: Oxford University Press, 1956), p. 277, note.

66. Marx, *Manifesto*, p. 496. With the launching of the theory of "Eurocommunism," the debate over the term *dictatorship of the proletariat* has become heated indeed. Although the literature is enormous, the two most representative texts are Santiago Carillo, *Eurocommunism and the State* (London: Lawrence and Wishart, 1977), and Etienne Balibar, *Sur la dictature du proletariat* (Paris: Maspero, 1976).

67. Marx, *Manifesto*, p. 504.

68. Ibid., p. 486.

69. Ibid., p. 505.

70. Marx, *German Ideology*, p. 47.

71. Marx, *The 18th Brumaire of Louis Bonaparte* (New York: International Publishers, 1969), pp. 112, 128.

72. Marx, *German Ideology*, pp. 76–77.

73. Ibid., pp. 77, 80.
74. Max Weber, "Class, Status, Party," in *From Max Weber*, ed. Hans Gerth and C. Wright Mills (New York: Oxford University Press, 1958), pp. 180–95.
75. A recent exemplification of this analysis is the article by Perry Anderson, "The Antinomies of Antonio Gramsci," *New Left Review* 100 (Nov. 1976–Jan. 1977): 5–81. To be sure, Anderson claims that the "reality" of the bourgeois state is its administrative, military apparatus, which must be "smashed." But parliaments, law, and the like are treated as ideology, as purely bourgeois mystifications whose sole function it is to trick the working class into believing bourgeois myths of popular sovereignty and the like—these will obviously be dissolved once the proletariat takes power and institutes its own state apparatus.
76. Marx, *Manifesto*, p. 505.
77. Such has been precisely the concern of Jürgen Habermas. Cf. my "Why More Political Theory?" *Telos* 40 (Summer 1979): 70–94.
78. Thus Marx chooses the opposite path to the dilemma of civil society already noticed by Rousseau. As is well known, Rousseau chose to limit production to prevent the accumulation of property and wage labor at opposite poles and to maintain an ideal society based on simple commodity production as the guarantor of political freedom. The historical materialist thinks in a directly opposite fashion—let the contradictions emerge and mature, and growth will be the basis for their resolution. Marx at his best never quite succeeded in reconciling freedom and abundance, although this was his ultimate concern.

Chapter 4   The Historical Writings

1. Marx, *18th Brumaire*, author's preface, p. 8.
2. I am referring to *Class Struggles in France, 1848–1850* (New York: International Publishers, 1964), a collection of articles written for the *Neue Rheinische Zeitung* in Hamburg; *18th Brumaire*; and *The Civil War in France* (Peking: Foreign Languages Press, 1966), which was written by Marx in April–May 1871 and published as a pamphlet in June.
3. Marx, *Class Struggles in France*, p. 10.
4. Cf. the preface to Marx, *18th Brumaire*.
5. For an excellent discussion of the different models of history to be found in Marx's writings, see Claude Lefort, "Marx: d'une vision de l'histoire à l'autre," *Les formes de l'histoire* (Paris: Editions Gallimard, 1978), pp. 195–233.
6. Marx, *18th Brumaire*, pp. 16–17
7. Ibid., p. 15.
8. Ibid., p. 18.
9. Ibid.
10. Ibid., p. 19.
11. Lefort, "Marx," p. 224.
12. These classes are defined not in terms of income or standard of living but in terms of their mode of appropriation, form of labor, and property according to the forces/relations model.
13. Marx, *Manifesto*, p. 509.

14. Marx, *Class Struggles in France*, p. 40.

15. Marx, *18th Brumaire*, p. 54.

16. "No one had fought more fanatically in the June days for the salvation of property and the restoration of credit than the Parisian petty bourgeois. . . . And when the barricades were thrown down and the workers were crushed and the shopkeepers, drunk with victory, rushed back to their shops, they found the entrance barred by a savior of property, an official agent of credit, who presented them with threatening letters: Overdue bill of exchange! Overdue house rent! Overdue promissory note! Ruined shop! Ruined shopkeeper!" Marx, *Class Struggles in France*, p. 63.

17. Marx, *18th Brumaire*, pp. 49, 50.

18. Ibid., pp. 50–51.

19. Ibid., pp. 52–53.

20. Lefort, "Marx," pp. 221–25.

21. Marx, *Class Struggles in France*, p. 41.

22. Marx, *18th Brumaire*, pp. 126–27.

23. "The small-holding peasants form a vast mass, the members of which live in similar conditions but without entering into manifold relations with one another. Their mode of production isolates them from one another. . . . Their field of production, the small holding, admits of no division of labour in its cultivation, no application of science and, therefore, . . . no wealth of social relationships. Each individual peasant family is almost self-sufficient; . . . and thus acquires its means of life more through exchange with nature than in intercourse with society." Ibid., pp. 123–24.

24. Ibid., p. 127.

25. Ibid., p. 128 (and Marx, *Class Struggles in France*, pp. 118–19).

26. Marx, *18th Brumaire*, p. 128.

27. Ibid., pp. 125–27.

28. Ibid., p. 130.

29. "Insofar as millions of families live under economic conditions of existence that separate their mode of life, their interests, and their culture, from those of other classes, and put them in hostile opposition to the latter, they form a class. Insofar as there is merely a local interconnection among these small-holding peasants, and the identity of their interests begets no community, no national bond, and no political organization among them, they do not form a class. They are consequently incapable of enforcing their class interest in their own name, whether through a parliament or through a convention. They cannot represent themselves, they must be represented. Their representative must at the same time appear as their master, as an authority over them, as an unlimited governmental power that protects them against the other classes and sends them rain and sunshine from above." Ibid., p. 124.

30. Ibid., pp. 121–33.

31. Ibid., p. 130.

32. Marx, *Class Struggles in France*, p. 40.

33. Ibid., p. 43.

34. Ibid., p. 54.

35. Ibid., pp. 50–52.

36. Ibid., p. 58.
37. Ibid., pp. 45, 126.
38. Ibid., pp. 33–38.
39. Marx, *18th Brumaire*, p. 36.
40. Ibid.
41. Ibid., p. 48.
42. Ibid., p. 49.
43. Marx, *Class Struggles in France*, p. 77.
44. Marx, *18th Brumaire*, p. 62.
45. I do not think that any of the recent attempts to produce a Marxist theory of the state help in this regard. Neither Poulantzas's structuralist category juggling nor Offe's far more sophisticated and clear-sighted attempt to develop an adequate theory of the state within a Marxist framework succeeds in getting out of the straitjacket of the Marxian model. Cf. Introduction and Conclusion, herein.
46. Marx, *18th Brumaire*, p. 62.
47. Marx, *Civil War in France*, pp. 65–66, 162–63.
48. Ibid., p. 165.
49. Marx, *Class Struggles in France*, p. 50.
50. Marx, *18th Brumaire*, p. 123.
51. Ibid., p. 124.
52. Ibid., pp. 128–29.
53. Ibid., p. 131.
54. Marx, *Civil War in France*, p. 66.
55. Ibid., p. 64.
56. Ibid., p. 69.
57. Ibid., p. 71.
58. Ibid., p. 72.
59. Ibid., p. 73.
60. Ibid., p. 176.
61. Marx, *18th Brumaire*, pp. 43–44.

Chapter 5 Historical Genesis and Class

1. Several analyses have attempted to articulate the specificity of the method and object of analysis of *Capital* as opposed to the earlier writings. Among the most important are Althusser, *For Marx* and *Reading Capital*; Reichelt, *Zur logischen Struktur*; Zeleny, *Die Wissenschafts Logik*; and Emil Oestereicher, "Marx's Comparative Historical Sociology," *Dialectical Anthropology* 3 (1978): 139–55. Among them, only Oestereicher has argued consistently for the break with the theory of historical materialism beginning with the *Grundrisse* in the late works of Marx. I accept and extend this point of view.
2. This is, of course, not Marx's own self-understanding. Throughout his life, Marx continued to identify the theory of historical materialism with the analysis of the capitalist mode of production. Cf. *A Contribution to the Critique of Political Economy*, in *The Marx-Engels Reader*, ed. Robert C. Tucker (New York: W. W. Norton, 1972), preface, pp. 4–5; *Capital*, 1:8–9.

In their critique of Marx, both Habermas and Wellmer accept this self-interpretation. Habermas, *Knowledge and Human Interests*; Wellmer, *Critical Theory*. Nevertheless, I think that an analysis of the texts will demonstrate that Marx's own self-interpretation does an injustice to the real breakthrough in his most famous work, *Capital*. The introduction to the *Grundrisse*, pp. 107–8, verifies my interpretation.

3. Chapter 6, herein, focuses specifically on the problem of the relation between the system logic of capitalist reproduction and social class.

4. Lukacs is the first to stress this point. Lukacs, "The Changing Function of Historical Materialism," *History and Class Consciousness*.

5. Mandel, *Formation of Economic Thought*.

6. Marx, *Grundrisse*, pp. 471–514.

7. Marx, *Capital*, 1:713–65.

8. Marx, *Grundrisse*, p. 471.

9. This idea, of course, permeates Weber's work from *The Protestant Ethic and the Spirit of Capitalism* (New York: Charles Scribner's Sons, 1958) to *Wirtschaft und Gesellschaft* (Tübingen: J. C. B. Mohr, 1972).

10. Marx, *Grundrisse*, p. 158.

11. Ibid., pp. 491–97.

12. Polanyi, *Great Transformation*.

13. Marx, *Grundrisse*, p. 471, 485.

14. Ibid., p. 485.

15. Ibid., p. 486.

16. Lefort, *Les formes de l'histoire*, p. 204.

17. Marx, *Grundrisse*, p. 489.

18. Lefort, *Les formes de l'histoire*, p. 203.

19. Ibid., and Marx, *Grundrisse*, p. 494. What is referred to here is not the transition from feudalism to capitalism but an abstract model of "traditional society" as opposed to modern society.

20. Marx, *Capital*, 1:714.

21. Marx, *Grundrisse*, p. 258.

22. Ibid., p. 460.

23. Marx, *Capital*, 1:713–14.

24. Marx, *Grundrisse*, p. 504.

25. Ibid., p. 471.

26. Ibid., p. 497.

27. Ibid., pp. 497–98.

28. Marx, *Capital*, 1:714, and *Grundrisse*, p. 507.

29. Marx, *Capital*, 1:502, and *Grundrisse*, p. 715.

30. Marx, *Capital*, 1:714, 750–52 (for example, merchant and usurer capital).

31. Marx, *Grundrisse*, p. 498.

32. Ibid., p. 158.

33. Ibid., pp. 158–59.

34. Ibid., pp 161–62.

35. Ibid., pp. 241, 243–44.

36. Ibid., p. 243.

37. Ibid., p. 245.

38. Ibid., p. 275.
39. Marx, *Capital*, 1:714.
40. Ibid., p. 732.
41. Ibid., pp. 717–41.
42. Ibid., pp. 741, 732–33. For an excellent analysis of this process, cf. Polanyi, *Great Transformation*, pp. 33–111.
43. Marx, *Capital*, 1:737.
44. Ibid.

Chapter 6   System and Class

1. Marx, *Grundrisse*; cf. in this context the Introduction, pp. 83–111, and the section entitled "Forms which Precede Capitalist Production," pp. 471–79.
2. Ibid., p. 184.
3. Heller, *Theory of Need*, and Cohen, "Heller's *Theory of Need*."
4. Marx, *Capital*, 1:564–97.
5. This "economistic" interpretation is typical of Paul Sweezy, Paul Baran, Paul Mattick, and Ernst Mandel.
6. Marx, *Capital*, 1:39.
7. Of the non-Marxists, Joan Robinson, *An Essay on Marxian Economics* (New York: St. Martin's Press, 1966), is the best example. The work of Cornelius Castoriadis, "Valeur, égalité, justice, politique: de Marx à Aristote et d'Aristote à nous," *Les carrefours du labyrinthe* (Paris: Editions du Seuil, 1978), pp. 249–311, is the best example of a Marxist critique of the value theory.
8. Castoriadis, "Valeur, égalité, justice," pp. 263–64.
9. Ibid.
10. I am probably alone in advocating this interpretation.
11. Castoriadis admits that at least half of the time Marx is such a theorist ("Valeur, égalité, justice," pp. 259–74).
12. Marx, *Capital*, 1:170.
13. Marx, *Grundrisse*, pp. 404–7.
14. Ibid., p. 76.
15. For a good discussion of the concept of abstract labor, cf. Johann P. Arnason, *Zwischen Natur und Gesellschaft* (Frankfurt: Europäische Verlagsanstalt, 1976), pp. 192–272.
16. Marx, *Capital*, 1:73.
17. Ibid., p. 10.
18. Ibid., pp. 84–85.
19. Marx, "Results of the Immediate Process of Production," *Capital*, trans. Ben Fowkes (London: Penguin, 1976), 1:989 (this edition is used only for citations from the Appendix).
20. Marx, *Capital*, 1:176.
21. Marx, "Results," p. 1015.
22. Ibid., p. 1009.
23. For an excellent critique of the Marxian concept of use value, see Baudrillard, *Mirror of Production*, pp. 22–25. The problem concerns the projection of the concept of use value, a moment of commodity production and historically spe-

cific to capitalism, to all of history. To universalize use value as the goal of all production considered in abstraction from historical production forms is to impose a capitalist signification on noncapitalist labor processes. Simply because other societies do not produce for exchange does not mean that production is oriented instrumentally to use—instead, it could be structured symbolically to serve a variety of cultural purposes.

24. Marx, *Capital*, 1:183–85.
25. Marx, "Results," pp. 989–90.
26. Ibid.
27. Marx, *Grundrisse*, pp. 303, 513.
28. Ibid., pp. 303–4.
29. Marx, *Capital*, 1:185.
30. Ibid., p. 607.
31. Ibid., p. 409.
32. Ibid., p. 436.
33. Ibid. At times the introduction of machinery for the purpose of breaking the back of skilled labor was quite conscious on the part of capital. Marx quotes the words of the inventor of the steam hammer before the Trades' Union Commission to demonstrate this point: "What every mechanical workman has now to do, and what every boy can do, is not to work himself but to superintend the beautiful labor of the machine. The whole class of workmen that depend exclusively on their skill is now done away with. . . . The result was a considerable increase in my profits."
34. Ibid., pp. 435–36.
35. Ibid., p. 427.
36. Ibid., p. 429; cf. also the footnote on p. 429.
37. Ibid., p. 407.
38. Marx, "Results," p. 1035.
39. Ibid., p. 1024; and *Capital*, 1:360–61.
40. Marx, "Results," p. 990.
41. Marx, *Capital*, 3:880.
42. Ibid.
43. Ibid., p. 827.
44. Ibid., p. 881.
45. Ibid., p. 830.
46. Ibid., p. 791.
47. Ibid., 1:484.
48. Ibid., p. 422.
49. Ibid., pp. 422–23.
50. Ibid., p. 487.
51. Ibid.
52. Ibid., p. 420.
53. Ibid., pp. 420–22.
54. Ibid., p. 424.
55. Ibid., pp. 487–88.
56. Ibid., p. 488.
57. Ibid., 3:819.

58. Ibid., pp. 256, 438–40, and 1:492–94.
59. Ibid., 3:211–60.
60. Ibid., p. 249.
61. Ibid., p. 250.
62. Ibid., p. 440.
63. Ibid., 1:488.
64. Ibid.
65. Ibid., 3:264.
66. Ibid., p. 820.
67. Ibid., pp. 885–86.
68. Ibid., p. 618.
69. Ibid., p. 821.
70. Ibid., pp. 617–20.
71. Ibid., p. 821.
72. Ibid., p. 646.
73. Ibid., pp. 645–48.
74. Ibid., p. 618.
75. Ibid., p. 886.
76. Ibid.
77. Ibid., p. 813.
78. Ibid., p. 812.
79. Stalin drew the obvious conclusions, ruthlessly collectivizing peasant property through the means of the state without waiting for economic developments to render them anachronistic.
80. Marx, *Capital*, 1:78–80.
81. For an excellent analysis of modern "socialist" societies as societies whose central legitimating ideological principle is "rational redistribution" of the social surplus, see Szelényi and Konrad, *Intellectuals on the Road to Class Power*. I reject, however, their use of the concept of class to identify dominant and oppressed groups in these societies.
82. Baudrillard, *Mirror of Production*, pp. 152–60.
83. New working-class theorists formulated a class theory that is most adequate to the *Grundrisse* model wherein scientists represent the most progressive productive force—the general intellect of society.
84. Baudrillard, *Mirror of Production*, p. 30.
85. Cornelius Castoriadis, "From Marx to Aristotle, from Aristotle to Us," *Social Research* 45 (Winter 1978): 667–739.
86. Ibid. For one of Habermas's most recent statements on the subject, see Jürgen Habermas, "Hannah Arendt's Communications Concept of Power," *Social Research* 44 (Spring 1977): 3–24.
87. Castoriadis, "From Marx to Aristotle."
88. For an excellent discussion of the mythological dimension of the principle of laissez-faire economics, see Polanyi, *Great Transformation*.

Conclusion

1. The works of Talcott Parsons in the United States and Niklas Luhmann in West Germany are the most significant. Parsons's most accessible work for the

nonspecialist is *The Evolution of Societies*. Luhmann's key work in this regard is *Legitimation durch Verfahren* (Berlin: Neuwied, 1969).

2. The works of Ted Gurr (*Why Men Rebel* [Princeton, N.J.: Princeton University Press, 1970]), Charles Tilly (*From Mobilization to Revolution* [Reading, Mass.: Addison-Wesley, 1978]), and N. J. Smelser (*Theory of Collective Behavior* [New York: Free Press, 1962]) are representative of the varied approaches to the analysis of collective behavior.

3. Although very few of his writings have been translated into English, Claus Offe's critical appropriation of systems theory is of the highest caliber. Cf. Offe, *Strukturprobleme*; "Political Authority and Class Structures: An Analysis of Late Capitalist Societies," *International Journal of Sociology*, Spring 1972, pp. 73–108; "Crises of Crisis Management: Elements of a Political Crisis Theory," *International Journal of Politics*, Fall 1976, p. 67; and "The Attribution of Public Status to Interest Groups: Observations on the West German Case," in Suzanne Berger, ed., *Interest Groups in Western Europe* (Cambridge: Cambridge University Press, 1979). See also Habermas, *Legitimation Crisis*, and *Communication and the Evolution of Society* (Boston: Beacon Press, 1979); and Alain Touraine, *Production de la société* (Paris: Editions du Seuil, 1973, *The Voice and the Eye*, and *L'après socialisme* (Paris: Grasset, 1980).

4. Offe, *Strukturprobleme*, pp. 66–68.

5. Offe, "Crises," pp. 52–54.

6. Nor could one proceed in the opposite direction and arrive at a concept of the system from the analysis of various conflicting interest groups. Offe, "Political Authority," pp. 73–82.

7. The term *selectivity* refers to event-generating sorting processes involved in the institutionalization of exclusion rules. But Offe wants to go beyond the general systems-theoretical assertion (Luhmann) that every social organization is based on exclusion rules serving to demarcate the boundary between what is internal and what is external (reduction of complexity). From Luhmann's standpoint, each social system is constituted by selectivity and consists in an infinite variety of exclusions. Niklas Luhmann, "System-theoretische Argumentationen," in Jürgen Habermas and Niklas Luhmann, *Theorei der Gesellschaft oder Systemtheorie?* (Frankfurt: Suhrkamp Verlag, 1971), pp. 271–380. According to Offe, this means that Luhmann has no criterion to refer to what the functions of political organization for maintaining order, boundaries, and stability are directed against. Just what is excluded, what is a relevant "nonevent," and how does the selectivity process favor certain interests over others? These are the concerns of Offe's critique. The analysis thus proceeds on a higher level of abstraction than the empirical question of influences on the state and/or the discussion of its specific decisions. A word of caution is necessary here. A discrepancy exists between the two essays devoted by Offe to the discussion of selectivity. The first, "Political Authority and Class Structure," focuses on the specific selectivity of the political system, transcending typical influence theories. The second, *Strukturprobleme des Rapitalistischen Staates* (pp. 65–107), attempts to prove the "class character" of the state. I do not believe that Offe ever succeeds in this goal. By analyzing the structure,

ideology, process, and repressive institutions of the political/administrative system, Offe is able to identify analytically a general selectivity of political institutions that both generates a private interest structure in its action radius and excludes systematically certain types of needs, motives, and groups. But it is only through a conceptual sleight of hand, which equates the overall system maintenance functions of the political subsystem, or the preservation of the capitalist economy, solely with the class interests of capital, that Offe is able to assert the capitalist class character of the political/administrative system. Since Offe insists that this subsystem is noncapitalist, although it functions to preserve the capitalist organizational principle, his effort to prove its class character is quixotic. Offe assumes he has demonstrated this by revealing the systematic protection by the state of capitalist forms and its continual attempt to conceal this organizational bias through processes of "counter-selectivity" or claims to generality, neutrality, democratic consensus, and the like. This is understood as a contradiction between the imperative of fulfilling capitalist class interests (accumulation) and democratic legitimation. But the tension between legitimation and the functioning of the administrative system also serves to indicate another noncapitalist selectivity or particularism—namely, the complex interest structure that constitutes the administrative system itself. Despite his recognition of its noncapitalist character, Offe never analyzes directly the interest structure of the state itself. It is perfectly plausible to view the maintenance of the capitalist organizational principle as part of the interest structure of the state itself. Only on a "lower" level of analysis, that of influence theory, could the class bias of this distinct interest structure be proven. But Offe is unable to methodologically demonstrate the class character of the state and is forced to revert to the assertion that it becomes evident only in practice. Offe, *Strukturprobleme*, pp. 85–90.

8. Offe, "Political Authority," pp. 82–93.

9. The organizational principle of the capitalist system is defined by Offe as exchange relationships. This implies the commodification of wage labor and capital and autonomous private investment decisions independent of the state. Offe, "Crises," pp. 33–34.

10. Offe, "Political Authority," pp. 82–93.

11. Offe, "Klassenherrschaft und politisches System: Die Selektivitat politischer Institutionen," *Strukturprobleme*, pp. 91–105.

12. Offe, "Political Authority," pp. 95–96.

13. Ibid., p. 100.

14. This distinguishes Offe's analysis from pluralist theories that view interests as being formed within society and influencing the state apparatus (usually parliaments) through lobbying.

15. This relates to the thesis that the classes analyzed by Marx (capitalist and proletariat) are, to a certain extent, disorganized through state intervention. See also Habermas, *Legitimation Crisis*, pp. 20–31.

16. From this standpoint, it must appear as if the motives, needs, and groups that do not or cannot address the state are truly marginal—i.e., pose no threat to the system. At most they entail a legitimation deficit, tamed to the extent to which it is spread over pockets of the excluded, those without power to chal-

lenge system functioning. To the extent to which marginalized groups muster enough momentum to "make themselves heard," they can be demarginalized and integrated as an interest group within the framework of the political marketplace.

17. Offe, "Crises," pp. 36–43.

18. Ibid., pp. 34–35, 47.

19. Ibid., pp. 48–52, 58–64.

20. Ibid. See also James O'Connor, *The Fiscal Crisis of the State* (New York: St. Martin's Press, 1973).

21. Offe, "Attribution of Public Status to Interest Groups."

22. Offe explicitly rejects what he refers to as "normative analyses." Cf. Offe, *Strukturprobleme*, pp. 85–86.

23. For the concept of "counterpowers" and "structural reform," see Gorz, *Strategy for Labor*, pp. 9, 8, 58, 60–62.

24. Habermas, *Legitimation Crisis*, pp. 1–31.

25. Ibid., pp. 95–143. See also Habermas, *Communication*, pp. 178–205. For a detailed analysis of Habermas's political theory, see Cohen, "Why More Political Theory?"

26. Habermas, *Legitimation Crisis*, passim. See also "The Dialectics of Rationalization," an interview with Jürgen Habermas, *Telos* 49 (Fall 1981): pp. 5–32, for a further elaboration on the crisis concept.

27. Habermas, *Legitimation Crisis*, pp. 7–8. This text is not comprehensible without prior knowledge of Parsons's work.

28. Ibid., p. 77.

29. Ibid., pp. 75–92. The thesis of a general culture crisis has of course been put forth by many "conservative" thinkers. The most serious version of this thesis is that of Talcott Parsons (*Evolution of Societies*, pp. 182–207). The most recent example of the antidemocratic interpretation of this thesis is Samuel Huntington, *American Politics: The Promise of Disharmony* (Cambridge, Mass.: Belknap Press of Harvard University Press, 1981).

30. Habermas, *Legitimation Crisis*, pp. 75–92.

31. For a discussion of moral development, see Habermas, "Moral Development and Ego Identity," *Communication*, pp. 69–95.

32. Habermas, *Legitimation Crisis*, pp. 88–90.

33. For a discussion of the concept of generalizability regarding interests and compromise, see ibid., pp. 111–17.

34. Ibid., pp. 86–92.

35. See Habermas, *Communication*, pp. 78–90, for the discussion of the theory of moral development and the analysis of Laurence Kollberg's stages model.

36. Ibid., pp. 82–90. See this text for the discussion of Habermas's "stage three" of postconventional morality, or the communicative ethnic. For an interesting critique of this theory of moral and legal development, see Guenter Frankenberg and Ulrich Rödel, *Von der Volkssouveränität zum Minderheitenschutz* (Frankfurt: Europäische Verlagsanstalt, 1981).

37. Habermas, *Strukturwandel der Öffentlichkeit*. See also Cohen, "Why More Political Theory?"

38. This point has been misunderstood by some of Habermas's critics. Seyla Ben-

Habib argues that Habermas offers a purely normative political theory of dis-cursive will formation that articulates postconventional ethics as a pure *ought*. Accordingly, it is claimed that the counterfactually conceived structure of dis-cursive rationality articulates an emancipatory ideal that cannot guide eman-cipatory praxis since it belongs to the life history of no societal subjects. I do not believe that this is the case, for Habermas makes the explicit claim that he is articulating a level of moral development that indeed is to be found in the social identity of present actors. See Seyla Ben-Habib, "Modernity and Ration-alization in the Tradition of Critical Theory," *Telos* 49 (Fall 1981): 38–60.

39. Habermas, *Legitimation Crisis*, pp. 90–91. In his earlier writings, Habermas clearly interpreted the social movements of the 1960s as important creative forces, trying to realize the cultural potential of modernity in new institutions. But once he developed his crisis theory (in part through a critical appropriation of Parsons), social movements were denuded of their creative dimension and were viewed primarily as carriers (träger) of cultural potentials. Cf. Habermas, *Toward a Rational Society* (Boston: Beacon Press, 1971).

40. Jürgen Habermas, "New Social Movements," "Dialectics of Rationalization"; and *Telos* 49 (Fall 1981): 33–37.

41. Ben-Habib, "Modernity and Rationalization"; and McCarthy, *The Critical Theory of Jürgen Habermas* (Boston: 1979), p. 386.

42. Habermas, "New Social Movements."

43. Touraine, *The Voice and the Eye*, pp. 31–36. The first work of Touraine dedi-cated to this action approach is *Sociologie de l'action* (Paris: Editions du Seuil, 1965). His most comprehensive statement of the sociology of action is *Production de la société*. It is clear that Touraine has been influenced by the pathbreaking work of Cornelius Castoriadis, *L'institution imaginaire de la société* (Paris: Éditions du Seuil, 1975).

44. Touraine, *The Voice and the Eye*, pp. 56, 81.

45. Ibid., p. 114.

46. Ibid., pp. 62–72.

47. Touraine's action theory is, of course, based on a reconceptualization of the Parsons's theory of the social system. The theory of social movements (class struggles) is conceptualized in a parallel manner to Parsons's theory of indi-vidual action. Thus the formula "*I-O-T*" refers to a collective identity (*I*), an antagonist (other or alter) (*O*), and a common field of action or a shared definition of a situation (cultural model) (*T* = totality). Here the social movement takes the place of ego and alter—hence the idea that there are always two social movements, if any, interrelated by a common cultural field. For a detailed explication of this, see ibid., pp. 77–102.

48. Ibid. Touraine is clearly relying on Castoriadis's emphatic concept of social creativity, as distinguished from the Marxian concept of production. Cf. Cornelius Castoriadis, *L'Institution Imaginaire*.

49. Ibid., pp. 109–15.

50. Presumably one could situate Offe's analysis on this level.

51. What immediately comes to mind here is Habermas's attempt to theorize communicative interaction as the third form of action (see Habermas, *Knowl-edge and Human Interests*). However, since Touraine seems to reject practical

philosophy or discourses of universality, he is left with a concept of communicative action that is entirely conflictual. But communicative interaction has many dimensions other than that of conflict between social movements. Without a linguistic theory of communication of the Habermasian type, Touraine cannot provide adequate underpinnings for the model of communication he is striving for.

52. Touraine, *The Voice and the Eye*, p. 82.
53. Ibid., p. 83.
54. Ibid., pp. 103–7.
55. Ibid., p. 94. A more serious difficulty with this approach arises, namely, the impossibility to distinguish between mass movements and social movements on the basis of pure action theory. What, one might ask, distinguishes Touraine's theory of social movements (with the stress on irreconcilable antagonism between the class actors, the apparent rejection of compromise between antagonists, and the focus on creativity vis-à-vis norms) from the theory of Georges Sorel, apart from the rejection by Touraine of a productivist bias? Georges Sorel, *Reflections on Violence* (New York: Macmillan, Collier Books, 1974).
56. Cf. Althusser, *Reading Capital*, and the various works of Poulantzas cited in the Introduction, herein.
57. Touraine, *The Voice and the Eye*, pt. 2, pp. 139–212.
58. It is not an alternative to simply abandon Touraine's two-class model and return to the multiplicity of movements or conflicts within a given society, for the problem of defining the relevant form of conflict and of selecting criteria for distinguishing social movements from other forms of social action remains.
59. Touraine, *The Voice and the Eye*, p. 115.
60. Touraine, *Production de la société*, pp. 117–42, and *The Voice and the Eye*, pp. 103–5.
61. Touraine, *Production de la société*, pp. 117–42.
62. Ibid.; also Touraine, *The Voice and the Eye*, pp. 6–8.
63. This is Touraine's version of the thesis regarding the decline of the workers' movement in late capitalism. I reject all versions of this thesis to the extent to which it implies that struggles at the point of production by workers over self-management issues are somehow not possible, not radical, or doomed to impotence vis-à-vis the organizing principle of a society. It is entirely different to criticize the Marxian class theory and its exaggerated claims vis-à-vis the proletariat. Touraine, *The Voice and the Eye*, pp. 10–12.
64. Ibid., pp. 6–13.
65. Touraine's own work on *La société post-industrielle* (Paris: Denoël, 1969) is a pertinent example.
66. Touraine, *The Voice and the Eye*, p. 94.
67. Ibid., p. 103. These societies differ in terms of their pattern of development, or type of state and relation between the state and the dominant class, according to Touraine. Be that as it may, the argument regarding social movements or class struggles is nevertheless very unconvincing.
68. Klaus Eder, "The New Social Movements in Historical Perspective," forthcoming in *Telos* 51 (Fall 1982).

69. Touraine, *The Voice and the Eye*, p. 2.

70. Eder, "New Social Movements."

71. I reject this thesis. Clearly it does not hold true for the social consciousness of actors in the United States regarding institutionalized norms (law, civil liberties, the constitution).

72. See Hans-Georg Gadamer, *Truth and Method* (New York: Continuum, 1975).

73. Castoriadis, *L'institution imaginaire de la société*, pp. 159–497. See also Dick Howard, *The Marxian Legacy* (London: Macmillan, 1977), pp. 262–301.

74. According to Castoriadis, creation in this sense is quite distinct from production. "Homo Faber" is not the adequate basis on which to develop a concept of human creativity in history.

75. I do not see how Touraine could escape the charge that he substitutes the idea of permanent social movement for that of permanent revolution. If compromise and institutionalization are not provided for within the framework of a theory of social movements, then the valid insight that every healthy society is animated by social movements degenerates into the embrace of conflictual action for its own sake.

76. It should be pointed out that by virtue of his rejection of all forms of democracy other than direct democracy modeled either on the Polis or on workers' councils, Castoriadis fails to articulate the specificity of the institutional framework of modern civil society. While he grants that the moderns, unlike the Greeks, have tended to put all institutions into question, that is, have extended the reflexive attitude toward all domains of social life, he does not say what it is about the modern social imaginary that allows for this advance in autonomy (or potential advance). Because he has not emphasized the plurality of forms of democracy within a given society, Castoriadis misses the most important innovation of the "imaginaire" of modern civil society—the toleration of difference and the principle of plurality. The democratic tradition of modern civil societies remains obscure in Castoriadis's work—struggles for democratization of society or economy appear as eruptions against heteronomy that recall or are similar to other such struggles in the past yet whose interconnection is unclear.

77. I am using Castoriadis's term to refer to what Castoriadis, too, has refrained from analyzing: modern civil society.

78. Castoriadis has focused his analysis of the modern Western social imaginary on the idea of rationality, carried by science, philosophy since Descartes, and institutionalized by capitalism. He is critical of this imaginary but does not engage in a thorough analysis of the other imaginary of modernity, namely, civil society, and the democratic tradition.

79. In using the term "civil society" I do not mean the system of needs described by Marx, nor the economy as understood by the utilitarians and economic liberals. Nor do I mean society against the state as postulated by the anarchists. For civil society implies legality, and hence has a political dimension to it, and requires the presence of the state for its own existence. A theory of civil society would require a reconceptualization of its constitutive moments such that the economic liberal, utilitarian, and anarchist orientation could be transcended.

80. Gorz, *Adieu au proletariat*. In a total about-face vis-à-vis his earlier work, Gorz has abandoned the project of reform for either the economy or the state, arguing that these constitute the realm of necessity, heteronomy, unavoidable hierarchy, etc. The proletariat has been bidden adieu, because the "Taylorization" of the workplace renders impossible nonalienating labor and, hence, worker subjectivity. Not having the possibility to overcome alienation at the workplace, the worker is denied the possibility of acting and of democratizing the structure of labor or the corporation. The same holds true for the state, according to Gorz. Thus any attempt to reform the economy and polity, such as introducing democratic decision making while not denying the functional importance of differentiated management or administrative structures, is foreclosed by Gorz. Freedom must occur elsewhere—in "civil society," understood as the pure social realm of countercultures, counterinstitutions, and free social, democratic communicative interaction. Such autonomous spheres are to exist alongside the economy and state, organized hierarchically and devoid of freedom or fulfilling activity. In short, having originally located the potentiality for freedom in nonalienating labor, Gorz now rejects the possibility of freedom in the realm of necessity because he has embraced the idea that labor in these realms cannot but be alienating. The confusion of the social with the economic thus takes its toll. Instead of insisting that the principles of civil society should enter into all spheres of social life, Gorz too quickly relinquishes some for the sake of preserving the purity of others. Thus, despite the call for a dualistic society, his schema is rather undifferentiated and, in the last instance, either antimodern or naive.

81. Ibid.

Index

Library of Congress Cataloging in Publication Data
Cohen, Jean L., 1946–
Class and civil society.

Includes index.
1. Communism and society.   2. Proletariat.   3. Social
classes.   4. Social conflict.   5. Marx, Karl, 1818–1883.
I. Title.
HX542.C6   1982   335.4′11   82-11104
ISBN 0-87023-380-7